DEDICATION

For Linnea

May your life be filled

with asset builders

Building Assets in Congregations

A Practical Guide for Helping Youth Grow Up Healthy

Eugene C. Roehlkepartain

Foreword
Peter L. Benson, Ph.D.
President, Search Institute

This book has been made possible with the generous support
of the DeWitt Wallace–Reader's Digest Fund, New York, New York.

This resource was developed as part of the Uniting Congregations for Youth
Development, a four-year initiative of Search Institute to equip youth workers
and congregations to build developmental assets in youth. Uniting
Congregations for Youth Development is underwritten by a major grant from
the DeWitt Wallace–Reader's Digest Fund, New York, New York. The Fund's
mission is to foster fundamental improvement in the quality of educational
and career development opportunities for all school-age youth, and to
increase access to these improved services for young people in low-income
communities.

The resource is also part of Search Institute's Healthy Communities • Healthy
Youth initiative, which seeks to unite individuals, organizations, and
communities for children and adolescents. Lutheran Brotherhood, now
Thrivent Financial for Lutherans, was the founding national sponsor for
Healthy Communities • Healthy Youth. Thrivent Financial for Lutherans
Foundation has provided Search Institute with generous support.

Building Assets in Congregations
A Practical Guide for Helping Youth Grow Up Healthy
By Eugene C. Roehlkepartain
Copyright © 1998 by Search Institute

10   9   8   7   6
Printed on recycled paper in the United States of America.

615 First Avenue Northeast, Suite 125
Minneapolis, MN 55413
612-376-8955
800-888-7828
www.search-institute.org

Credits

Editing: Jennifer Griffin-Wiesner, Kathryn (Kay) L. Hong, and Peter Kizilos
Design: Connie Baker
Cover illustration: Pepper Tharp
Production coordinator: Rebecca Manfredini

ISBN: 1-57482-113-X

Contents

Foundations for Asset Building

Putting Asset Building into Practice

List of Tipsheets and Worksheets

Chapter 5

Chapter 6

Chapter 7

Leading the Charge

Peter L. Benson, Ph.D.

uilding Assets in Congregations represents both affirmation and challenge. It affirms the power of all faith communities—regardless of type or size or location—to nurture centered, focused, and healthy youth by uniting and mobilizing all of their relational and programmatic resources. Indeed, I would argue that after the institution of family, the communities known as temples, synagogues, mosques, parishes, or churches have the greatest potential to help youth emerge into adulthood as caring, responsible, and committed citizens.

This book also offers a challenge. To take advantage of their power, congregations must change how they connect with, relate to, and include their young people. Much of a congregation's power rests with its people, in their becoming a vibrant intergenerational community that sees itself as an important actor in the lives of youth. This approach requires a different model of congregational youth work. Instead of a few professionals or volunteers leading the charge, all adults—and youth as well—become key actors. When each participant in a faith community activates her or his power to build developmental assets, a congregation becomes particularly effective in shaping a desired worldview.

Search Institute's framework of developmental assets, on which this book is based, has several other important implications. We know empirically and scientifically that the ability of a religious institution to pass on its specific faith tradition is enhanced when it mobilizes to meet youth's developmental needs for support, empowerment, boundaries, structure, competency, and positive identity. As assets increase in a young person's life, her or his openness and willingness to engage deeply and meaningfully with a tradition of faith increase.

The framework also provides a rationale—and, I hope, sparks a passion—for placing congregations within the larger sphere of civic life. Because all youth in a community need greater developmental-asset strength and because all social institutions have a role to play in asset building, congregations become viewed as teammates—not adversaries—in unleashing the capacity of a community to nurture healthy youth. We have seen many times how the vision of developmental assets links congregations with schools, youth organizations, businesses, and local government around a common purpose.

Gene Roehlkepartain has done a masterful piece of work in both conceptualizing the asset-building capacity of congregations and providing the kinds of practical strategies that help congregations activate this capacity. I highly recommend this significant work to all faith communities, and I hope you will journey with us in becoming wiser about how congregations can deeply touch youth both inside and outside the walls of our faith communities.

Acknowledgments

Though only one name is on the title page, this book reflects the contributions of many people. Thanks, first, to the Uniting Congregations for Youth Development project staff and consultants, as well as other Search Institute staff: Tom Berkas, Ann Betz, Jim Conway, Jennifer Griffin-Wiesner, Kay Hong, Colette Illarde, Peter Kizilos, Peter Scales, and Adell Smith. Your insights, questions, editing, careful reviews, and other forms of assistance made this book possible. Special thanks to Peter L. Benson, a colleague, friend, and mentor, who developed the framework of developmental assets and trusts me to share and expand these ideas through writing.

Many people also contributed to this book by sharing their stories through interviews and consultations. While some of them had not heard of developmental assets before the interview, their stories and effective work make up the patchwork quilt that illustrates the potential for asset building in congregations. Thanks to: T. J. Anderson, Zion Lutheran Church, Anoka, Minnesota; Karen Anway, Nativity Lutheran Church, Northfield, Minnesota; Luis Centeno, Bethel Temple, Philadelphia; Jonathan Cohen, Union of American Hebrew Congregations; Jimmy Cunningham, Liberty Hills Baptist Church, Little Rock; Jewell Dassance, Congress of National Black Churches, Washington, D.C.; Kenda Creasy Dean, Princeton Theological Seminary, Princeton, New Jersey; Paul Fleischmann, National Network of Youth Ministries, San Diego; Jeff Green, North Shore Synagogue, Syosset, New York; Rabbi Hayim Herring, Minneapolis Jewish Federation; James Moseley, First Presbyterian Church, St. Louis, Missouri; Ann Edenfield, LOGOS Program, Albuquerque, New Mexico; Art Erickson, Urban Ventures, Minneapolis, Minnesota; Janice Goodjoin, Central United Methodist Church, Albuquerque, New Mexico; Will Healy, Emmaus Baptist Church, Northfield, Minnesota; Roland Martinson, Luther Seminary, St. Paul, Minnesota; Matthew Ramadan, American Muslim Council, Minnesota Chapter, Minneapolis, Minnesota; Judi Ratner, Temple Emanu-El, Dallas; John Roberto, Center for Ministry Development, Naugatuck, New York; Rob Ross, Trinity Lutheran Church, Town and Country, Missouri; Glenn Seefeldt, Nativity Lutheran Church, St. Anthony Village, Minnesota; and Marilyn Sharpe, Mount Olivet Lutheran Church, Minneapolis. Many of these interviews were conducted by Sara Barron, whose help is greatly appreciated.

The leadership teams and congregations in the seven pilot sites in the Uniting Congregations for Youth Development initiative—where we are intentionally working to equip congregations for asset building—contributed many ideas and questions that helped to shape the content of this book. These communities are South Minneapolis/St. Louis Park, Minnesota; Durham, North Carolina; Albuquerque, New Mexico; Uptown and Edgewater, Chicago, Illinois; Bridgeport, Connecticut; Columbus, Georgia; and Santa Clara County, California. Thank you for your commitment to asset building and for being willing to be on the journey with us as we explore the implications of asset building for congregations.

I also want to acknowledge members of the Asset-Building Vision Team and the Youth Ministry Focus Group at St. Luke Presbyterian Church, Minnetonka, Minnesota. Thanks for your commitment to asset building, your willingness to experiment, and the opportunity to learn from putting some of these ideas into practice close to home.

In addition, this manuscript was strengthened considerably from its pilot form because of invaluable input from many youth workers in congregations and, especially, members of the Uniting Congregations for Youth Development national advisory committee.

Finally, I thank Pamela Stevens and her colleagues at the DeWitt Wallace–Reader's Digest Fund, not only for providing financial support for this book and the Uniting Congregations for Youth Development initiative, but for guidance, encouragement, and vision to see that congregations are critical resources for young people's healthy development.

I N T R O D U C T I O N

Making a Difference for Youth

hurches, mosques, parishes, synagogues, temples, and other communities of faith represent an invaluable—though often unrecognized and untapped—resource for today's children and adolescents. Think about the many things congregations do or could offer that all young people need:

- An intergenerational community of people who support, guide, nurture, and build relationships with one another.

- Opportunities to serve, lead, and contribute to their community.

- Clear values, beliefs, and commitments that guide young people, help them make wise and healthy choices, and give their lives purpose and meaning.

- Positive activities that engage and challenge young people and build their skills as they develop intellectually, physically, emotionally, socially, and spiritually.

- A safe place (physically and emotionally) where they can be themselves and where they can form positive relationships with their peers.

- Ongoing education, guidance, and support for their parents or guardians.

These opportunities only scratch the surface in naming the potential of congregations to enhance the positive development of young people. A report from the Carnegie Council on Adolescent Development points to the potential of congregations: "For many adolescents, their religious organization and its leaders are often as trusted as family. This sense of familiarity, combined with the commitment adult church leaders have to nurture young church members, lends strength to church-based youth programs."[1]

Critical Questions Facing Congregations

Clearly, congregations have tremendous potential for addressing the needs of youth. At the same time, they face serious hurdles that can leave youth workers and other leaders frustrated, overwhelmed, or burned out, wondering if there's anything they can do that will make much of a difference. Some questions we ask ourselves include:

1. How do we keep kids involved?

Typically, there's a mass exodus of youth from congregational involvement between 7th and 9th grade. For example, a Search Institute study of five mainline Protestant denominations found that, while 60 percent of 6th-grade youth are active in religious education, only 35 percent of 10th- to 12th-grade youth are actively involved.[2] Similarly, other researchers have concluded that three-fourths of Jewish 13-year-olds are involved in some form of Jewish education. By high school graduation, involvement in any organized Jewish activity has fallen below 25 percent.[3]

A report on Jewish education put the challenge this way: "There is a deep and widespread concern in the Jewish community today that the commitment to basic Jewish values, ideals, and behavior may be diminishing at an alarming rate. A substantial number of Jews no longer seem to believe that Judaism has a role to play in their search for personal fulfillment and communality. This has grave implications not only for the richness of Jewish life but for the very continuity of a large segment of the Jewish people."[4] With minor language changes, that statement could accurately describe other faith traditions as well. Many Christian denominations struggle to keep young people involved, and they face similar membership declines.

2. How can we get more support from the congregation?

In most congregations, a handful of people work with the youth, while youth are largely ignored by others in the congregation. The result is that many youth workers feel isolated, unsupported, overworked, and burned out.

3. How can we focus our work to make a real difference?

Adding to the sense of being overwhelmed is the fact that many congregations take a shotgun approach to youth programming. They offer lots and lots of activities, hoping a couple of them really hit home. The result is often a frenzy of activity with little sense of purpose. As Jonathan Cohen of the Union of American Hebrew Congregations put it, "What can you really give them that's going to stick in two or three hours per month?"

4. How can we touch the lives of more kids?

Many congregations don't tap their potential to reach and support youth in the community—to be a public voice in shaping society for the sake of all youth. Yet today more than ever, life in the community affects youth in the congregation. And perhaps even more important, young people who are not in a congregation desperately need the faith community to be a positive advocate and voice on their behalf.

These are difficult questions with no easy answers. Yet a growing body of research affirms that there are practical things you can do in your congregation that can have a tremendous impact for youth. These things don't cost a lot of money. They also don't require being a large congregation with a paid staff and ample volunteers. But, I believe, these things can begin to address the tough questions facing many congregations.

A Practical Guide for Asset Building

Building Assets in Congregations is a practical tool to help congregations recognize and unleash their capacity and potential for helping to provide young people what they need to grow up responsible, caring, and healthy.

At the heart of this book is Search Institute's framework of 40 developmental assets—positive experiences and qualities that young people need to grow up healthy. While these assets center on everyday relationships and activities, research shows that these positive experiences, when added together, provide a solid foundation for life. Young people from all backgrounds are more likely to be contributing, productive members of families, congregations, and communities when they have these assets in their lives. They are also less likely to become trapped in violence, alcohol and other drug use, too-early sexual activity, and other problem behaviors.

These assets offer a vision and focus for congregational work with youth. Congregations that take asset building seriously not only see the potential for using the asset framework in their programming with youth, but they also see how it can shape all areas of congregational life as well as outreach to the community. Just as important, everyone in the congregation—not just the youth workers or the volunteers or the clergy—has a role and a stake in asset building.

What's in the Book

Building Assets in Congregations calls on communities of faith to build these assets and gives practical strategies for creating an asset-building congregation. It begins by presenting the vision of developmental assets and talking about their implications for congregations ("Foundations for Asset Building," Chapters 1 and 2).

Chapters 3 through 7 ("Putting Asset Building into Practice") turn to the practical application. Chapter 3 highlights key tasks in introducing asset building to your congregation. Then the book looks at the implications for the congregation's structure and intergenerational activities (Chapter 4); programming for youth (Chapter 5); family education and support (Chapter 6); and outreach and partnerships in the community (Chapter 7).

In addition to solid information, the book has many practical tools, including summaries of each chapter, stories from congregations of many faith traditions, reproducible pages, and hundreds of tips and ideas. The appendixes provide 10 ready-to-use bulletin inserts, a list of resources to help you in your asset-building efforts, and a reproducible list of the 40 developmental assets (in English and in Spanish).

Because the vision of asset building is comprehensive and can touch many areas of congregational life—and because each congregation is different—this book includes many more suggestions and ideas that you can implement in your congregation. In a sense, *Building Assets in Congregations* is more like a cookbook than a single recipe. Some ideas and options might be appetizers—a chance to whet the congregation's appetite for asset building. Others may be entrées—the core strategies of the asset-building approach. And you'll also find some desserts— things that are fun and rewarding once you have the "entrées" working well!

Trying to do everything in this book at once would fill anyone's plate too full. Rather, after you understand the asset-building basics (in Chapters 1 and 2), use or adapt the process outlined in Chapter 3 for getting your congregation on board with asset building. Then pick the specific ideas out of the remaining chapters that fit your congregation's style, energy, priorities, and interests.

Who This Book Is For

Asset building can touch all areas of congregational life. That doesn't mean everyone in a congregation needs to read this book. However, a congregation is more likely to discover the potential of asset building if several people in the congregation have internalized the core ideas and the vision outlined here. Therefore, it may be appropriate for several congregational leaders or advocates to read and discuss this book together, identifying ways these ideas and strategies can strengthen your congregation. Each chapter includes a summary page with discussion questions for this study process. Here are some of the intended audiences:

- **Professional youth workers** and others who coordinate a congregation's work with youth (such as clergy, religious education directors) need to have the "big picture" that comes from reading the whole book. Then certain chapters will be most relevant to address specific areas of work for which you are responsible.

- **Clergy** (including ministers, pastors, priests, rabbis, imams) will also find it valuable to be familiar with the overall contents of this book, particularly if you have responsibility for programs for families and youth. Of particular interest (because clergy are often directly responsible for these areas) are Chapter 3—how to introduce asset building to a congregation; Chapter 4—strategies for integrating asset building throughout the congregation; and Chapter 7—how to integrate asset building into outreach into the community.

- **Volunteer youth workers** (including religious education teachers and leaders, parents, youth who are in leadership roles, as well as members of the congregation's youth committee) will also find the whole book useful as a way of understanding how your congregation can include young people. Certain sections, such as Chapters 2 and 5, are particularly pertinent because they speak directly to youth programming.

- Finally, **other congregational leaders** will find major portions of this book helpful in planning and supporting your congregation's work with youth, depending on areas of interest. For example, the congregation's board of directors should be familiar with asset-building basics and the key emphases spelled out in Chapters 1 and 2. The leaders of a congregation's mission/service/outreach area will want to review Chapter 7, and people responsible for family programs will be most interested in Chapter 6.

Notes on Language and Traditions

The choice of appropriate language is one of the challenges in developing materials that seek to build bridges across many faith traditions.[5] Thus, I have chosen language that is widely understood and inclusive of many faith traditions. For example, Search Institute uses the generic term "congregations" instead of talking about churches, synagogues, mosques, parishes, temples, and other specific terms for the gathered faith community.[6] Similarly, I have used the more inclusive term "youth work," as opposed to "youth ministry," which resonates in Christian congregations but not in Jewish or Muslim traditions.

It is also important to note that this book does not seek to make a theological case for asset building. Rather, it begins with an understanding of young people and the resources congregations have to help youth grow up healthy. The theological work, though important, must be done within each faith tradition, not by a nonsectarian organization such as Search Institute. However, people in many faith traditions find the asset framework highly compatible with their own theology and traditions. (I interviewed a variety of leaders who give insights on how asset building fits with their faith tradition. See pages 15–20.) I encourage you to reflect on the connections between asset building and the values and traditions of your own synagogue, mosque, parish, temple, or church.

Affirmation and Challenge

Many people find that the assets give them a new language for articulating and celebrating what they're already doing. As you read this book, you may discover many ways your congregation already builds assets—even if you don't call it asset building. Take time to celebrate and highlight those good things; all of the hard work and commitment you have given to youth in your congregation is really important.

In addition, you may find many things in this book that challenge you to question some things you're doing, to reshape some programs and activities, and to try some new things. That can be tough work. It can take a lot of time. And there will be barriers along the way. But such change is essential in your ongoing efforts to ensure that young people's experiences in your congregation are both life-shaping and life-affirming.

As you read, try to keep a balance in mind. Too much cheering, by itself, can lead to complacency and self-aggrandizement. Too much challenge, by itself, can lead to frustration and despair. A healthy mixture of the two gives you the energy and vision to sustain your efforts to contribute to the well-being of youth, both now and in the future.

Uniting Congregations for Youth Development

This book was written as part of the Uniting Congregations for Youth Development initiative, a four-year pilot project made possible by the generous support of the DeWitt Wallace-Reader's Digest Fund. This initiative was designed to equip religious youth workers and congregations to build developmental assets for youth in the congregation and community. Seven pilot sites have been part of this initiative: Southern Albuquerque, New Mexico; Edgewater/Uptown, Chicago, Illinois; Columbus, Georgia; Durham, North Carolina; South Metro, Minneapolis/St. Louis Park, Minnesota; San Jose, California; and Bridgeport, Connecticut. Through our partnership in these pilot sites, Search Institute has been testing several strategies for equipping youth workers for asset building.

They include:

- Opportunities to participate in interfaith networks of youth workers in their own community;

- Access to quality training and practical resources to strengthen their congregation's work with youth; and

- Community-wide activities for youth and youth workers that build assets.

Once the materials and training have been developed and tested in these seven pilot sites, they will be made available to religious youth workers and congregations in communities across the country. For more information on this initiative, call 800-888-7828. Or visit our Web site at www.search-institute.org.

Foundations for Asset Building

Helping Youth Grow Up Healthy

A New Vision for Congregations

hen you walk into the building, this congregation seems a lot like many others. People warmly greet each other. And most of the activities listed in the literature seem familiar: worship services, religious education, youth groups, social activities, service projects.

But then you begin noticing some differences. As people socialize, adults don't just talk to other adults. A senior citizen and teenager are laughing about a funny incident that happened the previous week. Kids say "hi" to the adults as they walk by—and the adults say "hi" back. It's clear that this is a place where everyone knows your name.

Then you sit down for the worship service. Something's different about it, too. You begin to understand what's happening when you notice that the children and youth are paying attention and participating actively, some in leadership roles. This isn't a service just for adults; this is a service for the whole intergenerational community of faith. And the announcements tell you that this intergenerational inclusiveness extends throughout congregational life. It's clear that all congregational activities are planned with an eye to building relationships across generations and including all generations in decision making.

You wonder whether any of this affects the youth programming. So you stop by a youth-group meeting. The first thing you notice is that it's clear the kids want to be there. It feels warm, friendly, and comfortable. You see ground rules posted on the wall: "No put-downs. No abusing property. Listen respectfully to each other. No chemical use." These young people have high expectations for each other.

What's going on here?

On one level, everything is so familiar. On another, it all seems so different from so many congregations. You see someone in the hall, so you ask.

"Oh, we're a congregation committed to building assets in children and youth."

"What does that mean?"

"It means we make it a priority to ensure that all young people in our congregation and community have the positive experiences they need to grow up healthy, caring, and responsible."

That's the kind of congregation you can create with the tools in this book. This vision doesn't depend on having a large staff, starting a costly program, being in a particular kind of community, or having a particular theological perspective.

Rather, it's a vision that invites congregations of all faiths and cultural backgrounds to a renewed focus and commitment to ensure that children and adolescents have access to the positive relationships, opportunities, and guidance they need to thrive in a challenging world.

A Vision for Congregations: Building Assets in Youth

At the heart of this vision for congregations is the concept of developmental assets. Identified by Search Institute, assets are positive building blocks for the healthy development of all youth, including youth of all racial and ethnic backgrounds, youth from all types of communities, and youth of any income level.

The asset framework gives a clear picture of things that are important for helping youth make healthy, positive choices and avoid problems. The framework is made up of 40 developmental assets, which are organized into eight categories (Chapter 2 examines the 40 assets in more detail):

- **Support**—Young people need to experience support, care, and love from their families and many others. They need organizations and institutions that provide positive, supportive environments.

- **Empowerment**—Young people need to be valued by their community and have opportunities to contribute to others. For this to occur, they must feel safe.

- **Boundaries and expectations**—Young people need to know what is expected of them and whether activities and behaviors are "in bounds" or "out of bounds."

- **Constructive use of time**—Young people need constructive, enriching opportunities for growth through creative activities, youth programs, congregational involvement, and quality time at home.

- **Commitment to learning**—Young people need to develop a lifelong commitment to education and learning.

- **Positive values**—Youth need to develop strong values that guide their choices.

- **Social competencies**—Young people need skills and competencies that equip them to make positive choices, to build relationships, and to succeed in life.

- **Positive identity**—Young people need a strong sense of their own power, purpose, worth, and promise.

The assets are more than just nice ideas. They represent the synthesis of extensive research into factors that prevent risky behaviors among youth, promote resiliency in kids in tough circumstances, or promote positive attitudes and activities by youth.[1] Together, these assets give young people the launch pad needed to become responsible, contributing members of society.

Focusing energy on building these assets is an important challenge and opportunity for congregations.

There are five major reasons to focus energy on building assets:

1. They have a powerful influence in young people's lives.

2. Most young people—regardless of their background—experience too few of these assets, leaving them vulnerable and unprepared.

3. Because assets focus on relationships and character, congregations of all faiths have tremendous potential to build assets for youth in the congregation and the community.

4. Asset building is integral to the mission of congregations from all major faith traditions.

5. Most congregations do not live up to their asset-building potential.

Let's explore each of these reasons in more detail.

Assets Shape Young People's Lives

While the 40 assets may look like "just plain common sense," they are actually powerful and critical building blocks for healthy development. Think of your own life for a moment. What did you experience as you were growing up that positively influenced your character and behavior? Was it several caring adults who believed in you? Was it a loving family? Was it a strong commitment to education or to certain values and beliefs? Was it opportunities to serve others? If so, you can readily relate these positive memories to the asset-building model.

Search Institute research bears out the power of these assets in young people's lives. Surveys of thousands of young people across the United States have found that the more assets young people experience, the more they engage in positive behaviors, such as volunteering and succeeding in school. The fewer they have, the more likely they are to engage in unhealthy risk-taking behaviors, such as alcohol and other drug use, antisocial behavior, violence, and others. This important relationship between assets and young people's choices has been documented for all types of youth, regardless of age, gender, region, town size, or race/ethnicity.

Take the issue of violence, for example.

Among youth who report having 10 or fewer assets, 61 percent report being involved in patterns of violent activities (which were defined as three or more acts of serious violence in the past year). But among those youth reporting 31 or more of the 40 assets, only 6 percent engaged in patterns of violence. This same pattern holds true for at least 10 different areas of high-risk behavior: alcohol, tobacco, and other drug use; sexual activity; depression and attempted suicide; violence and other antisocial behavior; school problems; driving and alcohol; and gambling.

The opposite pattern occurs when we focus on positive attitudes and behaviors, such as valuing diversity. Among youth with 31 or more of the 40 assets, 87 percent value getting to know people who are different from them. Yet only 34 percent of those with 10 or fewer assets express this positive attitude.

In addition to the assets' power to protect youth from negative behaviors and promote positive behaviors, the assets also help young people "bounce back" from adversity or trauma such as sexual abuse, alcoholism in the family, divorce, neglect, and poverty. Several prominent researchers in the field of resiliency have identified factors that make it more likely for young people to "beat the odds."[2] Many of these factors are included in the framework of assets, including caring family environments (assets #1–2), quality relationships with nonparent adults (asset #3), high expectations (asset #16), participation in structured activities (assets #17–20), success in school (assets #21–25), and a positive identity (assets #37–40).

This research tells us two things.

First, the assets are powerful influences on young people's choices. Their presence does not eliminate problems, but it could significantly reduce problems and increase positive behaviors among youth if more youth experienced more assets. Second, the assets are cumulative or additive—the more the better.

It is important to note that the 40 assets identified by Search Institute don't represent everything that young people need to thrive. (Even some of the young people with high levels of assets engage in negative behaviors.) Healthy development is influenced by many other factors as well, including economics, cultural norms, temperament, genetics, and traumas. Thus, while asset building is an essential strategy, it shouldn't be seen as a cure-all that will magically transform the lives of all youth.

Most Youth Experience Too Few Assets

If most young people already had the 40 assets, we could be relatively content with the status quo. Most youth would be getting what they need from their families, congregations, schools, and communities. In fact, the opposite is true. Most young people of all cultural backgrounds and in all types of communities experience far too few of these assets. Indeed, "asset gap" may well be the greatest crisis facing the future of our congregations and society.

Ideally, a community should strive to ensure that all youth develop 31 or more assets.

However, recent research shows that only 8 percent of youth have 31 or more of the 40 assets (see *Fast Facts*, "Levels of Assets Among Youth"). In virtually every community we have studied across the United States, the average young person experiences only about half of the assets. In our recent studies of 213 towns and cities in 25 states, the average young person has only 18 of the 40 developmental assets. Thus, the foundation for positive development is incomplete or fragile for 92 percent of 6th- to 12th-grade youth. This reality is true for all types of youth, both male and female, across all grades and racial/ethnic groups surveyed.

Our families, congregations, and communities pay a huge price for failing to provide the assets young people need. We see some of the costs in the violence, crime, hopelessness, chemical abuse, unplanned pregnancies, and other problems that have become almost normative for youth in this culture. Just as tragic are the lost potential, stolen dreams, and undeveloped gifts of our young people, resources our society desperately needs at the dawn of a new millennium. A report from the American Medical Association puts the situation this way: "For the first time in the history of this country, young people are *less* healthy and *less* prepared to take their places in society than were their parents. And this is happening at a time when our society is more complex, more challenging, and more competitive than ever before." The report continues:

> Far too many of our teenagers have lost their way and are engaging in destructive behaviors that imperil their immediate health, their future

The Impact of Developmental Assets

This table indicates the percentage of youth who report engaging in patterns of high-risk behaviors and in positive behaviors and attitudes, based on the number of assets they report having.*

	0-10 Assets	11-20 Assets	21-30 Assets	31-40 Assets
Patterns of Risk-Taking Behavior				
Illicit drugs	42%	19%	6%	1%
Used illicit drugs three or more times in the past year.				
Sexual intercourse	33%	21%	10%	3%
Has had sexual intercourse three or more times in lifetime.				
Violence	61%	35%	16%	6%
Has engaged in three or more acts of fighting, hitting, injuring a person, carrying or using a weapon, or threatening physical harm in the past year.				
Depression/suicide	40%	25%	13%	4%
Is frequently depressed and/or has attempted suicide.				
Positive Behaviors and Attitudes				
Helps others	69%	83%	91%	96%
Helps friends or neighbors one or more hours per week.				
Succeeds in school	7%	19%	35%	53%
Gets mostly A's on report card.				
Values diversity	34%	53%	69%	87%
Places high importance on getting to know people of other racial/ethnic groups.				
Maintains good health	25%	46%	69%	88%
Pays attention to healthy nutrition and exercise.				

*Based on survey data from 99,462 6th- to 12th-grade public school students in 213 towns and cities in 25 states.

well-being, and their prospects for living a fulfilling life. This crisis is not, as some people believe, confined to communities that are suffering from poverty and crime: Indeed, it involves millions of teenagers *in every neighborhood* across the nation. Without a doubt, it will destroy many young lives. Yet it goes beyond a concern for individuals, for when so many of our young people are affected by poor health or are engaging in risky health behaviors, it is the country as a whole that is at risk.[3]

This bleak picture of young people's lives suggests that our society has badly neglected—or forgotten how—to provide the basic, positive experiences young people need to grow up strong and healthy. Indeed, many factors in this society limit young people's access to the positive experiences and relationships needed to grow toward adulthood.

Levels of Assets Among Youth

This chart indicates the percentage of youth who have the different levels of assets.*

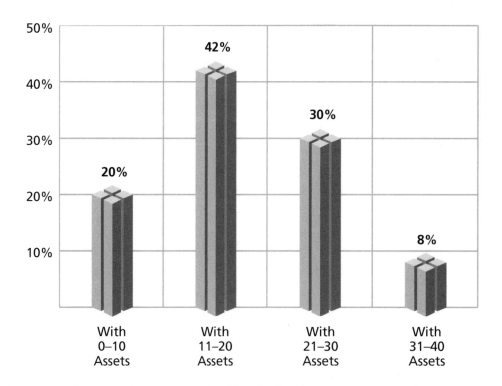

Based on surveys of 99,462 6th- to 12th-grade public school students in 213 towns and cities in 25 states.

While a deeper exploration of these factors is beyond our scope, four major themes emerge:

1. **Developmental deficits such as poverty, abuse, and neglect are among the most serious challenges limiting young people's access to these positive assets.** These pervasive social problems demand that young people focus on sheer survival, often leaving little energy or opportunity for the positive experiences that bring meaning and hope. Furthermore, young people caught by these injustices often do not have access to the caring relationships and opportunities that can help them beat the odds or bounce back from trauma.

2. Another reason young people do not experience these assets is that **society has become highly age-segregated.** Teenagers spend most of their time with other teenagers. Parents relate primarily with other parents their own age. Older adults relate primarily to older adults. As a result, outside of their family, teenagers rarely spend time with anyone older or younger than them. As Search Institute president Peter Benson writes: "The architecture and design of communities and neighborhoods isolates families, and virtually every program and institution is organized to meet age-specific needs at the expense of the richness of intergenerational community."[4] The result is that young people do not build the relationships across generations that provide support and care, guidance and challenge, and wisdom and insight. It's a sad reality, especially since research shows that the single most positive influence in a young person's life is regular time spent with a caring adult.

Many congregations reflect these cultural norms. In most faith traditions, youth work has focused almost exclusively on age-specific education and activities for youth. Youth have their own room (sometimes their own building), their own programs, their own worship services. Like our society in general, too many congregations have become age-segregated institutions that provide activities to "targeted" age groups. "Over the last century," writes Presbyterian author Mark DeVries, "churches and parachurch youth ministries alike have increasingly (and often unwittingly) held to a single strategy that has become the most characteristic of this [traditional youth ministry] model: the isolation of teenagers from the adult world and particularly from their own parents."[5] He concludes:

> Apart from the family (and perhaps the television), the church may be the only lifelong nurturing structure left. . . . All other communities (except, on rare occasions, neighborhoods) are essentially orphaning structures (for example, parachurch groups, schools, scouts and youth groups). Orphaning structures provide support and connection for people only so long as they fit into the age group of that particular organization. Many orphaning structures provide teenagers with a high degree of support and involvement. But, in the end, without the support of a lifelong nurturing structure, a young person's life becomes fragmented and rootless.[6]

To be sure, age-specific activities and relationships have a role in young people's lives, and building positive relationships with peers is an important part of growing up. But our society's almost exclusive focus on age-specific opportunities and interaction has numerous negative side effects.

3. A corollary to this age segregation is that **parents and youth-serving professionals (teachers, youth workers, counselors) have been given almost sole responsibility for raising young people.** Indeed, it is culturally acceptable— even expected—that people without children or whose children have grown up and left home should not "interfere" in parents' job of raising kids. When you ask

them to take some responsibility, a too-common response is "I've already done my time" or "I don't have anything to offer because I don't have kids."

As a result, a relatively small number of people are held accountable for doing all the work of raising society's youngest generation. Whereas young people might once have been guided and nurtured by a whole neighborhood or extended family, many families are now left alone to provide everything their children need. Adding to the isolation are work demands, single parenthood, divorce, and other challenges that make it even more difficult for parents to be there for their kids.

Beyond the family, we have enormous expectations for our youth-serving systems. We give them minimal resources, then count on them to somehow take care of or "fix" our kids. This pattern is common in congregations. A single youth worker or a small team of volunteers is charged with planning programs (with few volunteers) that will keep youth connected to and interested and involved in their congregation. This situation becomes a perpetual cycle, as professionals develop more and more specialized skills, while fewer and fewer adults are involved in the lives of youth as either volunteers or just caring friends.

4. Related to the age-segregation issue is the reality of **pervasive negative attitudes toward young people,** particularly adolescents. Most adults in this society now view young people with suspicion and fear. When adults were asked in a recent study to describe teenagers, two-thirds chose adjectives such as "rude," "wild," and "irresponsible."[7]

When I speak to groups and challenge negative stereotypes of adolescents, I often face a question like: "Well, isn't it appropriate to be suspicious of youth? After all, aren't kids responsible for a disproportionate amount of crime in our community?" I respond: "It's true that young people are more likely to commit a crime than older adults. But what percentage of crime do you think they commit? And what percentage of young people are involved in crime?" After taking a few answers from the group, I cite statistics from the U.S. Department of Justice: Young people commit about one in five of all crimes (19 percent). So 80 percent of crime is committed by adults over age 18. In addition, only 6 percent of all youth are arrested for a crime in a given year. That means that 94 percent of youth are not.[8]

To be sure, there are serious issues to address. Too many young people commit too many crimes. And there are other problems less serious than crime that deserve attention. But the point is that all young people are unjustly blamed for the misbehavior and misdeeds of a few. This view is wrong, and we need to acknowledge and work to change it.

5. Finally, providing these assets has become more difficult as **we have lost a clear vision of the values, priorities, and perspectives we seek to nurture in young people**. Indeed, young people often face a barrage of conflicting messages from different parts of society, such as the media, peers, schools, and family. The result is that different sectors of our society conflict and compete with each other for influence over young people, rather than sharing a positive vision of the common good.

Why can't we all get on the same page? Calls for a common vision may raise warning flags for some, especially religious and cultural minorities. There is a legitimate concern that the "common vision" not simply reflect the values and vision of the dominant culture, one that ignores some people's values, experiences, and priorities. Calls for a common vision can be used to promote narrow perspectives, intolerance, and bigotry.

It's important to remember and respect these concerns and to consciously include all people and traditions in any "common" vision. This is not necessarily easy in a diverse society. But the difficulty of identifying and promoting a consistent, positive vision for young people in a diverse culture should not dissuade us from such a critical task. Young people have too much to gain from a unified, consistent vision that supports their healthy growth and development.

Certainly, there will always be differences in how various religious or political perspectives approach these issues. And there will be some values and boundaries that are important to one tradition, but not to others. But in the midst of all the differences we can find common ground—shared perspectives, hopes, priorities, and values that we can build and promote together. For example, honesty, integrity, caring, and responsibility are important virtues in all faith traditions. Building a consensus on such values and reinforcing them throughout society could have a significant impact.

It's also important to build a consensus about the kinds of things that young people should *not* do. As caring adults, we need to set appropriate boundaries and limits on violence, chemical use, too-early sexual activity, and other health-compromising behaviors.

S N A P S H O T

Connecting to the "Real World"

The "real world" for teenagers in the Brother to Brother Program operated from **Liberty Hills Baptist Church in Little Rock, Arkansas**, is a world of high crime, gangs, violence, and racial isolation and stereotyping. But the program—which focuses its efforts on young African American males—doesn't seek to shield participants from this real world, says program director Jimmy Cunningham. Rather, it seeks to give them the skills, support, and sense of identity they need to deal with the world around them.

The program (which receives federal, state, and other support) weaves together social rituals, cultural information, and educational enrichment within the context of values. For four days each week, 50 boys, ages 6 to 18, come together for a meal, group activities, ceremonies, tutoring, computer classes, and other programs. They watch both educational and entertainment videos, but always take time to talk about what they see.

"In the context of talking about who they are, we talk about what that means in the real world," Cunningham says. "As black males [these young men] feel stigmatized in the school and community.

"In a world that is increasingly multicultural," he continues, "it becomes even more important to be comfortable and grounded in self so you can relate to other people. . . . What we offer is a holistic kind of approach to dealing with the multitude of issues they have to deal with."

Congregations Have Tremendous Potential for Asset Building

Congregations alone cannot address these critical issues and turn the tide for youth. Creating a better world for young people will require major commitments and shifts in priorities from virtually every person and every institution in our communities. Yet congregations already contribute significantly to young people's base of assets. Furthermore, there is even greater potential for congregations that focus energy on asset building.

As an institution in our society, congregations have a unique opportunity and capacity to build assets in youth. For example, congregations:

- Have potential for intergenerational relationships that can be sustained across many years;

- Provide opportunities for youth to understand themselves, their identity, and their world through leadership development, education, service, field trips, and other positive social activities;

- Reach and work with parents, partnering with them to support their crucial role in young people's lives; and

- Have a positive public presence, with the potential for leadership, advocacy, and service on behalf of young people in society.

In some instances, the faith community is one of the few institutions with the credibility and access to address these basic needs among youth. "In the contemporary world, the black church remains the primary, perhaps the only, institution capable of reaching effectively into African American communities and offering answers to some of the problems African American people face," asserts the Congress of National Black Churches. "In many cities, our young people—our most precious resource—are seriously at risk. It is vital that the churches act now to help young people and their families learn to function effectively in today's complex society."[9]

Congregations as "alternative cultures" are particularly relevant in communities of faith that have, historically, had to resist and challenge a dominant culture. The experiences of African American churches illustrate this potential, according to Robert Michael Franklin, director of the Black Church Studies Program at Candler School of Theology, Emory University:

> In response to horrific conditions of racial and economic oppression, black congregations emerged as alternative cultures wherein their affirmations of God, community, and selfhood provided the strength to resist exploitation and to love others. . . . But black congregations were not content merely to survive the horrors of the past; they also made claims upon the nation's identity, conscience, and moral obligation to practice fairness and mercy toward its most disenfranchised citizens. Their public mission was to compel America to become America for everyone. Hence the African-American religious narrative may offer clues to all sorts of congregations about how to renew hope and energize ministries that can positively transform society.[10]

This kind of alternative culture and positive vision is exactly the kind of "shining light" that young people need in today's society. Congregations of all faiths and in all settings have the potential not only to model the qualities of an asset-building community for youth, but also to call all segments of society to a renewed commitment to the youngest generation. Because they are, in a sense, communities within communities, congregations also have the potential to model what it means to be an asset-building, intergenerational community for all of society.

Asset Building Is Integral to Congregations' Mission

National leaders in many faith traditions are beginning to see asset building as a foundational framework for their work with youth. And no faith tradition has done more to integrate asset building into its foundation than the Roman Catholic Church, the largest religious body in the United States. In mid-1997, the U.S. Conference of Catholic Bishops approved a document that outlines the components of "a comprehensive ministry with adolescents," titled "Renewing the Vision: A Framework for Catholic Youth Ministry." In reference to Search Institute's developmental assets, the document states:

> The church's ministry with adolescents and their families has an important contribution to make in building healthy communities and in providing the developmental and relational foundation essential to a young person's healthy development. This model of healthy adolescent development offers practical direction for the church's ministry today and in the future. Ministry with adolescents will need to be more comprehensive and communitywide to take full advantage of the opportunities presented by this research. These assets focus our ministry by naming what the church seeks to achieve in the lives of young people.[11]

To illustrate how compatible the asset approach is with other major faith traditions in the United States, I interviewed six national leaders from various faith traditions: Christian, Jewish, Muslim. Though each places a different accent on asset building, all see it as an integral part of their tradition's work with youth. (See the "Assets and Faith" snapshots, pages 15–20.) As Kenda Dean writes in a major study of religious youth work in the United States:

> If spiritual growth is a matter of caring for the total person as a divine creation, then a religious youth program is inherently a multifaceted proposition. Yet religious youth programs often fail to express themselves through the full range of options available to them; developing spiritual identity often ignores the need to resolve personal struggles, and vice versa.[12]

Most faith traditions have a long history of, and commitment to, addressing the whole person. Often this commitment is expressed through congregational programs and activities designed to meet the basic physical needs of people in distress around the world, including food, housing, health, safety, and basic human rights. These traditions and values have been sustained and reinforced as core commitments by people of faith for thousands of years.

This same commitment also extends to meeting young people's needs for caring relationships, principled guidance, and opportunities to learn, grow, and contribute—the stuff of asset building. These needs may not be as concrete or tangible as the need for food, clothing, and shelter, but they are no less essential if we want to nurture young people.

Many of the things congregations commonly do in youth work also contribute to building assets. Search Institute surveyed 500 youth workers from many faith traditions about their goals in youth work (see *Fast Facts*, "How Developmental Assets Connect to Youth Workers' Priorities," page 21). Faith-specific goals are, as we would expect, the most widely shared priorities. In addition, though, we found that the vast majority of youth workers believe, for example, that providing a safe and caring place for youth and developing young people's skills and values are also important goals. These two statements—as well as many others in the list—are directly related to building developmental assets.

Furthermore, building assets can have a direct impact on young people's spirituality and faith commitment. In a study of more than 12,000 youth in a southwestern city, Search Institute found that the more assets youth experience, the more likely they are to place value on "being religious or spiritual." For example, youth who have little interest in being religious or spiritual average 15 of the 40 assets. In contrast, those who place a high value on spirituality average 21 assets. In interpreting this finding, Peter Benson turns to Abraham Maslow's hierarchy of needs and suggests that young people's spiritual interest (a high-order need) increases as their more basic psychological and social needs (which are reflected in the 40 assets) are met.[13]

Thus, while the developmental assets may not explicitly address the unique dimensions of a congregation's spiritual or faith commitments, building assets is integral to being effective in nurturing a faith commitment. Young people are unlikely to grow in their faith if the congregation is not a place where they experience support and care. They will not learn the lifestyle demands of their faith tradition without an articulation of boundaries. And similar statements could be made for the other categories of assets.

Most Congregations Don't Live Up to Their Asset-Building Potential

We've shown that developmental assets are vital for young people's healthy development, yet too many youth do not experience these assets. We've also shown that congregations have both the potential and priorities required to build assets. While many young people have positive experiences in, and perceptions of, congregations (see *Fast Facts*, "Young People's Perceptions of Congregational Life"), congregations rarely live up to their full asset-building potential. Consider these common realities:

- Youth programs are often segregated from other areas of congregational life so that young people have little contact with adults (or younger children) in the congregation. Only a small handful of adults (usually young adults and/or parents) see it as their responsibility to "be there" for youth.

- Parents are tangential to the congregation's work with youth; indeed, sometimes they are seen as adversaries who either "don't do their jobs" or "get in the way" of the congregation's youth work. If they are involved, it is so that they can support the youth program, not so that the congregation can support them in their crucial role as parents.

- Youth programs treat youth like passive "clients," trying to keep them involved without giving them opportunities to shape the programs and opportunities or to contribute to their congregation or community. One result is that activities are often boring, or they are eliminated because not enough youth participate.

- While some congregations do see their mission as reaching out to young people in the community and helping them address the realities of their daily lives, too many others have become fortresses against the community, hoping to keep the needs and problems of youth from invading their tranquil space.

Assets and Faith:
A Black Church Perspective

Condensed from an interview with Jewell Dassance, director of Children and Family Development, Congress of National Black Churches, Washington, D.C.

Why is it important for African American Christian congregations to focus energy on building developmental assets?

For a hundred reasons. First, it's a part of the church's mission to be responsible for children —to value children and to be concerned about their welfare. That has always been the case for black churches.

In addition, the black church has a tremendous capacity to have an impact. Historically, the church has been the center for African American activities for both the family and the people. The church is where people always go for support and comfort. Politically, that's where people had to go to try and respond to some of the things that were going on in the communities. The whole idea of valuing education and getting an education to be prepared to be a good citizen came from the black church— because it was the only institution that black people had access to.

Today, churches are in neighborhoods where children are—after many institutions have abandoned those areas. Because of their credibility in the African American community, churches have the capacity to lead people in the community into supporting children.

Are there any specific accents that the African American experience and culture bring to asset building that might not be true in other cultures?

One of the realities of our country is that painful history of African Americans in this country—the powerlessness, the slavery, the whole baggage associated with the experience. Because of that history, it's very, very difficult for a majority of African Americans to trust leadership that is primarily white.

There is also such a hunger on the part of African Americans for connecting with their history, and learning about our history and heritage. It has been lacking for many reasons. When cultural features are integrated into a program, African Americans tend to trust it more and feel more relevance to the activity. I believe it is critical for every child not only to be aware of her or his culture, but to accept it and feel okay about it.

In other traditions there is some resistance to focusing on asset building because it is not an explicitly faith-based framework. Do you see that in the congregations you serve?

No. Every single African American pastor that I have talked to about children's development and the community's responsibility sees this as an important role of the church. But the challenges they face are the resources: How do I get volunteers? These are real issues. Churches need more resources. They need to have people or a person who can take this and move it.

As you look at the framework of assets, what are some of the challenges you see it offering to African American congregations?

The primary challenge is access because of the demands on the clergy's time and then preparing the clergy to articulate that message. Rallying the congregation to support asset building requires that the clergy understand, recognize the issues, and make a decision to support this ministry, and then bring together key people to come up with a plan for doing it. That takes time, and it takes technical assistance and tools to do it. It takes a lot more than we probably had thought to get them up and going.

Assets and Faith:

An Evangelical Christian Perspective

Condensed from an interview with Paul Fleischmann, executive director, National Network of Youth Ministries, San Diego, California.

Why do you think it is important for Evangelical Christian congregations to focus energy on building developmental assets?

Well, I think that they need to define their target in youth work. A lot of times, people in congregations view youth ministry as baby-sitting, or keeping the kids off the street, or keeping kids busy. But these developmental assets give you a target to shoot for, and I think that's very biblical. Philippians 3:14 talks about "I press toward the mark of the prize by thy calling." And 1 Corinthians 9:24-26 talks about running in a race with a view to winning. So we ought to have an aim and I think this gives us some targets to aim for.

What are some of the themes that you think about in Evangelical theology and understanding of scripture that connect with some of the core ideas in the 40 assets?

The scriptures talk a lot about a balanced life—Luke 2:52, where Jesus grew mentally, physically, socially, and spiritually. So I think that it fits well from an Evangelical standpoint. 1 Timothy 4:12 talks about being an example to the believers in word, in conversation, in faith, love, and purity. The assets are one way to give definition to what does it mean to be an example.

As you look at the framework of assets, what are some of the challenges you see it offering to Evangelical congregations?

From one perspective, the asset framework is problematic for many Evangelicals because faith is not explicit. We see no other way to develop some of the values. At the same time, the assets stretch us to think through some things that maybe the Bible doesn't specifically relate to, for instance, our work in schools or in the larger community.

The assets challenge Evangelicals to reach and help our youth by every means possible. And though we are committed to reaching people for Christ, there are a lot of aspects of a person's personal development that can be helped by people who may not share our faith. But by exposing people to others, their own faith can be challenged—as well as other aspects of their development.

What are some of the reasons you see that Evangelical congregations might resist getting involved with the asset-building approach?

Evangelical churches tend to stick to themselves. They almost see people of other faiths as, if not the enemy, at least someone so different from them that they will be hesitant to cooperate. But the assets name 40 qualities that we all can agree on and say there needs to be community support to help that happen, no matter what. However, there may not be the trust built up because people may hesitate to cooperate when they don't see their faith being shared by those that they're working with.

If we're going to reach young people, we have to draw upon all of the tremendous wealth that has been given to us. We have a responsibility to be fully aware and involved in our communities and to not be cloistered away in a corner just mixing with the people who talk and believe only as we do. Jesus freely mixed in, because he had a love for all people.

Sometimes in youth ministry, we forget to connect with social service agencies and other youth programs because they're not doing their work from a faith-based background. The assets give us a reason to cooperate.

Assets and Faith:

A Jewish Perspective

Condensed from an interview with Rabbi Hayim Herring, director of identity and continuity, Minneapolis Jewish Federation, Minneapolis, Minnesota.

Why do you think it's important for Jewish congregations to focus energy on building developmental assets?

In the Jewish community we always talk about kids being the future. I'd like to share a wonderful teaching about our responsibility to children.

According to a legend, when God wants to give the Torah—the five books of Moses—to the Jewish people, he asks for some proof that they're worthy of it. What, God asks, can serve as surety or collateral for receiving the Torah? First the people offer to God the ancestors, Abraham, Isaac, and Jacob. "They can be our surety." But God says that's not good enough. Then the people suggest the prophets, but God says, "Not good enough." So the people huddle together and come back to God: "Our children will be our guarantors." God then accepts the offer and gives them the Torah.

That story has always been a very, very powerful reminder about how kids really are tied up with the future. They are our guarantee for the future. So how can we not work on building these developmental assets?

How do you see the developmental assets being a resource for congregations and organizations in the Jewish movements?

I see them giving us a comprehensive framework for evaluating everything we do. The Jewish community does a number of things that fit with the asset model. In fact,

there are very Jewish values in these assets. For example, we involve our older adolescents in working with our younger adolescents. Education is something we really promote heavily. A commitment to learning, developing a positive identity, developing skills and social competencies—these are all things that happen for kids within a congregation.

In addition, the assets challenge us to develop more intergenerational structures that offer youth more access to adult role models and relationships. Most synagogues have atomized the family so that there are programs for kids and programs for older adults. There are lots of adults who could play those roles, but they're not used in that way because we've got the structure that puts the kids in the youth department off to one corner. It isn't as if the congregations aren't investing in youth. It's just that they're investing in the youth in a way that doesn't really maximize their connections with adults in the congregation.

What advice would you give to Jewish congregations about whether and how to get involved in interfaith efforts for asset building in the community?

One of the complexities the Jewish community faces is the extent to which we can promote the goal of building assets in the broader community while promoting a sense of Jewish identity and culture. We get alarmed when we look at patterns of interdating and intermarriage. Yet we are not just an isolated community, and our kids don't live that way. So we need to struggle with how to participate in the broader community without sending a message that you can date whomever you want. It's a challenge, but I think we can do it.

Assets and Faith:

A Mainline Protestant Perspective

Condensed from an interview with Dr. Kenda Creasy Dean, assistant professor of youth, church, and culture, Princeton Theological Seminary, Princeton, New Jersey.

Why is it important for mainline Protestant congregations to focus energy on building developmental assets?

The first reason is theological. Out of a response to God's grace, we have a mission to serve others and make the world a better place and try to pay attention to the holistic health of all people, young people included. John Wesley believed that you cannot adequately nourish the soul if you leave the body unnourished, so you've got to pay attention to the whole person.

The other reason is practical. Churches are the social institution most available to young people. Churches are in every community, and anywhere kids are, the church technically is there also. But whether it's acting as the church in that community remains to be seen.

What are some ways the asset-building framework helps mainline Protestant congregations think about the way they care for youth?

I like to use the analogy of shepherding when I talk about asset building. A shepherd has two jobs: to keep the sheep safe and to lead them home. I see asset building as a concrete way of thinking about what it means to "keep youth safe" on their journey through adolescence, so that we can lead them home to their identity in Jesus Christ.

There is a tendency for churches to err on the side of either keeping youth safe or leading them home. They're either into the existential kinds of salvation—bring them to the altar at whatever cost—or we are on the other side

where we are interested in trying to save the world, as though we are responsible for salvation all by ourselves. My understanding of the faithful path is pulling those two together.

What are some of the reasons you see that mainline Protestant congregations might resist getting involved with the asset-building approach?

I see two strands of resistance. The first has to do with our understanding of the church. When we discuss asset building in class, the room will divide in half. On one side will be those who believe asset building is true to who we are theologically. A woman in one class who was involved in street ministry saw the assets as a great gift. You don't start with "churchy" stuff to reach an unchurched kid, she argued. The assets gave her a language to talk about forms of ministry that she could relate to—and some research that showed that this work was important. On the other side of the room was a woman who thought that the church is called to be a unique institution. The church is called to lift up issues through a lens of faith, and the assets don't do that. To me, they are not contradictory points of view and there is truth in both. But they have to be worked through to address the resistance.

The other challenge is that people who are new to youth ministry don't think in terms of community cooperation. You're so busy trying to get your feet on the ground that you too easily write off the idea of building support on a broader scale. But if you last long enough, you finally figure out: "Wait a minute. I don't have to do all of this by myself." Then you become much more open to thinking outside the traditional boundaries.

Assets and Faith:

A Muslim Perspective

Condensed from an interview with Matthew Ramadan, vice president of the American Muslim Council, Minnesota Chapter, Minneapolis, Minnesota.

Why do you think it's important for Muslim congregations to focus their energy on building assets?

I think it's imperative. Our faith begins with the premise that everybody starts with a clean slate and with the best makeup. But then factors within the life of the person tend to bring us down, so we need to constantly work to kind of keep the good we started out with.

The Prophet Mohammed said every child is born in the natural state of excellence, but then environmental factors make that child become something else. Because we start from the best, it's a matter of holding on to that which is best in us, as opposed to trying to start from the worst and then put something good in.

What are some challenges that the developmental assets offer Muslim congregations?

Our greatest challenge is almost like the ostrich-with-its-head-in-the-sand attitude. Many Muslim communities and congregations don't really believe that our children can be affected negatively by society. So when our children are being affected—and they are being affected—we tend not recognize the problems. We need to realize that we have some social problems within the Muslim community that have never been addressed because we always felt: "Well, we've got everything all together. We don't have drugs in our community. We don't have teenage pregnancy in our community." We're having those things now.

One of my big concerns is that we tend to do well with the very young and then with adults. But we don't have a lot of things for the adolescents in between. So it's important for the Muslim community to make sure that we have the mentors and supports that young people need. This need is sometimes difficult to understand, because many people immigrated from places with strong structures and norms in place that guided young people. That's not true in this country.

What are some of the reasons Muslim congregations might resist getting involved in asset building?

I think the biggest reason for resistance will be an interpretation that this is just a Western way of doing things—particularly if we don't do a good job of translating the ideas into Islamic reality. The challenge is even greater when you begin talking about interfaith cooperation. It's important to remember that Muslims have been particular targets of attack from the Christians attempting to convert them. So building these relationships will take a lot of time and rebuilding trust.

How do you see the assets being a resource for Muslim congregations?

The developmental assets suggest the best possible way to do things. When people immigrate to this society from other cultures, they don't realize that we're saying some of the same things are important (such as community building and intergenerational relationships) that they thought were old-fashioned in their home country and culture. The assets may offer a way for us to reclaim and rebuild those traditional strengths within the U.S. context.

Assets and Faith:
A Roman Catholic Perspective

Condensed from an interview with John Roberto, director, Center for Ministry Development, Naugatuck, New York.

Why do you think it is important for Catholic congregations to focus energy on building assets?

The assets really are the building blocks for solid religious growth—total growth as a person that blends skills, values, religious knowledge, and religious behavior. For example, the positive values assets reflect the kind of gospel lifestyle that we are trying to build in young people. Not that everything is in the developmental assets, but they point to some of the foundational building blocks. That's why assets are an integral part of the new statement on youth ministry that was adopted by the U.S. Conference of Catholic Bishops [summer 1997].

The developmental assets have been important for your work in the Catholic Church. How have the assets shaped your understanding?

The developmental assets give people an image of what we are trying to do in ministry with adolescents. Of all the research on adolescents, it's the most practical, usable knowledge. Not only has it got a long tradition of research behind it, but when you present this information, people grab it. They get it. It's something that names people's experience and moves them ahead.

We've had a very strong emphasis on family for the last decade and a half in the Catholic Church. But then the developmental assets really named what we were trying to communicate to people: You just can't work with the kids. Every time you're with a young person, you work with that young person in the context of his or her family, in the context of the community, the school.

What are some of the reasons you think Catholic congregations might resist getting

involved in asset building, and what might you do to deal with that resistance?

This is almost a different language for parishes that conceive of their ministry solely as either social/recreational or strictly educational. The folks who get the broader picture make the easiest transition into understanding all the challenges and the potential within the developmental assets framework. The people who are really centered on a program or on a narrow need—like social/recreational or just religious knowledge or reception of the sacrament—have the hardest struggle to see a broader context for ministry, even though that's what the church is teaching. For them it's a real struggle to move beyond that.

What advice would you give to Catholic congregations about whether and how to get involved in asset-building efforts in their community?

The natural fear is that people will lose their own congregational identity or denominational identity. In addition, people see it as an add-on, rather than a way of working. When churches have adopted it as a way of working, it becomes essential to what they do. They don't seem to have any problem between saying what things they do within their congregation and what things they do interchurch or interfaith. But if you don't have a comprehensive vision of what you're trying to do and if you don't have the grounding that the assets give you, you will have a harder time partnering.

My hope is that the assets will help move people toward more of a community-wide partnership model—where the whole congregation is seen as needing to be in ministry with adolescents and that congregations and synagogues need to work together for all the kids. If we can get to that model, this research will have done immeasurable good.

How Developmental Assets
Connect to Youth Workers' Priorities

A Search Institute survey of 500 religious youth workers from many faith traditions found that most of them share youth development goals, but they are dissatisfied with their ability to achieve those goals.[14] This chart show the connections of many of these top goals of youth workers to Search Institute's framework of 40 developmental assets.

GOAL IS "VERY IMPORTANT"	ACHIEVE GOAL "VERY WELL"	CONNECTIONS TO DEVELOPMENTAL ASSETS
Helping youth apply faith to daily decisions — 88%	25%	Asset #32: Planning and decision making
Nurturing a lifelong commitment — 88%	22%	Asset #39: Sense of purpose
Providing a safe and caring place for youth — 84%	64%	Asset #10: Safety, plus a caring climate (cf. #5)
Developing young people's skills and values — 81%	24%	Assets #26-31: Positive values; #32–36: Social competencies
Keeping youth involved in the congregation — 78%	21%	Asset #19: Religious community
Building caring relationships with other youth — 77%	30%	Asset #15: Positive peer influence
Encouraging self-respect and dignity — 76%	35%	Assets #37–40: Positive identity
Providing positive activities to help youth avoid negative behaviors — 69%	43%	Asset #18: Youth programs; Asset # 19: Religious community
Reaching out to serve youth at risk — 68%	9%	Potentially all assets
Helping youth build caring relationships with adults — 65%	25%	Asset #3: Other adult relationships
Nurturing a commitment to service in youth — 64%	22%	Assets #7–10: Empowerment; Asset #26: Caring

In short, congregations do have tremendous potential in the lives of youth—and many youth and adults can attest to the life-transforming influence of their congregation on their lives. But too often that potential is neglected, unrecognized, and untapped. Like the rest of our society, many congregations have lost a vision for being—or becoming—the kind of community that shapes and transforms young people's lives.

What Does an Asset-Building Congregation Look Like?

Suppose a congregation were intentionally to focus on building the 40 crucial developmental assets. What would it look like? How would people interact? What emphases and programs would it have in place? At the beginning of this chapter, we offered a scenario of how an asset-building congregation might look to an adult. It may be even more powerful, however, to imagine what it might feel like to

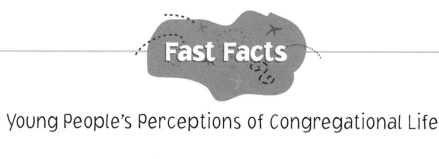

Young People's Perceptions of Congregational Life

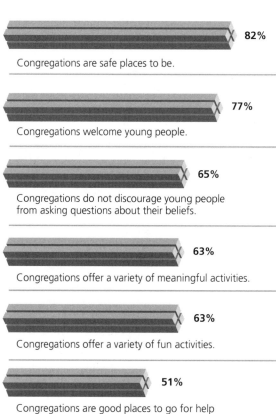

82%

Congregations are safe places to be.

77%

Congregations welcome young people.

65%

Congregations do not discourage young people from asking questions about their beliefs.

63%

Congregations offer a variety of meaningful activities.

63%

Congregations offer a variety of fun activities.

51%

Congregations are good places to go for help about serious issues like alcohol, other drugs, or sex.

As part of its Uniting Congregations for Youth Development initiative, Search Institute surveyed 1,100 young people in Minneapolis, Minnesota, Durham, North Carolina, and St. Louis, Missouri, about their perceptions of congregations in their community. Most of the youth surveyed were active in a congregation. Here are the percentages of youth who agree that each statement is true about congregations in their community.

a young person (let's call her Anita) when she participates in worship, education, and other congregational activities.

The asset-building commitment would be apparent as soon as Anita met the first person, a greeter. This week it's a senior citizen. Sometimes it's another teenager. As always, Anita is greeted warmly. In fact, many people in the congregation greet her by name and several adults ask her about the school test she had been worried about the week before.

As she walks toward the worship center, Anita notices some younger children leaning precariously over a stair railing. She doesn't hesitate to ask them to stop; the congregation has clear expectations of how everyone is responsible for looking out for each other's safety.

Youth are included

When she walks into the worship center, Anita is torn. Should she go sit with the group of youth who are clustered near the front on the left? Should she sit with her family? Or should she go sit with the Jacksons? They are always so warm and caring to her. This week, she opts to sit with the other youth.

As she sits down, Anita glances at the bulletin. One of her friends will be assisting with readings this week. The sermon will include stories and examples that relate directly to her and her life. And an intergenerational group will be providing the music.

As Anita reads through the announcements in the worship bulletin, she notices a number of places where she can get involved. An upcoming service project for families to do together interests her because she remembers how fun it was to be part of the intergenerational paint-a-thon this past summer. She's also interested in joining the youth council and notes that the deadline for applications is coming up. The updates section of the bulletin announces that the congregation has joined a coalition with other organizations that are coordinating after-school activities for children and youth in the community. Anita isn't surprised; her congregation sees itself as a resource to the community's young people.

Youth receive guidance

As she's walking into the youth-group meeting room later that week, the youth leader is just getting started. She asks group members to name some of the tough decisions they're facing right now. In the midst of the responses, Thomas, who is usually quiet, blurts out that he is trying to decide whether he should go to a party where people will be drinking alcohol. Everybody listens carefully as he explains that some school friends are putting a lot of pressure on him to go out partying every weekend. When he says no, they tease him mercilessly. He doesn't know how much more of it he can take. Maybe he should go just to get them off his back.

As Thomas finishes, Andrea, who is sitting next to him, gives him an affirming hug, and other kids ask questions. Pretty soon, the whole group is helping Thomas weigh his options. By the end of the discussion, Thomas feels pretty good about trying some new approaches to resisting the pressure he's feeling. He will let the group know how it goes when he comes back next week.

This illustration only scratches the surface of what an asset-building congregation could be like. It's important to note that this congregation could be any size. It wouldn't necessarily need to have a large youth group, and it doesn't have to have a large (or any) staff. It could just as easily be an inner-city congregation as a

All Sizes of Congregations Have Asset-Building Potential

Sometimes the comprehensive vision of asset building leads to the conclusion that asset building is more suited to large congregations. However, congregations of all sizes have potential for asset building. Here are some of the opportunities and challenges for asset building in congregations of different sizes.[15]

	ASSET-BUILDING OPPORTUNITIES	ASSET-BUILDING CHALLENGES
The Family Congregation *Average attendance:* Fewer than 50 People are bonded by relationships, not programs. Congregation has an informal structure, but a clear hierarchy, with a matriarch or patriarch as "gatekeeper." Special events are more important than programs.	• Everyone knows everyone. • Leaders and members tend to focus on relationships, not programs. • Congregational activities tend to be intergenerational. • Everyone has a chance to participate and contribute. • Festivals and other special events bring generations together.	• A small or nonexistent youth group limits opportunities for peer-to-peer relationships. • One or two leaders can control the congregation, making change difficult if they don't support it. • New young people may have trouble being assimilated or "adopted" into the "family." • Clergy generally work part-time, and there is often a high turnover rate.
The Clergy-Centered Congregation *Average attendance:* From 50 to 150 Two or three "clans" operate as extended family units. The congregation operates like a wheel, with the clergyperson at the hub of all activities.	• Young people have opportunities to build a relationship with the pastor, rabbi, or other leader. • Small enough so that youth can know everyone, but large enough that they can be selective in forming close relationships. • Potential for building caring relationships with more adults.	• Clergy often lead the youth group, which divides their attention. • It may be difficult for new young people to become assimilated into one of the "clans." • Because the clergyperson is at the center of all activity, asset building cannot move forward without her or his support and leadership.
The Program Congregation *Average attendance:* From 150 to 350 A more democratic structure, with work being shared more among members. People often connect to a specific area of the congregation, not the whole congregation.	• Often have paid staff to lead or coordinate youth activities. • Can offer numerous opportunities to meet specific interests and needs of youth and parents. • The congregation often has leadership and influence in the community.	• Tend to emphasize age-specific programming, making intergenerational contact less frequent and natural. • The youth program can become completely disconnected from other areas of the congregation. • Running lots of programs can consume resources that might otherwise support outreach.
The Corporation Congregation *Average attendance:* More than 350 Many specialized activities and programs characterize these congregations. Each area often has its own paid leadership and decision-making process.	• Lots of opportunities to meet specific needs and interests of youth and parents. • Often organize into small groups that provide strong relationships with compatible peers and adults. • Can have staff trained in specific areas of youth work. • Congregation has influence in the community and resources (people, facilities, money) to support asset-building efforts in the community.	• Members may not feel responsible for youth, since they can hire staff to address needs. • It can be easy for a young person to get "lost" and not form strong connections in the congregation. • If the youth program becomes "full service" (providing youth-only worship services, etc.), youth may have no opportunities for building relationships with adults beyond youth staff and volunteers.

suburban or rural one. While each congregation will have its own dynamics and emphases, all congregations can become asset-building congregations.

Each congregation and each faith tradition will shape its commitment to asset building based on its history, traditions, and culture. Tipsheet 1 highlights both challenges and opportunities for typical congregations of various sizes.

Transforming Youth Work Through Asset Building

Rebuilding the asset foundation for youth is not a matter of adding a new program or buying a different curriculum package. Rather, it involves a fundamental shift in the way we view young people and how we serve them in congregations.

In his book *The Seven Habits of Highly Effective People*, Stephen R. Covey writes: "It becomes obvious that if we want to make relatively minor changes in our lives, we can perhaps appropriately focus on our attitudes and behaviors. But if we want to make significant, quantum change, we need to work on our basic paradigms."[16] (See Tipsheet 2.)

Such a shift in thinking is exactly what needs to happen regarding today's young people. Instead of viewing adolescence as a disease to be avoided, we need to see it as an exciting, sometimes challenging, growth experience.

Instead of seeing youth as problems in our communities, we need to view them as resources with energy, fresh ideas, and much to contribute.

Instead of putting all our energy into trying to keep youth from doing something wrong, we need to provide them with the support, skills, opportunities, and values they need to do things right.

And instead of waiting to address youth needs when they erupt as crises, we need to provide young people with the foundation they need to make wise choices so that challenges will be fewer and more manageable.

The asset framework can be a lens for examining congregations' roles in the lives of youth—both those in the congregation and those in the community. Congregations can use this framework to strengthen their work with youth in at least five ways:

1. A shared vision and focus

Too often, congregational youth programs are like old buildings that through the decades are patched, repaired, or remodeled to the point that they are no longer recognizable. Congregations add a new idea here and resurrect an old idea there, depending on who is interested in what at the moment. At some point, it's important to step back and consider the big picture. Why are we doing all this stuff? What are we trying to accomplish?

The asset framework gives a lens or filter through which to set priorities, plan, and make choices. Instead of operating a grab bag of programs, congregations using the assets can see how the many areas of work are interrelated. As John Roberto of the Center for Ministry Development says, the assets "give people an image of what we are trying to do in ministry with adolescents."

While most congregations would want to integrate language from their own faith tradition into a purpose statement for youth work, the vision of asset building offers a good starting place. Many specific programmatic activities for youth, from recreation to formal education to counseling services to leadership development efforts, can be built upon this framework.

This benefit of a shared asset-building vision extends beyond the congregation. The framework is relevant and useful to a broad range of institutions and perspectives. Thus, it provides common ground for congregations, schools, government agencies, community youth organizations, and others to begin talking about their contributions to the asset base of young people.

2. Affirmation and celebration

When I tell people in congregations about the importance of building assets, I often hear people say, "This is really affirming. We've been building assets for years, and we didn't even know it!"

It's true. Congregations have always offered young people many of the positive things that are identified in the framework of assets: caring relationships, a sense of purpose, opportunities to lead and serve, and many other opportunities. What's new is that these themes are made concrete and specific through the assets. Furthermore, the research shows that these things are *essential* in young people's lives. Thus, the asset framework affirms and celebrates actions that may have been undervalued or taken for granted.

T I P S H E E T 2

What's Different About Asset-Building Congregations?

When congregations adopt an asset-building perspective, it can change many things about they way they work with youth and families. Here are some of the ways it may be different.

COMMON APPROACHES TO RELIGIOUS YOUTH WORK	AN ASSET-BUILDING APPROACH TO YOUTH WORK
• Program is made up of many seemingly unrelated activities without a clear mission or purpose.	• The framework helps to integrate diverse activities into a larger framework of positive goals.
• It's often unclear what to do in the program that will make a difference in the lives of youth.	• The framework gives concrete things the congregation can do to make a lasting difference for youth.
• The focus is primarily on youth-to-youth relationships.	• The focus broadens to building intergenerational community.
• Children and youth in the congregation are the responsibility of the youth leaders, volunteers, and parents.	• Everyone in the congregation recognizes her or his responsibility for children and youth and her or his power to build assets.
• Parents are only superficially involved in the youth program (providing refreshments or being informed).	• Parents are active partners in the youth program, through family activities and parent education.
• Energy is consumed by reacting to problems after they occur.	• Energy is put into nurturing skills and values that help to avoid problems before they start.
• The focus is almost exclusively on building the congregation's own youth program.	• The congregation becomes committed to reaching out to all youth in the community by cooperating with other sectors.
• The youth worker is primarily a program leader, planner, and mentor for youth in the congregation.	• The youth worker also serves as a networker and voice for youth in the community.

From Glenn A. Seefeldt and Eugene C. Roehlkepartain, *Tapping the Potential: Discovering Congregations' Role in Building Assets in Youth* (Minneapolis: Search Institute, 1995).

3. Support and justification

Because the asset framework affirms the importance of congregations' involvement in the lives of youth, it also can be a tool to gain support for your efforts. The assets give you a way to say, "What we're doing is important, and there's research that shows it."

4. Call to action

Youth workers have been given a huge task. In many cases, they are asked to provide young people with everything they need—relationships, teaching, guidance, modeling, activities, and much more. Asset building reminds us that hiring a youth worker does not get the whole community of faith "off the hook" in caring for young people. Building assets calls everyone in the congregation to join in the commitment to care for young people.

The asset framework also helps everyone see that they can play a positive role in the lives of youth. Because society has focused so heavily on the role of parents and professionals, other people—many of whom are deeply interested and concerned—have trouble seeing any significant role for themselves. The assets remind people of the simple, positive things they can do to make a difference.

5. Challenge and growth

Finally, the asset framework challenges congregations to reflect on and improve how they connect with and support young people. Most congregations already create opportunities and build relationships that nurture assets. But most congregations do not provide the well-rounded, positive environment and opportunities that consistently and systematically build assets for youth. If they did, I believe congregations would not face the exodus of young people that is common across most faith traditions. And young people would report much more positive experiences within their congregations than they currently do.

For example, while a particular congregation may be very good at offering young people a caring environment, it may not have considered the importance of also empowering young people through service and leadership. Thus, the asset model helps you shape congregational life to address the whole foundation for healthy development, not just a few components.

Sometimes the asset-building emphasis helps congregations see simple ways they inadvertently slight youth. For instance, many congregations have newsletters that highlight activities for the "whole congregation." But too often, those activities really are just for adults. The assets help them think about ways to ensure that everyone is truly welcome.

Getting Started with Asset Building

This chapter has outlined a challenging vision for congregational youth work. In the chapters that follow, we'll look in more depth at the assets and their implications for congregations. But you don't have to read through the whole book to begin asset building. Here are six specific things you can start doing to begin the asset-building journey.

Live

Live like an asset builder. It's hard to begin thinking about creating an asset-building congregation until you've done some asset building on your own. How can you—on your own—begin building assets? Whatever role you play in your congregation, community, neighborhood, or professional life, there are plenty of places to start.

For example, if you're a pastor or rabbi, consider being more intentional about greeting young people after a worship service. If you're a youth worker, consider spending time talking one-to-one with young people about the values that are important to them and to your tradition. If you are a parent, maybe it's simply making a commitment to being home for dinner with your family every night.

Learn

On one level, asset building seems simple. But the closer you look, the more depth you discover. So take time to learn about the assets. Also, learn about your congregation—its culture, its history, and the dynamics that would shape your asset-building efforts. This background will help as you begin exploring with others the potential for asset building in your congregation.

Listen

As you begin thinking about the potential of asset building for your congregation, it's important to listen to others—young people, members and leaders of the congregation, volunteers in the youth program, people in the community. They can help shape your sense of priorities and your cautions or concerns. Sometimes when we get excited about an idea, we start planning how to implement something new. It's important to take time to listen to ensure that your ideas are consistent with other people's experiences and priorities.

Using the asset-building checklist (see Worksheet 1) can help jump-start a conversation on how your congregation already builds assets and how asset building fits with your congregation's heritage and resources.

Link

Don't try to introduce asset building into your congregation by yourself. Find other interested, supportive people who will link with you. Share in the vision, the ideas, and the problem solving that will inevitably be needed.

Lobby

At some point, you'll want to get influential people to support asset building. For example, in some congregations, gaining the active support of a senior clergyperson (pastor, rabbi, imam) is essential for any effort to gain momentum. To begin with, it's probably enough just to talk informally with influential leaders to gauge their level of interest and to identify any concerns they may have. They can also help you identify other key leaders who can greatly influence your congregation's support for asset building.

Launch

Try some asset-building activities to see how they go. For example, you could lead a youth meeting that focuses on the assets or preach a sermon on the topic. Maybe you want to offer some kind of parent education related to assets. (Later chapters elaborate on these and other ideas.) See how well your initial efforts are received. It can tell you a lot about what will or won't work as you move forward.

Beginning the Journey

Becoming intentional about building assets in your congregation will not suddenly transform your congregation for youth or their families. It will take some time to build support for the ideas, internalize what asset building means for the congregation, and then gradually integrate the assets into many areas of congregational life.

In some ways, it would be much easier if asset building were a specific curriculum you could purchase and then just implement. But it's not. Asset building is more a way of life, a way of thinking about all that we do for young people in and through congregations. That makes it a challenging, sometimes difficult journey. But it is an important journey to begin—for the sake of all kids.

An Asset-Building Checklist for Congregations

How does the idea of asset building fit with your congregation's youth work? What assets do you already build? Which ones do you see great potential for building? Use this checklist to reflect on these questions with youth leaders, congregation staff, young people, parents, and others in the congregation.

This checklist includes the names and definitions of the 40 developmental assets identified by Search Institute. First, check all the assets that your congregation already builds effectively.

(Be sure to think beyond the traditional youth program to the ways the congregation supports families, builds intergenerational community, and reaches out to the community at large.) Celebrate the things you are already doing to build assets.

Then go through and mark all the assets your congregation is well positioned to build because those assets fit with your congregation's identity, mission, and resources. Talk together about what areas may be priorities for you.

Building This Asset Fits with Our Congregation's Identity, Mission, and Resources

Asset Name and Definition

Our Congregation Already Builds This Asset Effectively

Support

1. **Family support**—Family life provides high levels of love and support. ☐ ☐
2. **Positive family communication**—Young person and her or his parent(s) communicate positively, and young person is willing to seek advice and counsel from parents. ☐ ☐
3. **Other adult relationships**—Young person receives support from three or more nonparent adults. ☐ ☐
4. **Caring neighborhood**—Young person experiences caring neighbors. ☐ ☐
5. **Caring school climate**—School provides a caring, encouraging environment. ☐ ☐
6. **Parent involvement in schooling**—Parent(s) are actively involved in helping young person succeed in school. ☐ ☐

Empowerment

7. **Community values youth**—Young person perceives that adults in the community value youth. ☐ ☐
8. **Youth as resources**—Young people are given useful roles in the community. ☐ ☐
9. **Service to others**—Young person serves in the community one hour or more per week. ☐ ☐
10. **Safety**—Young person feels safe at home, at school, and in the neighborhood. ☐ ☐

Boundaries and Expectations

11. **Family boundaries**—Family has clear rules and consequences and monitors the young person's whereabouts. ☐ ☐
12. **School boundaries**—School provides clear rules and consequences. ☐ ☐
13. **Neighborhood boundaries**—Neighbors take responsibility for monitoring young people's behavior. ☐ ☐
14. **Adult role models**—Parent(s) and other adults model positive, responsible behavior. ☐ ☐
15. **Positive peer influence**—Young person's best friends model responsible behavior. ☐ ☐
16. **High expectations**—Both parent(s) and teachers encourage the young person to do well. ☐ ☐

Constructive Use of Time

17. **Creative activities**—Young person spends three or more hours per week in lessons or practice in music, theater, or other arts. ☐ ☐
18. **Youth programs**—Young person spends three or more hours per week in sports, clubs, or organizations at school or in the community. ☐ ☐

An Asset-Building Checklist for Congregations, Continued

Asset Name and Definition	Building This Asset Fits with Our Congregation's Identity, Mission, and Resources	Our Congregation Already Builds This Asset Effectively

19. **Religious community**—Young person spends one or more hours per week in activities in a religious institution. ☐ ☐

20. **Time at home**—Young person is out with friends "with nothing special to do" two or fewer nights per week. ☐ ☐

Commitment to Learning

21. **Achievement motivation**—Young person is motivated to do well in school. ☐ ☐

22. **School engagement**—Young person is actively engaged in learning. ☐ ☐

23. **Homework**—Young person reports doing at least one hour of homework every school day. ☐ ☐

24. **Bonding to school**—Young person cares about her or his school. ☐ ☐

25. **Reading for pleasure**—Young person reads for pleasure three or more hours per week. ☐ ☐

Positive Values

26. **Caring**—Young person places high value on helping other people. ☐ ☐

27. **Equality and social justice**—Young person places high value on promoting equality and reducing hunger and poverty. ☐ ☐

28. **Integrity**—Young person acts on convictions and stands up for her or his beliefs. ☐ ☐

29. **Honesty**—Young person "tells the truth even when it is not easy." ☐ ☐

30. **Responsibility**—Young person accepts and takes personal responsibility. ☐ ☐

31. **Restraint**—Young person believes it is important not to be sexually active or to use alcohol or other drugs. ☐ ☐

Social Competencies

32. **Planning and decision making**—Young person knows how to plan ahead and make choices. ☐ ☐

33. **Interpersonal competence**—Young person has empathy, sensitivity, and friendship skills. ☐ ☐

34. **Cultural competence**—Young person has knowledge of and comfort with people of different cultural/racial/ethnic backgrounds. ☐ ☐

35. **Resistance skills**—Young person can resist negative peer pressure and dangerous situations. ☐ ☐

36. **Peaceful conflict resolution**—Young person seeks to resolve conflict nonviolently. ☐ ☐

Positive Identity

37. **Personal power**—Young person feels he or she has control over "things that happen to me." ☐ ☐

38. **Self-esteem**—Young person reports having a high self-esteem. ☐ ☐

39. **Sense of purpose**—Young person reports that "my life has a purpose." ☐ ☐

40. **Positive view of personal future**—Young person is optimistic about her or his personal future. ☐ ☐

Helping Youth Grow Up Healthy:
A New Vision for Congregations

Key Points

- Developmental assets are 40 building blocks of healthy development for all youth. (See Tipsheet 3.)

- There are five reasons why congregations should focus attention on building these assets.

  1. They have a powerful influence in young people's lives

  2. Most young people experience too few of these assets.

  3. Because assets focus on relationships and character, congregations of all faiths have tremendous potential to build assets for youth in the congregation and the community.

  4. Asset building is integral to the mission of congregations from all major faith traditions.

  5. Most congregations do not live up to their asset-building potential.

- Assets offer congregations a shared vision and focus, affirmation and celebration, support and justification, a call to action, and challenge and growth.

Questions for Reflection and Discussion

- What parts of the asset-building vision excite and energize you?

- How does the asset framework affirm or challenge the way your congregation cares for youth?

- What do you see asset building offering your congregation?

- What challenges do you anticipate in introducing assets to your congregation?

Suggestions for Getting Started

- Decide one thing you personally will do differently because you know about the assets.

- Talk with others in your congregation about the assets. Get their buy-in.

- Ask young people to tell about their own experiences, then listen without judging.

- Study the assets in light of your faith tradition. Show people ways your congregation is already committed to building assets.

C H A P T E R   2

Developmental Assets

A Framework for Focusing Congregational Life

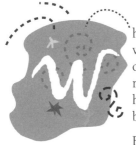

hen dinosaur teeth were first discovered in 1820 by Dr. Gideon Mantell, no one was quite sure what they were. As more bones were discovered, Dr. Mantell and other scientists began piecing them together into giant reptiles. Their work was revolutionary, but not always accurate. Dr. Mantell, for example, gave the creature he named "Iguanadon" a hornlike nose, using a bone that was later discovered to be a thumb spike.

Furthermore, our understanding of dinosaurs keeps changing as paleontologists explore and experiment. If, for example, you thought the Brontosaurus was the largest dinosaur, you'd be wrong. There were actually two larger dinosaurs: the recently found Seismosaurus and Ultrasaurus. And, by the way, the Brontosaurus has been renamed Apatasaurus!

In congregations, when new needs or issues arise, we often feel pressure to add more "bones" to the "skeletons" of programs created in the past. The result is that we get busier and busier and feel more and more fragmented in our efforts. Adding on to what we already have doesn't necessarily spell progress.

In some senses, the framework of developmental assets represents an effort to reconstruct a "skeleton" of positive human development. That is, it draws together into an understandable framework many sources of information about the positive things young people need in their lives. It doesn't necessarily identify all the "bones," and it is not the final or only helpful construct for understanding young people's needs. Yet it does provide a powerful model—a way of looking at youth development—that accurately reflects what we know, both scientifically and intuitively, to be true about young people's needs. This chapter gives a deeper understanding of these assets and explores their major implications for congregations.

Now that we've seen the power of the 40 assets and their relative absence in the lives of most adolescents (see Chapter 1), let's explore the eight categories of external and internal assets in more detail. A chart within each category shows the percentages of youth who report experiencing each asset. (For the definition of each asset, refer to Tipsheet 3 or the asset chart at the back of this book.) As we survey the assets, we will suggest some potential roles for congregations in building them.

Search Institute's 40 Developmental Assets

Search Institute has identified the following building blocks of healthy development that help
young people grow up healthy, caring, and responsible.

EXTERNAL ASSETS

Support

1. **Family support**—Family life provides high levels of love and support.

2. **Positive family communication**—Young person and her or his parent(s) communicate positively, and young person is willing to seek advice and counsel from parent(s).

3. **Other adult relationships**—Young person receives support from three or more nonparent adults.

4. **Caring neighborhood**—Young person experiences caring neighbors.

5. **Caring school climate**—School provides a caring, encouraging environment.

6. **Parent involvement in schooling**—Parent(s) are actively involved in helping young person succeed in school.

Empowerment

7. **Community values youth**—Young person perceives that adults in the community value youth.

8. **Youth as resources**—Young people are given useful roles in the community.

9. **Service to others**—Young person serves in the community one hour or more per week.

10. **Safety**—Young person feels safe at home, at school, and in the neighborhood.

Boundaries and Expectations

11. **Family boundaries**—Family has clear rules and consequences and monitors the young person's whereabouts.

12. **School boundaries**—School provides clear rules and consequences.

13. **Neighborhood boundaries**—Neighbors take responsibility for monitoring young people's behavior.

14. **Adult role models**—Parent(s) and other adults model positive, responsible behavior.

15. **Positive peer influence**—Young person's best friends model responsible behavior.

16. **High expectations**—Parent(s) and teachers encourage the young person to do well.

Constructive Use of Time

17. **Creative activities**—Young person spends three or more hours per week in lessons or practice in music, theater, or other arts.

18. **Youth programs**—Young person spends three or more hours per week in sports, clubs, or organizations at school or in the community.

19. **Religious community**—Young person spends one or more hours per week in activities in a religious institution.

20. **Time at home**—Young person is out with friends "with nothing special to do" two or fewer nights per week.

INTERNAL ASSETS

Commitment to Learning

21. **Achievement motivation**—Young person is motivated to do well in school.

22. **School engagement**—Young person is actively engaged in learning.

23. **Homework**—Young person reports doing at least one hour of homework every school day.

24. **Bonding to school**—Young person cares about her or his school.

25. **Reading for pleasure**—Young person reads for pleasure three or more hours per week.

Positive Values

26. **Caring**—Young person places high value on helping other people.

27. **Equality and social justice**—Young person places high value on promoting equality and reducing hunger and poverty.

28. **Integrity**—Young person acts on convictions and stands up for her or his beliefs.

29. **Honesty**—Young person "tells the truth even when it is not easy."

30. **Responsibility**—Young person accepts and takes personal responsibility.

31. **Restraint**—Young person believes it is important not to be sexually active or to use alcohol or other drugs.

Social Competencies

32. **Planning and decision making**—Young person knows how to plan ahead and make choices.

33. **Interpersonal competence**—Young person has empathy, sensitivity, and friendship skills.

34. **Cultural competence**—Young person has knowledge of and comfort with people of different cultural/racial/ethnic backgrounds.

35. **Resistance skills**—Young person can resist negative peer pressure and dangerous situations.

36. **Peaceful conflict resolution**—Young person seeks to resolve conflict nonviolently.

Positive Identity

37. **Personal power**—Young person feels he or she has control over "things that happen to me."

38. **Self-esteem**—Young person reports having a high self-esteem.

39. **Sense of purpose**—Young person reports that "my life has a purpose."

40. **Positive view of personal future**—Young person is optimistic about her or his personal future.

Factors That Shaped the List of Assets

Before exploring specific assets, it's useful to understand a little more about how they were selected. Here are some key reasons why these particular assets are included in the framework.

1. The assets are accessible.

Many people note that the asset framework doesn't directly address issues of poverty, economic security, and other economic infrastructure issues. While these are important issues, the selected assets focus on the "human development" infrastructure. They were selected because they are accessible: it is in the hands of everyday people to nurture these assets through caring relationships and meaningful interaction. These assets are things we actually *can do*. They need to go hand in hand with economic development, yet do not depend on anything but our own willingness and ability to act.

2. The assets are supported by research and experience.

There are many more than 40 things that are good for youth. Those included in the asset model either have a strong research foundation or have been singled out by youth workers or other practitioners as particularly powerful. Still, many things that are good for youth are not included. Some have not yet been identified or fully understood; others are more deeply rooted in certain cultural or religious traditions.

3. The assets are inclusive.

A number of people from the religious community—many of whom see the assets as a valuable framework—question why religious faith is not listed as one of the assets (other than the inclusion of involvement in a faith community as a constructive use of time asset).

The assets were designed to form a framework for healthy development that will be widely accepted in many settings, including schools, community organizations, community-wide coalitions, congregations, and others. Including assets that focus specifically on religious beliefs and practices would limit how and where the framework could be used. For example, these assets would not be appropriate tools for public schools, where most data on young people's assets are gathered.

Similarly, it would be difficult to identify and measure the specific faith assets that could be widely shared across faith traditions and cultural and ideological perspectives. For example, while some religious traditions consider prayer to be a central spiritual discipline, it is much less important in others. As a result, inclusion of faith-specific assets within this basic framework would only serve to perpetuate differences and fragmentation.

Finally, there are also philosophical reasons for not identifying specific faith assets in the list, since faith can infuse all or most of the assets. For example, young people's boundaries and values are often significantly shaped by their faith commitments. Naming separate faith assets would give the false impression that young people's lives are compartmentalized, with faith being just one of the compartments rather than a filter or worldview through which young people experience all dimensions of life.

Now, let's take a closer look at the eight categories of developmental assets.

The External Assets

External assets are positive experiences that surround youth with the support, empowerment, boundaries and expectations, and opportunities for constructive use of time they need to guide them to make healthy choices. These experiences and opportunities should be provided by each of many socializing systems in a community, including families, schools, congregations, youth organizations, and neighbors.

The Support Assets

Support refers to the ways people show love, affirmation, and acceptance to young people. Sometimes we show support with a hug or other appropriate touch. Sometimes we show it by listening to them, including them, showing interest in them, and remembering things that are important to them.

While the asset framework names six support assets, young people need to experience support wherever they go and in all their relationships. Certainly they need to experience it at home, as suggested by the first two assets: family support and positive family communication. (When they don't, the challenge of providing support is even greater for others in their life.)

The support assets particularly highlight the need for positive intergenerational relationships outside the immediate family (asset #3). Adults can nurture informal relationships with youth in their neighborhood (asset #4), in the congregation, at work, and many other places. In addition, intentional mentoring relationships can be invaluable sources of support for youth.

While most young people report having caring parents, they are much less likely to say that other adults "really care about me," according to a survey of 10- to 17-year-olds by the National Commission on Children.[1] Here are the percentages of youth who indicate that each group of people really cares about them:

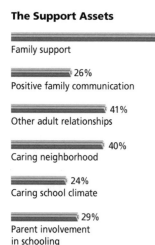

The Support Assets

64%
Family support

26%
Positive family communication

41%
Other adult relationships

40%
Caring neighborhood

24%
Caring school climate

29%
Parent involvement in schooling

- Grandparent   43%
- Aunt, uncle, cousin, or other relative   41%
- Teacher or coach   33%
- Adult friend or neighbor   16%
- Youth group leader, or priest, rabbi, minister, imam   15%

In addition to relationships with caring individuals, young people need to experience caring institutions. This we measure by the asset of caring school climate. Similar assets could be added for caring congregation, caring youth club, and other settings where young people spend their time. Everywhere young people go, they need to feel welcomed, valued, and supported.

Congregations have the potential to increase young people's experiences of support in all three areas: family, intergenerational relationships, and caring institutions. For families, it may mean educating parents about new ways to show support to teenagers who no longer respond to the ways they were supported when they were younger. Members of the congregation represent an often-untapped source of intergenerational relationships, both formal and informal. Finally, congregations can examine their own culture to discover whether young people feel welcomed and cared for when they participate.

In fact, providing some forms of support may already be a strength for congregations. Search Institute's study of religious youth workers found that 64 percent say their congregation does "very well" at providing a "safe and caring place" for youth. However, only 30 percent say they do very well at helping youth build caring relationships with other youth. And only one in four (25 percent) say they do very well at helping youth build caring relationships with adults in the congregation.[2]

The Empowerment Assets

Young people need to feel valued, to know that they are important. They need opportunities to contribute through leadership and service. The empowerment assets highlight this need, focusing on community perceptions of youth and opportunities for youth to contribute meaningfully to society. In addition, a sense of empowerment is only possible in an environment where young people feel safe.

The Empowerment Assets

20%
Community values youth

24%
Youth as resources

50%
Service to others

55%
Safety

Empowerment can occur in many ways. Part of it grows out of supportive relationships; when young people are noticed and paid attention to, they are more likely to feel valued. In addition, they need opportunities to contribute in acts of service and leadership. Service and leadership are two important themes in asset building, not only because they are assets in and of themselves, but because they provide opportunities to nurture many other assets, from building supportive relationships to teaching important social competencies.

Through a wide range of service and social action projects and leadership opportunities, many congregations actively give youth these kinds of empowering experiences. Efforts begin by providing a climate that is both physically and emotionally safe, where youth feel comfortable risking and possibly failing. In addition, there are dozens of ways to involve youth in service and leadership, inside the congregation as well as in the community.

The Boundaries and Expectations Assets

For healthy development, boundaries and expectations need to complement support and empowerment. Young people need clear signals about what behavior is expected and what is unacceptable—what is "in bounds" and what is "out of bounds." Once set, boundaries need to be monitored and enforced with appropriate and consistent discipline. These boundaries begin at home and should extend to other settings where young people spend their time, including neighborhood, school, congregation, and places of employment and entertainment.

Two key sources of boundaries are adults who model responsible behavior and peers who exert a positive influence. In some senses, expecting young people to live within boundaries is an extension of the support that they need from caring adults and peers. Unfortunately, too few young people have adults in their lives who are willing to share their wisdom by articulating boundaries. Philosopher Robert Bly contends that, in this age of self-indulgence, adults refuse to articulate their wisdom about what matters, choosing instead to extend their own adolescence indefinitely.[3]

Along with promoting healthy boundaries, it's important to have high expectations for young people. High expectations challenge young people to excel and can enhance their sense of being capable. While high expectations are typically associated with education, we need to have high standards in other areas of life: in their social relationships, how they spend time, and how they live their beliefs.

Building Support Assets:
"We Are a Community at the Synagogue"

North Shore Synagogue in Syosset, New York, has a large youth program that serves close to 400 youth in a congregation of 900 families. As a result, a lot of Youth Director Jeff Green's job is keeping track of schedules, going to meetings, and dealing with paperwork.

But even with the large size, the synagogue seeks to be a warm, close community for young people. "We want everyone to be part of the community . . . and to feel comfortable in this environment." All the activities and opportunities are designed for youth to "learn from one another and grow with one another."

A lot of the youth-to-youth relationships are formed in the congregation's youth lounge, which is designed with relationship building in mind. For example, all the games in the lounge are for at least two people to play together. Furthermore, youth-group programming (which is planned and led by youth) has a strong emphasis on building friendships and having fun together.

Green summarizes: "We are a community at the synagogue. We want to teach these kids where they can belong in the overall community."

For some in society, negative or restrictive boundaries are associated with religion. As a result, some congregations shy away from being explicit about boundaries. Some are reluctant to place expectations on youth for fear of scaring them away. The framework of assets challenges congregations to begin articulating boundaries and expectations, not in a punitive, condemning way, but as a positive way of passing on wisdom to young people. In a keen critique of society's inability to articulate and uphold legitimate moral authority, David Elkind presents a challenge:

> It is all-important for youth leaders to appreciate how necessary it is for them to exercise such [unilateral] authority. They must state their own position clearly and decisively with respect to sexual activity, substance abuse, foul language, and pornography. Some youth workers tell me that they want to be friends with their teenagers and do not want to exert unilateral authority for fear of being associated with the adult world that young people reject. I believe that this is a mistake, and that youth leaders must be leaders. That does not mean proselytizing to our point of view, but only making clear where we stand and why.[4]

In addition, because of their rich heritage and tradition in reflecting on ethical and lifestyle issues, communities of faith also have a great deal to offer others who need to set boundaries. Parents, for example, need knowledge and skills to articulate and enforce boundaries that are consistent with their beliefs. And the community at large needs leadership from congregations as society struggles with how to recover, articulate, and enforce common boundaries and expectations for youth.

The boundaries and expectations assets raise provocative questions for youth workers. I recently participated in a discussion with youth workers during which Mark Conway, youth worker from **Annunciation Catholic Church in Minneapolis, Minnesota,** described a policy in his congregation: any young person who becomes a peer minister must agree to be completely chemically free

The Boundaries and Expectations Assets

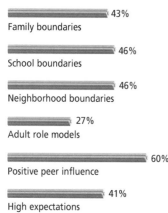

43%
Family boundaries

46%
School boundaries

46%
Neighborhood boundaries

27%
Adult role models

60%
Positive peer influence

41%
High expectations

all year. The belief is that the youth-group leaders should model responsible behavior everywhere, not just in the congregation. Conway noted that while many young people choose to make the commitment, others decide not to be leaders because of this policy.

The Constructive Use of Time Assets

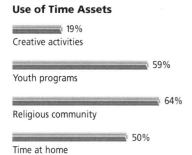

The Constructive Use of Time Assets

19% Creative activities

59% Youth programs

64% Religious community

50% Time at home

The fourth type of external assets emphasizes the importance of providing young people with opportunities to grow through programs and activities. Participation in activities such as the arts, sports, and religious groups have always been important, but they take on even more significance in a time when so many young people are home alone after school. These activities not only help build young people's peer relationships and skills, they also connect youth to principled, caring adults who nurture skills and creativity.

An important study of urban youth reached the following conclusion: "What distinguishes the hopefuls from other youth engaged in inner-city survival is their active involvement in some kind of neighborhood youth organization. These young people have 'ducked the bullet' and build hope through their participation in neighborhood-based organizations that offer safety, support, guidance, companionship, opportunities for growth, and engagement."[5]

Such opportunities for growth in constructive activities not only keep youth from getting bored (and in trouble), they also become the context in which youth build caring relationships, learn positive values, develop skills and competencies, and find opportunities for leadership and service. These activities can occur in many settings, from cocurricular activities in schools to youth clubs to creative arts and music activities to congregational youth programs.

Many young people today do not participate in these positive activities. Search Institute research has found that only 54 percent of all youth spend six or more hours per week in clubs, teams, or organizations in schools, youth programs, or religious institutions.[6] Access is lowest among low-income, urban youth. A report from the National Commission on Children found that only 52 percent of low-income urban youth had access to clubs and organizations, compared to 77 percent of low-income, nonurban youth.[7]

S   N   A   P   S   H   O   T

Empowering Youth:
Growing in Leadership Abilities

Each summer, **First Chinese Baptist Church in San Francisco** sponsors a day camp for children in the Chinatown community. About 100 children attend, and most of the leaders are youth-group members. Youth leader Jerald Choy says the day camp is "where they first learn to be more responsible . . . as part of the church."

The program's success is partly due to its progressive training structure, which is based on experience. The first year, kids are counselors in training. The next year, they become junior counselors. "By the time they've been in the program three years, they're ready to be senior counselors," Choy says. "They can take a whole group of kids and plan the program with the junior counselors and counselors in training."[8]

Setting High Expectations: Recognizing Outstanding Youth

There are many ways congregations can set high expectations for youth. **Mount Gideon Missionary Baptist Church in St. Louis, Missouri,** sponsors a program to recognize outstanding young people in the community through membership in "Youth on a Mission." The program is open to youth who:

- Maintain a grade point average of at least 3.25;

- Submit a letter of reference from both a teacher and their home church pastor; and

- Participate in a monthly community service project.

The rigorous membership requirements are an incentive for local youth to work hard in their school, congregation, and community. One particularly popular aspect of the program is the annual ball, where the youth are honored with a formal "introduction" to the assembled gathering.

The need for positive activities must also be balanced with the reality of busyness in the lives of many youth, particularly those in suburban and middle- or upper-class communities. Young people need positive time alone and with their family (asset #20), relaxing, reconnecting, and doing other things that are important for growing up.

The issue here is balance, which is highlighted in research by Reed W. Larson, who has found that young people spend as much as one-fourth of their waking hours alone. He has also found that adolescents who spend a moderate amount of time alone (25 to 45 percent of their waking hours when they are not in school) are better adjusted than those who spend little time alone or those who spend a lot of time alone. This time is used for emotional renewal and coping.[9]

If, however, the time alone is too high, young people are more likely to become bored or lonely. For example, considerable research has highlighted the dangers of young people spending too much time alone after school without adequate structure or adult supervision and guidance.

Congregations clearly have an important role to play in providing structured, positive, and enriching activities for youth. This may include traditional activities such as religious education or youth groups, or it may extend to an array of after-school and summer recreation, athletic leagues, academic enrichment, and service opportunities.

In addition, congregations can help to coordinate activities with others across the community to ensure that there are multiple opportunities for every young person to get involved in something that matches her or his talents, interests, and schedule. As the Carnegie Council on Adolescent Development challenged: "In a youth-centered America, every community would have a network of affordable, accessible, safe, and challenging opportunities that appeal to the diverse interests of young adolescents."[10]

There is also another important message for congregations in the constructive use of time assets: Young people need time at home. They need time to be by themselves. Thus, overprogramming in ways that take young people away from home several evenings each week can interfere with young people's need for balance and varied opportunities for involvement.

The Internal Assets

Internal assets involve the internal strengths, commitments, and values young people need to guide their choices, priorities, and decisions. They are grouped into the categories of commitment to learning, positive values, social competencies, and positive identity.

The Commitment to Learning Assets

Curiosity, the ability to internalize new knowledge, and the discipline required by learning are all important to healthy development. The ability to connect school with other aspects of life is vital in our ever-changing society.

This kind of commitment can be nurtured in all young people, not just those who are particularly good at schoolwork. Sometimes it begins when someone focuses attention on helping kids discover the joy of learning. And it's the kind of commitment we seek to instill in youth in our congregations so that they—and we—will continue to study, grow, and learn.

The commitment to learning assets address young people's educational commitments and the informal learning that occurs when young people read for pleasure.

Commitment to learning is the category of assets that religious leaders sometimes have the most trouble connecting to their own priorities (unless their congregation sponsors a parochial school or other formal educational endeavor). However, there are a number of places where congregations can and do address educational commitments beyond involvement in formal or parochial schools. Some possibilities are:

* Developing computer labs for neighborhood youth and their parents.

S N A P S H O T

Providing Constructive Activities:
Books, Bikes, and Buddies

Members of **First United Methodist Church in Albuquerque, New Mexico,** didn't have to look hard to uncover the needs of youth in the community. A look out the window easily revealed the need for after-school activities for youth and a safe place for them to go.

In cooperation with the schools, the congregation developed a variety of after-school activities to help build developmental assets in the youth in their congregation as well as in the community. Having been introduced to the asset-building framework, they knew the importance of intergenerational relationships and tried to integrate that element as much as possible.

Every Monday afternoon, the church opens its doors to youth from the local middle school for recreation, help with their homework, and movies. Soon the congregation will launch the Longfellow Publishing Company for elementary school children to write, illustrate, and bind their own books. The congregation also plans to start a bicycle club where kids will learn basic repair skills.

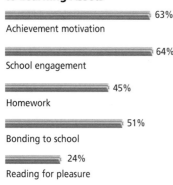

The Commitment to Learning Assets

63%
Achievement motivation

64%
School engagement

45%
Homework

51%
Bonding to school

24%
Reading for pleasure

- Enriching young people's formal education by offering space for studying after school with congregation members and/or neighborhood adults volunteering as tutors.

- Affirming young people's educational commitments through recognition for academic achievement.

- Respecting students' study needs in scheduling activities.

- Supporting parents in playing an active role in their young person's education.

- Encouraging continuing education beyond high school with college and vocational school tours and other preparation activities.

- Cultivating a love for learning beyond formal education, providing interesting reading material and opportunities for growth, and encouraging students to delve deeply into topics that interest them in ways that develop learning skills.

- Supporting young people's educational involvement and commitments.

The Positive Values Assets

Positive values are important "internal compasses" to guide young people's priorities and choices. Though there are many positive values that various traditions seek to nurture in young people, the asset framework focuses on six widely shared values. Many others could be added. These six values can be grouped into two categories.

- The first two assets are *prosocial values* that involve caring for others and the world. For the well-being of any society, young people need to learn how and when to suspend personal gain in order to enhance the welfare of others.

Fast Facts

Instilling a Commitment to Learning: Denominations Join National Efforts

When the U.S. Department of Education launched the America Reads Challenge (to ensure that all children can read well and independently by the end of third grade) in early 1997, the religious community was challenged to recruit volunteers for the effort. Many denominations quickly got involved.[11] Some of the ways denominations have supported literacy:

- **The Presbyterian Church (U.S.A.)** declared 1998 the "Year of Education" to

focus congregations' attention on reading and tutoring.

- **The Progressive National Baptist Convention** focused on the challenge at its annual convention of 15,000 delegates.

- **The Union of American Hebrew Congregations** plans to mobilize 100,000 volunteers.

- **The United Methodist Church** is publishing resources for churches to use in supporting education in their community.

The Positive Values Assets

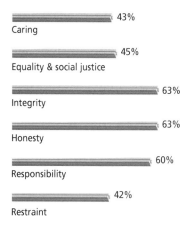

Caring — 43%

Equality & social justice — 45%

Integrity — 63%

Honesty — 63%

Responsibility — 60%

Restraint — 42%

The Social Competencies Assets

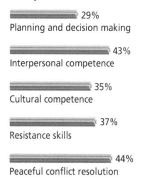

Planning and decision making — 29%

Interpersonal competence — 43%

Cultural competence — 35%

Resistance skills — 37%

Peaceful conflict resolution — 44%

• The four remaining values assets focus more on *personal character* (though they clearly have societal implications). These values provide a foundation for wise decision making.

Both types of values assets connect directly with all major faith traditions, which emphasize service, compassion, social justice, and an ethical lifestyle guided by personal values such as those listed in the asset framework. By nurturing positive values, congregations help to shape young people's life choices. These values can become a foundation for discussions of the life choices young people face regarding sexuality, alcohol and other drugs, and other current issues and concerns.

In addition, congregations can offer their wisdom to the larger community, which is now struggling with how to articulate values in a pluralistic society. The challenge is to discover ways to offer the wisdom of the faith tradition without imposing the particulars of that tradition on the community at large.

The Social Competencies Assets

Social competencies include the skills young people need to put their commitments, values, and beliefs into practice. While they are not enough, in and of themselves, to guide behavior, they are essential tools for making decisions and putting those decisions into practice. Two of the social competencies assets (planning and decision making, and resistance skills) emphasize personal choice making, and the other three (interpersonal competence, cultural competence, and peaceful conflict resolution) focus more on healthy interpersonal relationships.

A lack of skills in both areas among many adolescents raises troubling questions about how well young people are equipped for life. Research by Father Flanagan's Boys' Home in Boys Town, Nebraska, has found a lack of social skills to be strongly linked to aggression and antisocial behavior, juvenile delinquency, child abuse and neglect, mental health disorders, loneliness and despondency, and learning disabilities and school failure.[12] Tom Dowd of Boys Town concludes: "Youth need to become increasingly skilled as they face the developmental tasks of adolescence, such as identity and value formation, independence from family, and appropriate group affiliation. Without a strong social and psychological base from which to develop, many adolescents fail to negotiate these tasks successfully."[13]

Congregations have many opportunities to nurture social competencies in youth, ranging from providing leadership and service opportunities that focus on these skills to including skills development as a component of their curriculum for youth. For example, in talking about faith traditions' expectations regarding the use of alcohol or other drugs, discussions can include specific skills young people need to resist pressure from peers and the media. Similarly, discussions of a tradition's views on racial reconciliation can include an emphasis on skills for communication and understanding between people who are very different from one another.

The Positive Identity Assets

Identity formation is one of the critical tasks of adolescence, as young people ask: "Who am I and who do I want to become?" The eighth type of assets focuses on young people's views of themselves—their own sense of power, purpose, and promise. Without these assets, young people can become powerless victims without a sense of initiative and direction.

Promoting Positive Values:
Congregations Partner in "Year of Values"

It may not be unusual for congregations in a community to work together on something called "The Year of Values." It could easily be an effort sponsored by a national interfaith or ecumenical organization. But it is unusual for schools, grocery stores, and other institutions in a community to work with local congregations in launching such a focus.

That's what happened in **Northfield, Minnesota**, a college town in the southern part of the state. The school district and the community's ministerial association worked together to identify and promote seven important values: equality, self-control, promise keeping, responsibility, respect, honesty, and social justice. Then other groups began joining in. Some of the things that have happened in Northfield as a result of this emphasis include:

• Elementary children designed posters about four key values: giving, honesty, respect, and responsibility.

• A grocery store printed information on the Year of Values on 50,000 grocery bags.

• The parent-teacher organization offered workshops to help parents learn how to talk with their children about values.

• Congregations throughout the community featured sermons on each of the key values, culminating a month later in an ecumenical Thanksgiving service.

• A national speaker came to town to talk about the media and values.

Concerns about religion in schools are always present in these kinds of initiatives. But, says Northfield school superintendent Charles Kyte, "This is not teaching religion in schools. . . . This is just helping kids and families know that values are important."

Most concerns eased as the initiative became concrete and people saw the values being promoted. In fact, it was so successful the first year that the community then launched "The Year of Values 2: Civility and Respect."

The Positive Identity Assets

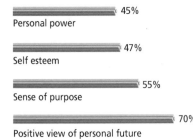

Personal power — 45%

Self esteem — 47%

Sense of purpose — 55%

Positive view of personal future — 70%

Two identity assets deserve particular note. The first is self-esteem. No other subject related to young people has gained as much attention as self-esteem. Indeed, many people view it as the single most important asset. Hundreds of books and articles have been published that say essentially what a subtitle claimed in a parenting magazine: "Self-esteem may well be the most important trait you can develop in your child."[14]

However, research by Search Institute and others finds that self-esteem, though important, is by no means the most powerful asset.[15] Rather, it is one element of a larger formula of healthy development for youth. Furthermore, self-esteem is not a simple concept; it involves young people's perceptions of themselves in many areas. And researchers have found that it is very difficult to change a young person's self-esteem unless a program is unusually intensive and comprehensive.[16] So while attention to self-esteem is important, this emphasis should not overshadow a commitment to building the range of assets young people need.

The other positive identity asset that merits individual mention is a positive view of personal future. A healthy sense of optimism about the future can be a driving influence in young people making positive choices. Thus, stories of youth who are not even sure they have a future because they live in communities haunted by daily violence and cycles of unending poverty become even more disturbing. Giving these young people reason for hope represents a vital challenge to congregations.

Many faith traditions draw their energy from a heritage that offers hope, meaning, and purpose. These traditions can help young people discover that they can make a difference (personal power) and that they are valuable people (self-esteem). However, it is not enough to just say these things. Youth need meaningful opportunities to experience (and thus internalize) this positive identity.

Extending the Assets to Younger Children

This book and chapter have intentionally focused on asset building in adolescence. However, the asset-building paradigm also has implications for younger children in the congregation and community. Indeed, asset building is more difficult (though not impossible) in adolescence if it does not build on a foundation of asset building started in childhood.

Search Institute has begun developing frameworks for developmental assets for infants, toddlers/preschoolers, and elementary-age children.[17] These frameworks show how the experiences of early childhood form a foundation for assets in adolescence and beyond. This framework will provide further guidance and direction for asset building in a child's earliest years.

As congregations begin introducing asset building in their work with youth, connections should also be made to the congregation's work with children. What foundations need to be in place in childhood programming that will enhance asset building in adolescence?

Furthermore, many of the activities a congregation undertakes for youth will also benefit children. For example, as congregational members learn of the importance of forming relationships with youth, they will inevitably do the same thing for younger children.

Implications of the Asset Framework for Congregations

The implications of the asset framework for congregations are profound and far-reaching. If taken seriously, the framework can have a powerful, transforming effect on your congregation's ability to serve and include youth. Tipsheet 4 offers a conceptual overview of the qualities of congregations that become committed to building developmental assets. It highlights three broad themes in asset building:

1. Asset-building congregations have an explicit commitment to building assets, and they seek to shape all areas of congregational life and the congregation's culture to support this commitment within the congregation as well as in the community.

2. Asset-building congregations use the asset framework as a lens for evaluating and strengthening programs and activities in the congregation, particularly those for children, youth, and families. The congregations also emphasize intergenerational activities.

3. Asset-building congregations call all individuals—youth, adults, parents—to intentionally build assets in their everyday life. Congregations can play a major role in encouraging and supporting these intentional commitments to care for young people.

Nurturing Positive Identity: Connecting with a Cultural Heritage

"Imani Circle." "Kuumba Class." "Lion's Den." While these phrases aren't common names in youth programs, they represent some of the core elements and the philosophy of the Brother to Brother Program at **Liberty Hills Baptist Church in Little Rock, Arkansas.** The program—which serves a neighborhood facing high rates of poverty and crime—builds on a philosophy that helping young African American males recover their cultural roots and identity is critical to their healthy development.

Thus, every aspect of the program is carefully designed to provide young men with the structure, support, and opportunities they need within a context of positive identity and cultural heritage. Imani Circle ("Faith" Circle, in Swahili) is a sharing and affirmation time. In Kuumba Class (Swahili for "creativity"), the boys make masks, molded figures, and other artistic crafts. And the Lion's Den is a recreation room.

Because of significant funding from federal, state, and private sources and a partnership with a local college, the Brother to Brother Program has access to extensive evaluation resources. And Jimmy Cunningham says they are seeing a real difference in young men's lives.

Cunningham tells about one boy who was suspended for 100 days for fighting in school. When he began the program, he had a 1.3 grade point average (GPA) and scored low on a scale of racial identity. After one and a half years in the program, the boy now has a 3.1 GPA and his scores on the racial identity scale have improved dramatically. Cunningham concludes: "We're talking about a kid who has become much more grounded and much more rooted."

Underlying these themes are several important shifts in congregational life and youth work. Here are some of the major implications:

Asset building calls congregations to unite around a positive vision for youth

Asset building does not focus on addressing problems. Rather, it focuses on recognizing and building strengths and assets that enable young people to make positive choices in all areas of their lives. This perspective goes against the grain in a culture that views youth with suspicion and falsely presumes that adolescence is, by definition, a stormy, turbulent period in life. How do congregations promote a positive vision?

- Cultivate positive attitudes toward youth in the congregation. Educate congregational leaders and members about the positive things they can expect from youth.

- Give adults a chance to get to know "real-live" young people. It can be amazing how quickly negative stereotypes fade as people actually get to know each other.

What Do Asset-Building Congregations Look Like?

This chart gives an overview of the qualities of congregations that
intentionally build developmental assets among youth.

CONGREGATION-WIDE COMMITMENTS AND ACTIONS

Building developmental assets is an explicit priority for the congregation.	• The vision of asset building is connected to the congregation's theology, identity, heritage, and mission. • The congregation's commitment to asset building is communicated regularly to all members. New members are quickly socialized to the commitment. • The congregation celebrates asset-building actions both within the congregation and in the community. People who work with youth have a high status in the congregation.
The congregation's policies, systems, and structures support asset building.	• The congregation's leader (pastor, rabbi, priest, imam) and governing board endorse and actively support asset building. • Young people are active participants in the congregation's decision-making structure. • Congregation-wide policies, systems, and activities are developed with a clear understanding of their impact on young people.
The congregation's climate and culture reinforce asset building.	• The congregation feels welcoming, warm, and accepting for all children, youth, and adults. • The congregation's climate challenges young people to think and grow. • Young people are celebrated as gifts for the congregation and community. • The congregation articulates and reinforces a core of shared values, norms, boundaries, and expectations. • People trust each other. The congregation is free of destructive conflict.
Congregation-wide programs and activities are shaped to be asset-building opportunities.	• Young people are intentionally included in all congregation-wide activities and events, including worship services, fellowship activities, and service projects. • Communication from the congregation regularly addresses young people's interests. • The congregation regularly plans intergenerational activities that intentionally build relationships among the generations. • Adults have opportunities to learn skills for asset building.

PROGRAMMATIC COMMITMENTS AND ACTIONS

Programming for children and youth intentionally builds developmental assets.	• Religious education, youth groups, recreation, service projects, special events, and other activities explicitly address developmental assets on a regular basis. • All youth activities nurture positive, caring relationships among youth. • Young people play key roles in planning, organizing, and leading youth programming. Their gifts and talents are discovered, nurtured, and celebrated. • There are clear ground rules that promote a positive, safe, and respectful environment. • Youth programming consistently addresses the real-life issues young people face. • Adult leaders (professional and volunteers) understand their role as asset builders. • Adult leaders include people of all ages within the congregation, not just parents or young adults.

What Do Asset-Building Congregations Look Like? (Continued)

The congregation supports parents in their role as asset builders.	• Parents have access to educational events that equip them to build assets. • Parents have opportunities to receive support from peers and leaders in the congregation in addressing parenting issues.
The congregation integrates asset building into its outreach to the community, nation, and world.	• Service and advocacy for children, youth, and families emphasize building on strengths and nurturing assets. • The congregation cooperates with other congregations for learning, mutual support, advocacy, and, when appropriate, shared programming. • The congregation partners with other organizations in shaping a positive vision for children and youth in the community.

INDIVIDUAL COMMITMENTS AND ACTIONS

Congregation adults take personal responsibility to build assets among children and youth.	• All members understand the assets and how they can build them. • Adults model and articulate their values and appropriate boundaries. • Members know young people by name. They build caring relationships with youth in the congregation, in their neighborhood, and other places they spend time. • Children, youth, and adults regularly spend time together. • Adults advocate on behalf of young people in the community, nation, and world.
Parents are supported and guided to build assets.	• Parents see themselves as asset builders for their own and other children. • Parents receive support and guidance from others in the congregation for asset building.
Young people build assets for themselves, their peers, and younger children.	• Children and teenagers know the developmental assets. • Most youth take action to promote assets for themselves and for their peers. • Young people feel comfortable and included in congregation-wide events and rituals. • Young people are active leaders in the congregation and its youth programming.

- Provide opportunities for youth to contribute to the congregation through leadership and service, which can counterbalance negative images of young people. Publicly affirm and celebrate their contributions.

- Be clear about boundaries and expectations with youth. Leaders unwittingly feed negative images when they do not insist that youth act within appropriate boundaries in the congregation. People have a right to be upset with youth if they damage property in the congregation or do not respect the rights of others.

- Challenge negative stereotypes of youth whenever and wherever they arise.

Keep in mind that a positive vision does not mean closing your eyes to the negatives. Nor does it imply a Pollyanna-like, "don't worry, be happy" attitude. Young people do face difficult, sometimes tragic problems. And some youth do get into serious trouble. These issues must be addressed. But the way you deal with them will be profoundly different from an asset-building perspective. While conventional thinking says, for example, that deviant behavior is normal for adolescent males ("boys will be boys"), an asset builder views the behavior as a sign that something is not right and seeks to understand and address the situation by offering support, boundaries, or another appropriate response.

From another perspective, the reaction to problems may be to impose stricter sanctions. If a lack of clear boundaries is the issue, this approach may work. Yet the problem is just as likely to stem from a lack of positive support or a lack of positive opportunities, leaving the young person idle, bored, and susceptible to negative pressure from friends and/or the media. As a result, the young person may turn to a gang for validation and support instead of parents or other caring adults. In such cases, an asset builder looks for ways to supply some of the missing pieces in the young person's life.

Asset building reshapes programming for youth

Just because asset building calls for finding ways to integrate young people into the life of the whole congregation does not mean that asset-building congregations should abandon age-specific programming for youth. These activities can be important opportunities to build peer relationships, focus on specific developmental needs, and create a sense of community. Many programmatic offerings for youth can be strengthened and focused by examining them through the asset framework. Some questions highlight the potential:

- What would be different about religious education classes if we were intentional about making them places where youth feel empowered and supported, where they struggle with issues of values and personal identity?

- How do we include youth in running programs so they have opportunities to lead and serve? How do we integrate them in leadership for the whole congregation?

- How do we shape service projects, social action trips to Israel, and other experiences so they have maximum impact on building these assets?

These are only some of the possibilities. Chapter 5 focuses on transforming youth programming from an asset-building perspective.

Asset building expands the vision from youth-group-only to youth-in-congregation

The asset-building approach highlights the critical importance of reconnecting youth to all generations, with everyone in the congregation (not just young adults and parents) claiming their responsibility for nurturing youth.

Part of the problem is that congregations have adopted a model of youth work that delegates responsibility for young people to one or a few youth "specialists" or "experts." They hire a youth worker and expect her or him to take care of everything to do with young people. Dr. Roland D. Martinson, a Lutheran seminary professor, describes this as the myth that youth work is "the responsibility of the pastor or youth director or church member who is good with kids." He continues:

> This "Lone Ranger" myth is adopted by churches who believe they can pay or appoint one or two people to do youth ministry for them. The congregation abdicates its responsibility and sits back to judge how well the pastor, the youth director, or the youth sponsor is doing with youth. This view of youth ministry centers in one leader and his or her personality. At its worst, this myth leads to a personality cult. At its best, it makes ministry dependent on one person. Where this is the case, the congregation's youth ministry often "leaves" when that person leaves.[18]

And, I would add to Martinson's critique, it fails to provide youth with the kinds of relationships and support they need from many adults, not just one or two who are designated to spend time with them.

The experiences of **St. Joan of Arc Catholic Church in Columbus, Ohio,** illustrate the potential when everyone in a congregation begins to see their role with youth. A year ago, fewer than 10 adults were involved in leading the youth program—which was growing rapidly. So Donna and Tom Berg, part-time youth ministry coordinators, began a program called "It Takes a Whole Parish." Berg spoke before mass, affirming people's abilities and challenging them to get involved. Before long, 40 people had expressed interest in helping. Each person has been trained and then given manageable, concrete responsibilities. The result is that many different people in the congregation are regularly involved with the youth.

With an emphasis on youth being empowered, valued, and connected, asset building challenges congregations to explore new ways of integrating youth more fully into the intergenerational community of faith. Chapter 4 suggests some possible ways to get started.

Asset building emphasizes links to families

A central component of an asset-building effort in a congregation is engaging families through participation, education, and support. Such efforts not only strengthen the program because parents support the work, but it helps equip parents to play their vital role in nurturing the assets of their children.

This education and support become particularly important for youth from vulnerable families that may be experiencing serious stress (e.g., due to divorce, abuse, unemployment) or where parents are poorly equipped with parenting and coping skills. While parents in these situations may be the most difficult to reach and serve, the efforts can pay off handsomely in positive impact on the young person and the family.

Broadening the Sphere of Youth Work in Congregations

In typical congregations, youth work focuses almost exclusively on the center circle in this diagram: the youth program. Asset building calls youth workers in congregations to expand their vision for youth work to include all of the circles shown here. The three inner circles represent life within the congregation. The outer circle represents outreach into the community.

Asset building reaches out to all youth

Everyone talks about the importance of engaging families, but the reality is that it can be quite difficult. Chapter 6 suggests ways the asset-building approach can extend the circle of youth work to include families.

Most youth workers see it as their calling to pay attention primarily to the young people who are part of the congregation. If the congregation pays attention to other youth, it is through service efforts that are disconnected from other areas of youth work.

If congregations are to be significant voices in addressing the needs of children and youth in the United States, it is imperative that they broaden their understanding of youth work to include youth beyond the families who attend week after week.

Complicating the issue, much of the community programming for youth in the past 20 years has focused on particular populations. Young people have been given labels (e.g., at-risk, gifted, challenged), then highly focused programs have been designed to address those specific issues. A similar thing has happened in many congregations. Some focus almost exclusively on providing opportunities for youth from the congregation, while others (a much smaller percentage) put all their energy into reaching out to those who have little or no commitment to the religious community.

While the goals of each of these approaches may have been laudable, both fail to live up to the potential of congregations to meet the needs of youth in a wide range of situations. The first approach ignores the fact that the young people most in need of positive opportunities are often the least likely to have access to those opportunities. In the introduction to *A Matter of Time,* the landmark study of young adolescents' nonschool time use, Wilma Tisch writes:

> A clear pattern emerged as we looked systematically at the many subsectors within the large universe of organizations and institutions that we had selected for analysis: Without exception, the young people in greatest need had the least access to support and services. Whether our particular focus . . . was publicly funded recreation programs, religious youth groups, sports programs, or private, nonprofit youth organizations, we found that young people in more advantaged circumstances had greater access to current programs and services.[19]

The second approach ignores the needs and interests of youth who are already connected and committed, and it may end up driving them away.

Part of the answer is to make the congregation's resources (human, physical, and financial) available to the community for after-school activities, job training, parent education, counseling, support groups, and other programs. Part of the answer is to become intentional about designing opportunities that reach out to youth in the community who are disconnected from any congregation (rather than relying on attracting youth from other congregations to increase participation in the youth program).

An asset-building approach recognizes that all youth need these assets and thus makes efforts to reach out to many different groups of youth, particularly those with less access to asset-building resources. Thus the asset-building perspective challenges congregations to reach out to youth beyond the congregation's families, particularly those with few opportunities. It also calls congregations to cooperate with others in the community on behalf of youth. Chapter 7 focuses on this challenge.

Asset building challenges leaders to develop new roles and skills

Many youth workers (paid or volunteer) took their position on the assumption that it was their job to "spend time with the kids." In an asset-building congregation, the whole congregation has that responsibility. (Note: Youth workers must still emphasize maintaining strong relationships with youth. They often remain key adult contacts for many of the young people in the congregation. What's different about the asset-building approach is that they are not the only ones in the congregation who are intentional in building these adult-youth relationships.)

Clearly, the asset-building vision calls for youth workers and other leaders to develop or assume new roles in the congregation and community. For example, some new (or newly emphasized) roles to be negotiated and integrated into job descriptions of both professionals and volunteers may be:

- Supporting and educating parents.

- Helping plan congregation-wide activities that involve youth.

- Advocating for youth within the congregation as well as in the community.

- Educating and equipping all adults in the congregation to build supportive relationships with youth as mentors and friends.

- Training adult volunteers to be more effective asset builders for youth.

Reaching Out in Missouri

"Who we are is just one piece of the pie," says Nancy Going, Director of Youth and Family Ministry at **Trinity Lutheran Church in Town and Country, Missouri.** So far, the rest of the pie in this suburb of St. Louis consists of the school district, police department, and hospital leaders who together want to make a difference in the lives of youth. And the pie is growing.

Trinity originally introduced the asset-building framework to Parkway School District, which, in turn, planned an educational meeting for clergy, hospital personnel, business and industry leaders, and others. These meetings led to a survey of youth to get a handle on their needs.

Rob Rose, former senior high youth minister at Trinity, believes the congregation is at the heart of the initiative. "Part of our church's philosophy is that Trinity needs to be a community center. We need to be more than just a building. We need to go out into the community and work in the community to make it better. That's what we're doing with assets."

- Coordinating youth leadership opportunities in the congregation and equipping youth for those roles.

- Partnering with other congregations to coordinate activities and services for youth in the community and to advocate on behalf of youth.

- Spending time in schools, youth organizations, and other settings to provide asset-building opportunities for youth in the community.

- Participating in community-wide efforts that benefit youth.

Some of these new roles may be unfamiliar and uncomfortable. Most youth workers get involved with youth work because they like "being with kids," and they may be really good at building those relationships. These new roles require other skills: networking, educating adults, advocacy, educating parents, working in the community. To be comfortable and effective in these roles, youth workers will need to develop new skills.

Before the new roles and skills start to feel overwhelming, it is important to remember that *the* youth worker doesn't have to do all these things alone. That would only exacerbate the high levels of frustration and burnout that are too common in congregations. Rather, by creating a larger vision for youth work (based on the assets) and expanding the definitions of what could be considered youth work, we can begin to find ways to involve more people with diverse gifts and talents in the lives of youth.

For example, while you may never have thought of the gray-haired community organizer as an ally for youth work, he or she may be just the right person to network with other organizations to discover how your congregation can partner in the community. Similarly, the people in charge of adult education in the congregation can be allies and resources in efforts to educate all members of the congregation about how they can be asset builders for youth.

Avoiding the Pitfalls

As Search Institute has worked with congregations and other organizations and communities to integrate the assets into their systems, we've seen several dangers or pitfalls surface. Here are four tendencies that can derail asset-building efforts in congregations:

- Since congregations already build some of the assets, it can be tempting to conclude that "we already do this, so we don't need to worry about it anymore." Certainly there are congregations that are very effective in serving youth and building assets. However, there probably are some challenges embedded within the asset framework that can strengthen all congregations.

- It is also tempting to pick one or two of the assets, then not worry about the rest. While it may be appropriate to focus your initial efforts on a few assets, the true power of asset building comes with their cumulative power. I would challenge you to develop a broader vision of how to shape congregational life to build as many assets as possible in all eight categories.

- Third, it's tempting to put asset building into a particular box. Often we think a new idea needs a new program or curriculum. Or we delegate asset building to a committee with limited responsibility. The result is that the assets have an impact in a focused area, but they don't become a vision that helps to transform the whole congregation for youth.

- A fourth danger is to become overwhelmed by the comprehensive vision of asset building. Sometimes it's easy to assume, for example, that a small congregation or a congregation with just a few youth can't really build assets in a comprehensive way. So it's important to start with simple steps that fit your particular context. The little things can make a real difference for young people.

Stepping Forward

While the asset-building vision may seem overwhelming, it can also be invigorating. Many veteran youth workers have expressed frustration that there are few new challenges for them in their work. They do the same things year after year with a revolving set of youth. Certainly the relationships are enriching and rewarding. But they feel stagnant in their work.

For these people, asset building opens new vistas to explore and new skills to build that will increase their effectiveness in serving youth. This exploration can renew energy and commitment to youth work, and raise awareness of and respect for the role of the youth worker in the life of the *entire* congregation.

At this point, we have examined the 40 developmental assets and their overall implications for congregations. We turn now to the nuts and bolts of integrating an asset-building focus into your congregation.

Developmental Assets:
A Framework for Focusing Congregational Life

Key Points

- The assets are organized into eight categories. Four categories are "external assets": support, empowerment, boundaries and expectations, and constructive use of time. The other four categories are "internal assets": commitment to learning, positive values, social competencies, and positive identity. Congregations can help build assets in all eight categories.

- While the 40 assets research has focused on assets for adolescents, the same kinds of assets are also important for younger children.

- The assets call congregations to broaden their vision of youth work to include not only youth programming, but also support for families, congregation-wide involvement, and a commitment to build assets for youth in the community.

Questions for Reflection and Discussion

- What has your congregation already done to build assets in each of the eight asset categories?

- What does your congregation already do to include youth as part of a vision that extends beyond the youth program? What challenges does this vision offer?

Suggestions for Getting Started

- Take time to study and discuss the eight categories of assets. Brainstorm a list of ways your congregation already seeks to build assets in each category.

- Talk to young people about the assets and the vision of asset-building congregations. What rings true for them and what doesn't?

- Examine how well your congregation already builds assets in the four contexts for asset building: youth programming, family support, congregation-wide involvement, and the broader community.

Putting Asset Building into Practice

C H A P T E R   3

Eight Steps for Nurturing Your Congregation's Commitment to Asset Building

very congregation is different, depending on size, faith tradition, location, congregational priorities, and many other factors. So there is no proven, step-by-step formula for integrating asset building into all areas of congregational life. This chapter does, however, outline some key steps toward building the interest and enthusiasm that lead to asset-building action and changed attitudes toward youth. The ideas can be shaped to fit the particular dynamics of your congregation.

Drawing from experience as well as from research on organizational and congregational change, we have identified eight key steps for nurturing a commitment to asset building in your congregation. They are:

1. Share the asset-building vision with allies and stakeholders.

2. Build a "vision team."

3. Listen and learn.

4. Develop a vision for asset building.

5. Shape your asset-building messages.

6. Create awareness, energy, and commitment.

7. Set up systems for success.

8. Network with others.

Integrating asset building into a congregation is tough work—because change is tough work. Many youth workers and other leaders don't have experience in introducing change into a congregation, so it's easy to be overwhelmed by the process, which can easily take several years to be fully implemented. In addition, sometimes they don't feel they have the power to influence change.

These realities highlight the necessity of building a team of people with the skills, personalities, and influence needed to bring about change. Don't try to do it alone. This chapter is designed to take you and a team through the change process.

We now turn to the specific steps. If you wish, use Tipsheet 7 to plan ways to take these steps in your congregation. Keep in mind that the recommended steps and the order in which they are presented may not fit every congregation. For example, a small congregation may be able to take many of these steps informally, while a large congregation might need a more formal process.

1. Share the Asset-Building Vision with Allies and Stakeholders

A first step in asset building is to personally understand the vision, then share it with others who will be allies and partners in integrating the vision into your congregation. Because asset building represents a new paradigm, or model, for understanding and working with youth, it's important that you take the time to internalize the basic concepts and make a personal commitment to building assets yourself.

It is also important to bring others on board early to share in gathering information, shaping the vision, and introducing the vision to the congregation. Otherwise, the idea can become trivialized into a "let's be nice to kids" fad or another "how to deal with the youth problem" approach, not a rethinking of the way our society—and your congregation—cares for young people.

New ideas catch on in different ways in different congregations, depending on their structure and culture. Let's look at the kinds of people you may want or need to involve in the process. (At this stage, it's more important to have a small, committed

---

T I P S H E E T 7

Brainstorming Ideas for Nurturing Your Congregation's Commitment

Use these prompter questions to identify the opportunities and strategies for getting started with an asset-building focus in your congregation.

1. Share the Asset-Building Vision with Allies and Stakeholders

- Which leaders in our congregation need to be informed and/or involved in planning?
- Which other stakeholders need to be included (e.g., youth, parents, volunteers)?
- Who are the informal "opinion shapers" in the congregation who need to be informed?
- What do we see as the key benefits of asset building for our congregation that address the specific concerns of each of these individuals and groups?
- What is the best way to introduce these ideas to and get feedback from these individuals and groups?

2. Build a "Vision Team"

- Who should be involved to represent the various stakeholders in asset building?
- What do you see as the group's primary purpose?
- How does the vision team connect with other groups in the congregation?

3. Listen and Learn

- What type of information do we need in order to plan well?
- What sources do we have for gathering that information?
- What strategies could we use to gather the information?
- What are the key things we are learning from the information we gather?

4. Develop a Vision for Asset Building

- How are we going to involve others in shaping the vision so that it is widely shared in the congregation?
- What do we hope our congregation will be like in five years if we really focus on asset building?
- How does our vision connect the resources, opportunities, strengths, and traditions of the congregation with the needs of youth in the congregation and community?

(Continues on next page)

Building Assets in Congregations

group than to have a large group that includes people who aren't "on board." You'll have chances to broaden the involvement later. At the same time, avoid the common tendency not to include youth in these kinds of leadership groups.)

Use Worksheet 2 to help identify the various people who might be interested in helping to initiate this effort. Tipsheet 8 presents an outline of an agenda you can adapt to share asset building with these individuals and groups.

As you consider the specific people in your congregation, think about the roles they could play in introducing asset building to your congregation. A team that seeks to introduce change into a congregation must include people who fill the following roles.[1]

Vision bearer. Someone who can help the congregation see the potential of asset building and who can ensure that planning is consistent with that vision.

Stakeholder. Someone for whom this idea is critically important.

T I P S H E E T   7

Brainstorming Ideas for Nurturing Your Congregation's Commitment (continued)

5. Shape Your Asset-Building Messages

- What are our core themes for asset building (e.g., building adult-youth relationships, youth leadership, involving youth in service)?
- Who are the key individuals and groups to which these themes need to be communicated?
- How do we make our asset-building themes meaningful and relevant to specific groups within the congregation and community?

6. Create Awareness, Energy, and Commitment

- How will we introduce the asset framework to different groups in the congregation?
- What low-risk opportunities can we offer or support that will give people a taste of asset building?
- How will we create and celebrate early successes?
- How can we apply positive social pressure that encourages people to build assets?

7. Set Up Systems for Success

- What opportunities do we have (or could we develop) to offer continuing education to members about asset building?
- How will we train youth and adults to be effective asset builders?
- What opportunities do we need to put in place that give people a chance to practice asset building?
- How do we want to recognize and affirm individuals for asset-building efforts?
- How will we monitor and evaluate our systems to be sure they are effectively supporting and nurturing people in asset building?

8. Network with Others

- What opportunities and resources are there in the community that can support our congregation's asset-building efforts?
- How will we balance working in the community with a commitment to integrating asset building into the congregation?

Decision maker. Someone who knows how to get decisions made in the congregation.

Networker. Someone who is good at building support for ideas by networking and relationship building.

Manager. Someone who can keep the group on task and moving forward.

Several people can fill one role or one person may fill multiple roles. The point is that the balance of these skills will, over time, be needed as you introduce change to the congregation. So if these skills are not readily apparent in your initial group, think of ways to expand your team to include them. Here are some of the kinds of people to identify:

Informal allies

Introducing asset building is not—and should not be—a one-person job. If you don't already have a small group of people interested in exploring asset building's potential in your congregation, identify two or three trusted people who will be partners with you in getting this effort started. (Or the initial impetus may come from an existing group in the congregation.) Meet informally to identify who needs to be informed, who will take responsibility for contacting different groups, and how best to introduce the idea into your congregation. Working together not only spreads the workload, it also increases the number of people really committed to this process.

Congregational leaders

Because asset building has implications for the entire congregation, it's important to have the support and involvement of leaders within the congregation. These leaders probably will not be able to do the work of planning the effort, but they need to be fully aware and supportive of what you are doing. These leaders may include:

- The congregation's head of staff (rabbi, pastor, priest, imam) as well as other staff members.

- The congregation's leadership group (e.g., board of directors, elders, session).

- The committee or group responsible for youth work in the congregation.

- Any planning or advisory group of youth.

- Other committees whose work potentially overlaps with asset building. The most obvious potential committees include those with responsibility for education, fellowship, care for members, community service, and worship.

- In some traditions, the effort may need to be endorsed by a congregational meeting.

- In some traditions, you may need to seek the support and encouragement of denominational or judicatory leaders in your community.

In most congregations, the clergyperson must be an active supporter—sometimes even initiator—of the asset-building effort, or it will never gain much support from others. Having her or his open support may well be the most important factor in helping your asset-building effort be accepted within the congregation. For example, in an open letter to a senior pastor, Group Books publisher Thom Schultz writes: "Youth workers invariably learn that their ministry's success

Identifying Potential Partners in Introducing Asset Building to Your Congregation

TYPES OF PEOPLE	POSSIBLE NAMES	ROLES THEY COULD PLAY	
Informal Allies		☐ Vision Bearer	☐ Stakeholder
		☐ Decision Maker	☐ Networker
		☐ Manager	
		☐ Vision Bearer	☐ Stakeholder
		☐ Decision Maker	☐ Networker
		☐ Manager	
		☐ Vision Bearer	☐ Stakeholder
		☐ Decision Maker	☐ Networker
		☐ Manager	
Congregational Leaders		☐ Vision Bearer	☐ Stakeholder
		☐ Decision Maker	☐ Networker
		☐ Manager	
		☐ Vision Bearer	☐ Stakeholder
		☐ Decision Maker	☐ Networker
		☐ Manager	
		☐ Vision Bearer	☐ Stakeholder
		☐ Decision Maker	☐ Networker
		☐ Manager	
Key Stakeholders		☐ Vision Bearer	☐ Stakeholder
		☐ Decision Maker	☐ Networker
		☐ Manager	
		☐ Vision Bearer	☐ Stakeholder
		☐ Decision Maker	☐ Networker
		☐ Manager	
		☐ Vision Bearer	☐ Stakeholder
		☐ Decision Maker	☐ Networker
		☐ Manager	
Opinion Shapers		☐ Vision Bearer	☐ Stakeholder
		☐ Decision Maker	☐ Networker
		☐ Manager	
		☐ Vision Bearer	☐ Stakeholder
		☐ Decision Maker	☐ Networker
		☐ Manager	
		☐ Vision Bearer	☐ Stakeholder
		☐ Decision Maker	☐ Networker
		☐ Manager	

depends on a number of crucial factors. You're a major one of those. What you believe, what you say, and how you spend your time have larger effects than you may fully realize—on your youth workers and on the young people in your church."[2] His words are relevant for other faith traditions as well.

You may want to approach these individuals and groups in different ways, depending on the particular dynamics in your congregation. Some individuals may merit a one-to-one conversation. Others who are less central could be informed through a letter or a large meeting, with opportunities for follow-up conversations.

In talking with these individuals and groups, think through how an asset-building framework would most benefit them and their causes and concerns. For example, the congregation's head of staff (pastor, rabbi, priest, imam) may be concerned about a lack of young families in the congregations. You might suggest that this approach has the potential of attracting families. Or if the congregation is concerned that only a small percentage of youth participate in the congregation after bar/bat mitzvah or confirmation, you might suggest that asset building has the potential of addressing youth needs in ways that keep them interested, involved, and connected.

Key stakeholders

In addition to the leadership, it is important to inform and involve several other groups of people early in the planning process. These include young people, parents, volunteers who work with youth, and other interested members of the congregation. As you develop plans for asset building, these people can become important allies and new congregational leaders. Their buying into and shaping of the vision is also essential to the success of your congregation's efforts.

Opinion shapers

There are always specific individuals within a congregation who are highly influential, even if they don't hold official leadership positions. They may be founding or longtime members, respected teachers, or active networkers. These people can become the best allies for asset building—or they can sabotage the effort if they perceive that it undercuts something they believe is important in the congregation.

For example, if they are passionate about programs for senior citizens or a particular social or theological emphasis, they may perceive that asset building would deflect energy and resources from these efforts. Thus, it is important to identify these people, tell them individually about what you are trying to do, listen to (and try to address) their concerns, and find out how they might want to be involved in asset building. You can probably identify specific ways that they can benefit from asset building. Senior citizens, for example, will also benefit from positive relationships with children and youth.

2. Build a "Vision Team"

Once you have a sense that many people in the congregation are interested in or committed to moving the asset-building vision forward, identify or assemble a team to take the lead in developing and implementing your plans. In Search Institute's work with communities that become committed to asset building, we call this group a "vision team" because its primary responsibility is to catch, shape, share, and keep alive the vision for asset building.

You may have already assembled a small team that introduced the asset-building concept in ways described in Step #1 above. Depending on its dynamics, this initial team may be the right group to continue as the formal vision team. However, there is an important reason for not formally establishing the team until after many segments of the congregation have bought in: you may discover important new allies during your conversations with individuals and groups and want to include them on the vision team. Some congregations and cultures may not want a formal vision team at all. An informal group can introduce the change and assume the role of the vision team.

Membership

Include a cross-section of members from youth through senior citizens, from infrequent attendees to congregational leaders. If possible, include people with responsibility for specific areas of congregational life that are particularly relevant for asset building (such as education, service in the community, social activities).

Concentrate on including people who have caught and support the asset-building vision for your congregation. While it is important to listen to the views of detractors, they are unlikely to be constructive members of a leadership group and can drain energy from those who are committed.

Keep in mind that a vision team does not need to be large. Sometimes three or four people may be all you need to move the vision forward, particularly in a smaller congregation.

T I P S H E E T 8

Suggested Agenda for Getting Support for Asset Building from Congregational Leaders

The following agenda can be adapted to introduce the asset-building idea to key leaders and stakeholders and for an individual conversation or a larger group.

1. **Introductions:** Be sure each person knows everyone else in the room.

2. **Asset Building and Its Potential in Your Congregation:** Briefly describe the asset-building approach and what excites you about it. Use information from Chapters 1 and 2. Distribute the list of the 40 assets (from page 34 or the back of this book) or the bulletin inserts in Appendix A.

3. **How Asset Building Fits with the Congregation's Mission:** Show connections between the asset-building approach and things the congregation already values and does. Emphasize the ways asset building enhances current goals and programs and addresses current concerns and interests of the person or group with whom you are sharing information.

4. **Listen to Hopes and Concerns:** Listen closely to what interests people and groups about asset building—any concerns they may have. Keep notes on their ideas and assure them that their concerns will be explored in the planning process.

5. **Brainstorm Potential and Connections:** Together, brainstorm ways asset building might be integrated into your congregation as well as current areas of congregational life that could contribute to asset-building efforts. (This brainstorming process often creates a tremendous amount of energy and enthusiasm for the asset-building process.)

6. **Seek Counsel on Process:** Tell the individual or group about how you are exploring the potential for asset building in your congregation. (Use steps outlined in this chapter as a starting point.) Get their counsel about dynamics in your congregation that need to be addressed in the process.

7. **Ongoing Involvement:** Find out if and how they want to be involved in the ongoing planning and implementation process.

8. **Thanks:** Thank the group or individual for their time and interest. Encourage them to contact you if they have other ideas and/or concerns.

Purpose

The group's purpose is not to start a myriad of new programs but to shape the asset-building vision and keep it alive, and to help existing structures align and coordinate their efforts with that vision. (Some possible tasks for this group are included in Tipsheet 9.) In my own congregation, for example, an asset-building group became a bridge between the youth program, religious education, a community partnership initiative, and other focus areas of congregational life. As a result, these different efforts are becoming mutually supportive and integrated.

Connection to existing groups

Established groups in the congregation could assume the responsibilities outlined in Tipsheet 9 for the vision team. In some cases, assigning asset building to an existing group may be appropriate because the group may already be functioning well. A related issue that sometimes arises is whether you really need a vision team at all. Once the congregation is aware of the assets, why not just let all the existing groups do this work on their own? In both cases, the real question is, why add yet another committee?

These concerns are legitimate and may override the benefits of a new vision team. There are, however, important advantages to forming a separate, new vision team.

- Because asset building is a new, cross cutting way of framing the congregation's work with youth, it may be difficult to fit it comfortably into an existing structure. If asset-building leadership draws only from a particular area of the congregation, a perception quickly develops that this is "a youth program effort" or "a religious education effort," not a vision for the entire congregation.

- Experts in congregational change find it takes three to five years to integrate new ideas into the congregation's life, and that a key factor in making that integration happen is having a particular group serve as the advocate and "vision keeper" for the new idea. The vision team can play this role.

- You avoid the danger of the planning getting set aside for the group's more "urgent" week-to-week assignments.

- Most congregations are not set up in ways that effectively coordinate various areas of congregational life. With intentional and strategic efforts, a task force designated to build connections can help overcome some of these barriers.

Ideally, asset building would be so well integrated into all areas of congregational life that a vision team would be redundant. Asset building would happen naturally, and everyone in the congregation would see their place on the asset-building team. That day is a long way off in most congregations. Lacking a group dedicated to the asset-building vision, the congregation is likely to lose its focus on asset building, and it will become the province of a particular area, not an overarching framework that informs and transforms all areas of congregational life.

At the same time, there may be ways to connect the vision team directly with existing groups. For example, the vision team could include people who also sit on other committees. The goal is to keep communication open and frequent.

3. Listen and Learn

Once a vision team is together, the first task is not to talk but to listen. Your effectiveness in engaging people and structures in the congregation in asset building will depend largely on how well you understand their perspectives, dreams, concerns, and capacities. Unless you listen closely to the people who will be most affected by your strategies, they are not likely to support your efforts.

Consider this example. Often when advocates for children try to motivate people to get involved in children's lives, they begin with the assumption that people don't really care about kids and aren't aware of the difficult challenges children face. As a result, they focus on all the problems children face and plead for people to show concern and get involved.

Though well intentioned, these messages may have little impact or even hurt the cause. Focus groups conducted by Public Agenda found that most people are

---

T I P S H E E T   9

Sample Job Description for an Asset-Building Vision Team

The purpose of the Asset-Building Vision Team at _____ (congregation's name) is to shape and keep alive a vision for asset building for youth and to assist other structures and committees in the congregation in aligning and coordinating their activities with this vision.

Team Responsibilities

- To seek input from leaders and other members of the congregation in shaping a vision for asset building in the congregation.

- To keep the asset-building vision alive as an underlying philosophy and priority in the congregation through awareness raising and education.

- To deepen the congregation's understanding of the developmental assets, how they are nurtured, and their implications for the congregation.

- To stimulate, coordinate, and support asset-building action and activities by the other committees and structures in the congregation (e.g., education, service).

- To sponsor training and other activities that increase the congregation's asset-building capacity and skills.

- To monitor activities and climate within the congregation and recommend changes to strengthen the asset-building emphasis.

- To serve as a link with asset-building efforts in the community at large (if present).

- To sponsor or cosponsor special asset-building activities that do not fall within the mission of other committees in the congregation.

- To lead or be a partner in conceptualizing and advocating major new efforts that focus on asset building in the congregation or community.

- To keep the congregation's leadership informed about asset-building efforts in the congregation, seeking formal approval for these efforts when needed.

- To monitor and evaluate asset-building efforts in order to improve efforts in the future.

Expectations of Team Members

- To be committed to the congregation, its mission, and its core beliefs.

- To be committed to enhancing the well-being of young people in the congregation and community.

- To become familiar with the concept of developmental assets and the congregation's potential role in building these assets.

- To serve faithfully on the vision team for at least one year, including regular attendance at monthly meetings and involvement in specific team tasks such as gathering information, publicity, and working with other committees.

---

deeply concerned about children and aware of many of the problems. But they don't take action because they feel powerless in the face of huge, intractable problems. "Their tolerance for the problems of children stems, in other words, not from indifference but from a feeling of helplessness," the researchers concluded.[3] If that conclusion is correct, emphasizing the crises facing children may only increase a sense of helplessness among the very people who are called to action.

Though it may not feel very productive, gathering information is an essential part of developing your congregation's asset-building plan. This information can be gathered in a variety of different ways, depending on how precise you want the findings to be and how much energy you put in. Tipsheet 10 outlines some of the possibilities.

Information from a number of different areas can inform and shape your plan. No congregation can do a thorough assessment in all of these areas. However, try to gather at least some information in each of the following areas.

Congregational emphases and priorities

What does your congregation see as priorities for its overall mission? Where is it headed? These are important questions as you consider how asset building fits into the congregation's overall mission. If you try to start an initiative that doesn't fit the overall mission, you will receive, at best, little active support or, at worst, active resistance to your plans.

Youth in the congregation

Who are the young people in your congregation? What are their needs, interests, and capacities? What do they like and not like about the congregation? What kinds of interactions do they have with adults in the congregation? What is their reaction to the asset-building model and its potential? In what ways could they see themselves participating in and contributing to an asset-building approach? Worksheets 3 and 4 provide short surveys that may be useful in gathering from youth information related to asset building.

Parents and other adults in the congregation

In addition to gathering information on youth, it is equally important to gather information on parents and other adults. How do they feel about young people in the congregation? How much do they interact with youth? What kind of education and other opportunities would they value? Where might they be interested in contributing their time and energy? What would their reaction be to a congregational focus on asset building? The questionnaires in Worksheets 3 and 4 can also be useful in gathering information from parents and other adults in the congregation.

Leadership and program areas in the congregation

Because asset building has the potential of touching all areas of congregational life, gather information and perspectives from the congregation's leadership in multiple areas, including, for example, worship, education, fellowship and care, operations, and community service.

The goal is for each of these groups to get excited about the vision and discover ways to integrate it into their existing efforts. If, however, you do not involve them early in the process, they are likely to resist any recommendations you have on how they can make their work more focused on asset building. On the other hand, in talking with them you may learn that they already have plans underway that will naturally fit with an asset-building focus.

Needs and opportunities in the community

Since asset building has an emphasis on serving youth in the community and being a resource to the community, it is important to know about the needs and opportunities that exist there. You may be able to find this information from existing sources, or you may want to gather some additional information.

Youth workers from several congregations could work together to gather this kind of information. This joint effort could be as simple as assigning each youth worker to gather information from a particular place (e.g., the library, city hall), or it could involve having the congregations work together to sponsor a study of youth or youth programs in the community.

Gathering information will do little good, however, if you don't take time to analyze, interpret, focus, and apply it. What does all this information mean for asset building in your congregation?

T I P S H E E T 1 0

Possible Information-Gathering Strategies

You can gather information to guide your asset-building efforts from a number of sources. Here are some possibilities.

- **Written surveys**—Ask youth, parents, and other congregation members to complete surveys that give you information on needs, interests, and priorities. These can be distributed through the mail (though many people won't return them) or during other activities (e.g., youth group, adult education, worship). Keep in mind that the surveys will probably reach primarily your most active members.

- **Focus groups and informal conversations**—Get people together to talk about the issues you're interested in learning about. You may want to use existing meetings (committees, education, youth group), though you will again only reach those who are actively involved. Or you could host conversations in members' homes, inviting people who live nearby to participate.

- **Telephone interviews**—Volunteers in the congregation can call members to get their feedback on a set of well-written questions.

- **Personal visits**—Some congregations have traditions of visiting in members' homes (for example, at pledge time). Some questions can be asked in these settings that can yield valuable information because people (particularly those who are less involved) may be more comfortable.

- **Existing information in the community**—Your community probably has a wealth of information already available about youth. Some may have conducted a survey of youth assets using Search Institute's *Profiles of Student Life* survey. Other information may be available through your public library, school district, mayor's office, or chamber of commerce. In addition, you could interview youth workers, city officials, and others in the community who watch trends. (One caution: Many cities only gather information on the problems of youth, such as crime and delinquency. This information must be balanced with a sense of their strengths and the opportunities for them in the community.)

- **Observation**—You can learn about your congregation by standing back and observing what happens in various programs and activities. Often an outsider can offer a particularly helpful perspective. (A great way to get an outside perspective is to ask a youth worker in another congregation or tradition to come observe your congregation and share her or his observations.)

- **Congregational records and history**—Your congregation may have a great deal of information in its records that would be invaluable in shaping your efforts. (For example, the congregation may have developed a strategic plan in recent years that would help you tie your efforts to congregational priorities.)

Worksheet 5 provides a place for jotting notes about key things you're learning as they relate to the four contexts of asset building. If you're using a group process to interpret the findings, you could break into smaller groups, assigning each to focus on one of the four contexts listed and present what they are learning to the larger group. As you note questions that still remain, think of ways to go about getting the information and answers you need.

Often when people sort through this kind of information, the first reaction is to problem solve. "What can we do about _____?" While it is useful to keep possible solutions in mind, don't jump too quickly to adopt any specific idea until you have gone through the next step of shaping a vision. Otherwise, you risk creating yet another flurry of unfocused activity.

4. Develop a Vision for Asset Building

Once you have a sense of the current reality in your congregation and some of its priorities, you can begin to shape asset building in your congregation. Focus on the kind of congregation you hope to become.

While there are many strategies for guiding a planning process, vision-based planning has a number of benefits for congregations seeking to integrate asset building into their life. First, the assets themselves offer a vision for youth. The vision you create for your congregation can then complement the vision of the assets. Second, our experience has been that a vision-based planning process tends to be hopeful, energizing, and bridge building. Finally, a vision can often have power right away—before you start planning anything else. That's because the vision sticks in people's minds and starts to guide their priorities and actions.

One way of creating a vision is to ask the people who have been reflecting on the information you gathered to each write down what they want their congregation to look like in five years if an asset-building initiative were in place right now. Encourage them to be concrete and specific. Then gather all these individual vision statements and compile them into themes. You may find that five or six themes emerge consistently. These can be reviewed, revised, and ranked in priority to ensure that they capture the spirit and priorities of the congregation. Then they can be used as a focus for planning.

As an example of the themes that emerged for one congregation, Tipsheet 11 shows five asset-building themes and priorities identified by **St. Luke Presbyterian Church in Minnetonka, Minnesota,** my own congregation.

With a vision (or several vision themes) in place, begin identifying the goals and strategies you need to move toward that vision. (See Tipsheet 12 for an example of the goals that emerged in St. Luke's planning process.) As you do so, keep the following tips in mind:

- Focus on areas that are consistent with the congregation's history, values, and commitments. A suggestion for something that breaks with tradition is unlikely to gain wide support.

- Include a mixture of priorities that are relatively easy to address (such as ways to integrate asset building into current programs) as well as some bigger dreams (such as new initiatives that the congregation could undertake).

Youth's Experiences of Assets in Your Congregation

Use this survey to explore what your congregation does to nurture the developmental assets young people need to grow up healthy.

1. In what ways do young people experience care and support in the congregation? What are areas where they are unlikely to experience care in the congregation?

2. What kinds of opportunities does this congregation provide for youth to lead and serve?

3. How clear is the congregation in teaching young people what behaviors are acceptable or unacceptable?

4. In what ways does the congregation provide young people with opportunities and activities that are positive, safe, and enriching—both within the congregation and in the larger community?

5. How does the congregation nurture a commitment to learning among young people?

6. What kinds of values are important to this congregation? How does the congregation intentionally nurture these values in young people?

7. In what ways does the congregation nurture young people's skills (such as decision making and conflict resolution)?

8. What does the congregation do to nurture a sense of hope and possibility in youth?

Identifying Asset-Building Priorities for Your Congregation

This worksheet can be used for personal reflection or with youth
and adults to develop a shared vision for asset building.

	HOW IMPORTANT DO YOU THINK THIS OUGHT TO BE? (1 = not important; 5 = top priority)	HOW WELL DO WE DO NOW? (1 = not well at all; 5 = very well)
1. Identify how important you think each strategy ought to be for your congregation (1 = not important; 5 = top priority).		
2. Evaluate how well your congregation is already doing in each area (1 = not well at all; 5 = very well).		
1. THE VISION FOR YOUTH IN THE CONGREGATION		
Seeing youth as a top priority for the whole congregation.		
Having congregational leaders who are committed to an emphasis on children and youth.		
2. PROGRAM OPPORTUNITIES FOR YOUTH		
Connecting all 6th- to 12th-grade youth to a weekly program.		
Providing social opportunities for youth and their friends.		
Providing a safe place where youth can gather after school, on weekends, and in the summer.		
Nurturing caring relationships among youth.		
Engaging every young person in at least one service-learning activity every year.		
Intentionally nurturing life skills and values through education programs.		
Involving youth in leadership for the youth program.		
3. SUPPORT AND EDUCATION FOR PARENTS		
Providing opportunities to enhance parents' skills in raising healthy children.		
Providing opportunities for families to serve others together.		
Providing opportunities for parents to build supportive relationships with other parents in the congregation.		

(Continues on next page)

Identifying Asset-Building Priorities for Your Congregation, Continued

	HOW IMPORTANT DO YOU THINK THIS OUGHT TO BE? (1 = not important; 5 = top priority)	HOW WELL DO WE DO NOW? (1 = not well at all; 5 = very well)
4. THE WHOLE COMMUNITY OF FAITH		
Nurturing a youth-friendly environment throughout the congregation.		
Having many members who intentionally seek to provide care and support for children and youth.		
Building sustained relationships between adults and youth in the congregation.		
Building sustained relationships between teenagers and children in the congregation.		
As a congregation, articulating core values to pass on to the younger generations.		
Connecting adults and youth in service projects.		
Providing opportunities for youth to lead and make decisions in the congregation.		
5. RELATIONS IN THE COMMUNITY		
Developing strategies for connecting with youth in the community who are not involved in a congregation.		
Working with clergy and youth workers in other congregations to promote positive opportunities for youth in the community.		
Supporting community efforts to nurture healthy youth through strong schools, strong parks and recreation programs, enforcement of underage drinking laws, etc.		
Serving as a partner in or a catalyst for a community-wide youth initiative.		

Focusing What You Have Learned About Your Congregation and Community

Use or adapt this worksheet with your vision team or planning group to distill the key things
you learn from the information you gather on your congregation and community.

	THINGS THAT PLEASE US	THINGS THAT TROUBLE US	REMAINING QUESTIONS
Youth Involvement in the Whole Congregation			
Programming for Youth in Our Congregation			
Family Education and Support in Our Congregation			
Opportunities for Youth in Our Community			

- Look for places where opportunities and resources intersect with identified needs. For example, several members of your congregation may be adept with computers and could provide job-skills training in an after-school program (either through your congregation or in partnership with an existing program).

- Find ways to enrich existing opportunities. For example, where in the congregation are there natural opportunities to build assets? How can these opportunities be strengthened and enhanced with the asset-building framework?

- Identify partnership opportunities. Perhaps your congregation could be a resource to existing programs serving youth in the community. Or you could work with other congregations to provide joint programming for youth focused in a specific area.

- As you develop strategies, regularly evaluate them against the framework of assets as well as your vision. Identify whether you are adequately balancing the contexts for asset-building action.

Developing and implementing strategies for asset building can be a long, complex process. While planning is important, it is just as critical that you not bury the enthusiasm for asset building in a pile of papers and laborious meetings. Getting started in some simple ways may be what's needed at first, with the larger vision being held in front of you to guide your progress. Chapters 4 to 7 give more ideas on how to integrate asset building into each of the four contexts.

5. Shape Your Asset-Building Messages

Once you've developed a sense of your congregation's priorities for asset building, you can begin shaping your asset-building messages for various groups within the congregation (and community). It may be tempting to simply tell everyone in the congregation your overall vision and goals. While that may be important as a way of informing them of an important initiative in congregational life, it will do little to get individuals moving toward a personal commitment to asset building.

Individuals will begin to commit when they see that the congregation's asset emphasis is "about me." If you want individuals (leaders and others) to become personally committed to asset building (which may mean changing their own actions and behaviors), you must fine-tune your specific asset-building themes to fit their particular needs and interests. Tipsheet 13 gives examples of how one potential theme could be tailored to different audiences.

One important point: You'll be most likely to shape messages that "hit home" if you involve people from the targeted group in developing the message. For example, if you want all adults in the congregation to take time to notice youth, get some adults who don't work with youth to help shape the messages and strategies.

6. Create Awareness, Energy, and Commitment

Before your congregation can become committed to asset building, leaders and members need a basic understanding of the ideas and motivation behind it. In other words, you have to move people from having little knowledge of asset building or their role in young people's lives to a point where they see they can make a difference and *want to* get personally involved. Only then can you move people into concrete action and commitment.

The goal at first, then, is to introduce the ideas in ways that spark interest. Then you can solidify the commitment by involving people in low-risk, convenient ways, celebrating and affirming early successes, and making it "socially desirable" to build assets.

Introduce the basic asset framework

Often a congregation will have difficulty seeing the potential for asset building until people understand it more fully. Find opportunities to educate the congregation (adults, parents, youth, youth workers, staff, board) about the idea of assets and how congregations can get involved. Also, focus attention on the ways individuals in the congregation can be asset builders even without a special program or training.

Use many opportunities to talk about asset building and its potential for your congregation. These may include adult education, youth-group meetings, newsletters, and other communication vehicles. Share the list of assets and have groups brainstorm about how this approach fits with your congregation's

---

T I P S H E E T 1 1

Themes for Asset Building in One Congregation

The following themes and images are condensed from a vision-building session by members of St. Luke Presbyterian Church, Minnetonka, Minnesota. Meeting participants each wrote a vision of St. Luke as an asset-building congregation based on what they would like to see in five years. The following five common themes were identified through these vision statements.

THEME #1: Nurture a shared responsibility for children and youth among all members of the congregation.

IMAGES: The whole community of faith takes seriously the promises it makes at baptism to nourish young people in the faith. Everyone—not just parents—her or his responsibility for caring for the young people of the church. Leadership for children and youth activities is broad based, including parents, nonparents, and youth, in Sunday school, recreation, youth group, and other activities. Being with teenagers is "in" for adults!

THEME #2: Create an inviting, intergenerational community where children and youth feel "at home."

IMAGES: Every child and youth has a "second family" at St. Luke. Youth feel comfortable here and feel comfortable bringing their friends. The congregation intentionally nurtures intergenerational relationships through programs such as intergenerational education, congregational conversations, adopt-a-grandparent programs, mentoring relationships, and weekly church meeting and fellowship nights. People have opportunities to learn the skills they need to build these relationships.

THEME #3: Equip and engage young people as leaders within the congregation and beyond.

IMAGES: Children and youth are valued as resources in the congregation and are regularly given opportunities to use and

develop their gifts through music, help with younger children, service in the community, and other activities. They hold leadership positions in the congregation as elders, deacons, and committee members, and they lead a Children/Youth Giving Team in which they decide how to contribute money to youth-specific causes. They also have opportunities to participate in the Presbytery, Synod, and General Assembly.

THEME #4: Become active in community leadership and partnerships for asset building.

IMAGES: St. Luke partners with schools, other faith communities, day-care providers, shelters, and other organizations in the suburbs and Minneapolis to strengthen the assets of all children and youth in the community. It sponsors or cosponsors programs and activities for young people, such as an after-school program or teen center (especially for 9- to 13-year-olds), a community center for all ages, and social events for youth and for all ages of community members.

THEME #5: Emphasize asset building in advocacy and social action for children, youth, and families.

IMAGES: St. Luke continues its tradition of advocacy with a focus on changing systems so that they provide children, youth, and their families around the world with the foundation they need for healthy development. The advocacy emphasis is matched with opportunities for direct involvement in the lives of children and youth in the community, metropolitan area, nation, and world.

A Congregation's Goals for Asset Building (Sample)

1. Young people feel valued, important, and "at home" in the congregation. They look to the congregation for support and guidance as they shape commitments, values, competencies, and sense of personal identity.

2. Building assets becomes an ongoing focus for the congregation's sense of mission. It becomes a visible framework that shapes the culture, structure, and programming.

3. Programs and initiatives in the congregation are designed and evaluated in light of their impact on asset building.

4. All members of the congregation recognize and act on their individual roles and responsibilities as asset builders in the lives of children and youth.

5. The congregation is known in the community as a congregation committed to the healthy development of children and youth.

philosophy and theology as well as ways your congregation currently can and does build assets in youth. Use the following tools:

Workshop. Tipsheet 14 gives an outline for a one-hour workshop for groups in your congregation.

Communication opportunities. Tipsheet 15 gives several ideas on how to share the asset-building message in your congregation.

Bulletin inserts. Appendix A includes 10 reproducible bulletin inserts you can use or adapt to share the basic asset framework within your congregation.[4]

At this point in the awareness-raising process, emphasize the benefits of asset building to the specific audience to which you are presenting the information. That's how you get them interested. It is also important not to overwhelm them with too much information. Present straightforward ideas, success stories, and a basic call to action. Later, when people are more interested and committed, you will have opportunities to explore in more depth all the implications and challenges inherent in the approach. Spending too much time up front talking about the costs will make people lose interest before a real commitment has begun to form.

Provide low-risk opportunities for involvement

One of the best ways to motivate people to commit to something new is for them to have a good experience in actually doing it. People can't be asset builders just by thinking about it. They have to take some kind of action.

As people are first getting involved, it may be tempting to ask them to "jump into the deep end" with, for example, a long-term mentoring relationship. Certainly, some people are daring and will do it. Most, however, prefer to start with less daunting involvement. To ensure early success, develop and promote opportunities for building assets that are:

* Easy and convenient (something people can do without training and without adding to an already busy schedule is ideal);

* Low cost (in terms of time, energy, and money); and

* Highly likely to succeed (you don't want to have to patch up failed efforts at this stage).

When my congregation began focusing on asset building, one of the first things we wanted to do was make young people more visible in congregational life. We wanted adults to notice them! We asked adults to think about how many kids in the congregation they knew well. We asked kids how many adults they knew, and we reported to the adults how few of the youth felt connected to adults. Then, during announcement times, we starting encouraging adults and youth to greet each other. We asked everyone to wear name tags to make the process easier.

A number of activities were sponsored to begin building relationships as well. The middle school youth organized a buddy system in which they invited adults to sit with an assigned young person for a month's worth of worship services. Several intergenerational educational classes focused on having adults and youth get to know each other and tell each other their stories. As a result, many members in the congregation who rarely paid attention to youth now make a conscious effort to learn names and greet the youth when they see them.

Create and celebrate early, visible successes

One way to generate momentum is to find simple ways to have early successes that show that asset building can make a difference. In my congregation, we realized early in our planning process that only adults had name tags. ("Kids would just lose them" was the given reason.) The asset-building vision team quickly arranged

---

T I P S H E E T   1 3

Translating an Asset-Building Theme into Audience-Specific Messages

Here is an example of how an asset-building theme could be translated for specific groups within a congregation. Such a list should be tailored to each individual congregation.

Sample Theme	The congregation seeks to have everyone committed to and engaged in asset building for youth.
Sample Messages for Congregational Leaders	• Leaders play an important role in modeling asset building for the congregation. • Involving members in building assets empowers them and gets them more actively involved in congregational life. • Nurturing a congregation-wide commitment to asset building creates a greater sense of community in the congregation.
Sample Messages for All Members	• Take time to notice and be with young people. • We all share responsibility for young people in our congregation. It's not just the job of parents and youth workers.
Sample Messages for Parents	• What you do can make a huge difference in your child's life. • You are not alone. The whole congregation seeks to be there for you and your child.
Sample Messages for Youth	• This community of faith cares about you and wants to be there for you. • For the congregation to be there for you, you also have a responsibility to reach out and build relationships with adults. • You can be a positive asset builder for yourself, your friends, and younger children.
Sample Messages for Youth Program Volunteers	• You are key asset builders for the congregation. You serve both as role models and teachers of others. • The whole congregation is here as a resource for building assets in youth. You don't have to do it alone.
Sample Messages for the Community	• This is a congregation in which everyone is committed to kids. • Young people who come to this congregation will be cared for by an intergenerational community.

for all children and youth to get name tags, just like the adults. This action was acknowledged in a worship service that highlighted the place of young people in the congregation.

Another key way to highlight early successes is to use the asset-building language when describing programs and events that already occur in the congregation (assuming they really do build assets!). Similarly, calls for youth teachers and volunteers can include a message like "Here's a great opportunity for you to build assets for our youth."

As people get involved in asset building, find ways to celebrate and affirm those commitments. Certificates and public recognition not only help to solidify an individual's own commitment, they also provide an opportunity for others to learn about asset building and think to themselves, "I could do that!"

Apply positive social pressure

Finally, an important way to raise awareness and build commitment is to have influential people in the congregation advocate for asset-building involvement. An obvious example is to have the congregation's spiritual leader speak about asset building during worship services and in other settings. In addition, it may be appropriate to have the congregation's governing body "endorse" asset building and commit themselves to it individually.

In addition to people in official roles, other influential people in the congregation can help create positive pressure to get involved. For example, an esteemed "pillar" of the congregation might be encouraged to share with the congregation why he or she believes asset building should be a priority in people's lives. Just as powerful may be having young people advocate asset-building involvement to their parents and other adults in the congregation. These endorsements should not be carefully scripted, but should be from the heart.

7. Set Up Systems for Success

Getting people interested and committed is only half of the equation. Your efforts will only have a long-term impact if you establish systems that support, strengthen, deepen, and renew people's commitment. Put another way, asset building will not become part of the congregation's culture unless it is integrated into programs and systems within your congregation.

Educate people about asset building

Part of the challenge is to keep the message fresh and visible. In addition, new people who enter the congregation need to learn about it. And, most important, people need opportunities to delve more deeply into the philosophy so that their understanding of it grows over time.

For example, once people become committed to and involved in asset building, it is important to balance the discussion of benefits with the costs and implications— particularly with those who will be leading the efforts. A thorough discussion of the first three chapters of this book, for example, may be appropriate with some groups. Others will need to be challenged to examine their own lives and priorities in light of this approach. Otherwise, asset building can devolve into a simplistic or trite theme that has little lasting impact on youth.

Train youth and adults with specific skills for asset building

I've separated education and training to highlight the need for focusing on equipping youth and adults with specific skills for asset building. One reason some adults don't talk with youth is that they don't really know how. Religious education leaders may not have the skills they need to nurture positive values in young people. Or parents may struggle with how to set appropriate boundaries.

Therefore, in addition to education to deepen their understanding of asset building, people need opportunities to be trained as asset builders. This involves asking people to identify areas where they feel inadequate, then providing very concrete help and practice in the skills they need to become more comfortable and effective.

Provide opportunities for people to practice asset building

Education and training are not enough. They need to be coupled with concrete opportunities for the people in the congregation to practice and live out their commitment to asset building.

Ideally, people would do asset building naturally in their everyday lives. Ideally, we would not have to talk about asset-building efforts, because people in congregations would do asset-building things without thinking about it. All of the programs in a congregation would build assets.

But the reality is that many parts of asset building have been neglected—and could even be considered countercultural. Too many people have forgotten how to build caring intergenerational relationships. Too many programs have become adult centered and do not meet the developmental needs of youth. As a result, congregations need to provide concrete, explicit opportunities for people to develop asset-building habits. Chapters 4 to 7 explore some of the kinds of opportunities that can be created.

Recognize people for their asset-building efforts

Asset building is intrinsically enriching and rewarding. Most of the time, people enjoy it and do it for its own sake. But it's not always easy and the impact is often not immediate. Therefore, one way to reinforce people's commitment and involvement is to publicly recognize and affirm their efforts.

An "Asset Builder of the Month" column in the congregation's newsletter, an asset builders picnic, recognition during a worship service, or other forms of affirmation can provide opportunities to celebrate both individual commitments to asset building and the whole congregation's.

At the same time, it is important that recognition not become the driving force in people's involvement. When that occurs, people's commitment dwindles unless the external rewards become more and more prominent. Recognition should be the surprise bonus that is added to an already enriching and rewarding experience, not the expected reward.

Monitor and evaluate your efforts

Finally, the long-term success of your asset-building efforts can be greatly enhanced if you keep track of how things are going and reshape your work when you detect rough spots.

For example, let's suppose your congregation is emphasizing service involvement as a key asset-building theme. It is not only important to see if people are actually getting involved, but also to see if those experiences have been positive and rewarding for everyone. If so, you have something to celebrate. If not, you can work to improve the system before too many people get discouraged or disillusioned.

8. Network with Others

One of the key messages of asset building is that everyone and all sectors in a community can play a role in building assets. Take advantage of this opportunity to learn from others and support others. Their insights and resources can be invaluable in your own congregation's efforts, and they can help to extend your congregation's reach into the community. Furthermore, knowing you are part of a larger effort can bring energy and enthusiasm to your congregation's work. Here are some ideas for how to network in your community.

• Partner with other youth workers for support, ideas, problem solving, and renewal.

• Work with other congregations to sponsor joint programs that your congregation could not do alone.

• Contact community-based youth workers and educators who can be resources to your efforts, offering insights into young people's needs and how to meet those needs.

T I P S H E E T   1 4

An Outline for Introducing Assets to Groups in Your Congregation

Adapt this outline for a one-hour workshop on asset building for various groups in your congregation, including adult education, parent groups, and youth groups. It can also be adapted to raise awareness among others in your community.

1. Introductions   **(5 minutes)**

Have people form pairs (with someone they don't know well), introduce themselves, and tell about a young person in their life (e.g., a child, a friend, a grandchild, a neighbor).

2. What Do Kids Need?   **(10 minutes)**

Ask pairs to brainstorm things that make a difference in that young person's life. Encourage them to think about things in the family, neighborhood, congregation, and other settings. Ask volunteers to report some of their ideas. List them on newsprint.

3. Introduce Developmental Assets   **(10 minutes)**

Distribute the list of 40 assets (from page 34 or the back of this book). Explain that these assets were identified by Search Institute as being powerful shapers of young people's behavior. Have people go through the list and mark all the assets that connect to the things they identified in activity #2.

4. Why Asset Building Is Important   **(15 minutes)**

Briefly summarize the information in Chapter 1 about why congregations should focus attention on asset building. If you wish, distribute the Chapter 1 summary on page 32.

5. What We Can Do   **(15 minutes)**

Explain that asset building calls for three types of commitments within the congregation: individual commitment and action, programmatic commitment and action, and congregation-wide commitment and action. If you wish, distribute Tipsheet 4, which shows a vision of an asset-building congregation.

Form pairs or trios. Ask them first to brainstorm one thing they each can personally do to build assets "before the sun goes down." Encourage volunteers to share their commitments. Then have the teams brainstorm what they'd like to see happen in the congregation to build assets. Have them report on their ideas to the larger group.

6. Closing   **(5 minutes)**

If there are specific ways workshop participants can plug into asset building in the congregation, highlight those opportunities. Tell them what they can expect to happen next in the congregation. Thank people for their participation.

- Build connections with other organizations in your community that are committed to the asset-building vision.

Many of the congregations that have learned about asset building see it primarily as a vehicle for working in the community. Congregation leaders serve on community coalitions. The congregation contributes funding to the local effort. And the congregation highlights its commitment to the community through sermons and newsletters.

All of these activities can be worthwhile components of an asset-building commitment. A concern, however, is that energy placed exclusively on efforts in the community will have little impact on the congregation itself. The challenge is to build bridges between this commitment in the community and the internal transformation of the congregation.

T I P S H E E T   1 5

Ideas for Creating Awareness About Asset Building in Your Congregation

- **Newsletters, bulletins, and bulletin boards**—Tell about your congregation's commitment and give ideas of how people can get involved. Use the information in the bulletin inserts in Appendix A for ideas. Tell how individual members are building assets. (See resource listing, Appendix B.)[5]

- **Announcements**—Include the asset-building language when talking about appropriate activities and opportunities in the congregation. Periodically have an Asset-Building Minute when a congregation member tells about what he or she (or someone else) is doing to build assets. Or occasionally have someone remind members what they can do to build assets. For example: "Before you leave today, I hope every adult will take an opportunity to greet at least three young people, and every young person will say 'hi' to at least three adults."

- **Worship services**—Work with worship leaders to include information about asset building in the worship service through special presentations, liturgical responses, music, or sermons. In some traditions, it may be appropriate to design a complete worship service around the asset-building theme. An opportunity for this is Children's Sabbath, coordinated by the Children's Defense Fund (for more information, contact CDF, 25 E Street NW, Washington, DC, 20001, 202-662-3652).

- **Religious education for both youth and adults**—Introduce asset building in educational settings for both youth and adults. You may want to use the video *A Foundation for Success* and the accompanying leader's guide (see page 193) to start up a discussion. Or adapt the workshop outline presented in Tipsheet 14.

- **Special events and celebrations**—Plan a special party, picnic, fair, or other event that highlights asset building. Have banners, balloons, and intergenerational activities that carry through the theme. Or integrate an asset-building focus into an ongoing event in the congregation, such as an annual picnic or banquet.

- **Presentations to small groups**—There may be a variety of small groups and committees that meet in the congregation (women's circles, men's groups, etc.) with which you could share an asset-building message. You might work with several youth to develop a skit to use with these different groups. After the presentation, have people brainstorm about how their group does or could build assets.[6]

- **Congregation's marquee**—If your congregation has a marquee sign on the street, display simple asset-building messages on it.

- **Individual conversations**—Never underestimate the power of one-to-one conversations. Ask everyone who is committed to asset building to talk to at least two other people about it.

- **Electronic communication**—Many congregations are now developing Web pages and electronic mail. Use these vehicles to communicate about asset building. If your congregation has a Web page, connect it to Search Institute's Web page on asset building.

A Long, Creative Process

This chapter describes the asset-building process as if it is linear, straightforward, and clear. Yet the reality of most people's experience with asset building is usually not so cut-and-dried. In the real world you have to deal with quirks and politics and personalities that make everything much messier! Some of the ideas suggested here may not work in your congregation. Other approaches may fit much better. Thus, the process and ideas in this chapter are more of a springboard than a road map. They may get you headed in the right direction, but your team must "complete the dive."

As already noted, experts in organizational change say it generally takes at least three to five years for a significant change to become fully integrated into an organization. That is certainly true for congregations that rely on volunteer members whose other commitments make it impossible to move quickly on everything that needs to be done to embody the many dimensions of asset building.

The goal, then, should not be to achieve everything you hope for immediately. Rather, it should be to equip yourself and your congregation for a journey toward creating a community of faith that truly makes a lasting difference in the lives of many young people.

Eight Steps for Nurturing Your Congregation's Commitment to Asset Building

Key Points

- **Introducing asset building is tough work and it takes time. There are eight steps:**

  1. Share the asset-building vision with allies and stakeholders.

  2. Build a "vision team."

  3. Listen and learn.

  4. Develop a vision for asset building.

  5. Shape your asset-building messages.

  6. Create awareness, energy, and commitment.

  7. Set up systems for success.

  8. Network with others.

Questions for Reflection and Discussion

- Who are the people in your congregation that it's important to inform about and involve in asset building?

- What information do you need about youth, families, your congregation, and your community to help you plan your asset-building efforts?

- What parts of the asset-building vision resonate the most with your congregation's heritage, values, and priorities?

Suggestions for Getting Started

- Identify people in your congregation who can form a core team to shape asset-building efforts.

- Schedule a series of team meetings to plan your asset-building efforts. Use Tipsheet 7 to guide your planning meetings.

- Make opportunities to talk with congregational leaders, youth, and other members about the potential of asset building. Distribute the 10 bulletin inserts found in Appendix A.

Integrating Asset Building Throughout Congregational Life

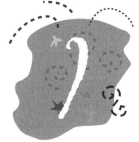

n his book *Black and White Styles of Youth Ministry,* William R. Myers reports on in-depth studies of youth ministry in two mainline Christian congregations, one black and one white. One characteristic that distinguishes the "style" of the black congregation is the way youth are integrated into the whole congregation. While there are many programs specifically for children, their work with youth is quite different. He writes:

> As children entered adolescence, however, things changed. Adolescent youth were reminded of their "pilgrimage" when they joined a choir carefully demarcated as the young *adult* choir. Here youth were treated very nearly as peers by adults. Adult advisors advised but did not lead this group. Leaders were the youth themselves who not only assumed major responsibility for the choir, but who also led worship in every way, including preaching Sunday's sermon. Grace Church seemed to say that by the time children reached adolescence they should be encouraged to make major contributions within the church community.[1]

This story from Grace Church stands in sharp contrast to the dominant models of youth work in the United States. As reflected in the majority of resources and training for youth work, the typical congregation has a distinct structure that runs essentially independent of any other congregational activities. Youth rarely, if ever, interact meaningfully with more than a handful of adults who are designated to work with youth. Connections to other areas of congregational life are coincidental or serendipitous. Almost the only time the youth program is discussed by the congregation's board is when there is a problem.

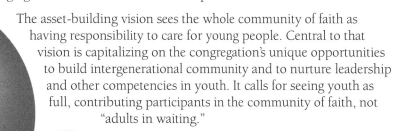

The asset-building vision sees the whole community of faith as having responsibility to care for young people. Central to that vision is capitalizing on the congregation's unique opportunities to build intergenerational community and to nurture leadership and other competencies in youth. It calls for seeing youth as full, contributing participants in the community of faith, not "adults in waiting."

If you were to draw a diagram of youth work in the typical congregation, it might look something like the one at left.

This chapter—and the asset-building framework—suggests a different diagram.

In this second diagram, youth are certainly a distinct part of congregational life. There are age-specific opportunities for them to build their knowledge, skills, and relationships with peers (the focus of Chapter 5). They spend time with their peers, just as adults spend time with other adults who share a similar place or experience in life (parents with other parents, singles with other singles, etc.). But the difference implied by the second diagram is profound: Youth are seen as integral, not tangential, to congregational life. The congregation is not equated with adult activities; rather, the congregation is viewed as an intergenerational community that includes all people, giving them opportunities to be with people their own age while also forming relationships across generations.

This theme will be familiar to veterans in youth work, particularly in the mainline Christian traditions. Charles R. Foster recalls efforts in the 1960s (prompted by ecumenical discussions through the National Council of Churches and the World Council of Churches) to fully integrate youth into congregational life. His description of the dialogues from 30 years ago sounds remarkably current:

> The developmental character of adolescence meant that youth could no longer be described as "the church of tomorrow." Neither could the task of church ministries for youth be seen simply as "inducting young people into the Christian fellowship and preparing them for future responsible roles" in church life. Instead, they must be seen as having the ability to participate with increasing sophistication in the full range of church life and mission.[2]

While many congregations have made important strides toward realizing this vision, many continue to operate youth programs that isolate youth from the larger congregation and that underestimate the capacity of young people to contribute to the congregation's life and mission. Mark DeVries puts the challenge bluntly: "There are worse things a church can do to its teenagers than providing miserable programs for them—patently isolating teenagers from Christian adults is at the top of the list."[3] (And, I would add, the same critique could apply to many other faith traditions as well.)

In addition, this asset-building vision challenges congregations to evaluate many aspects of their life to determine how various activities either enhance or impede asset building. This self-examination might include examining budget priorities, integrating youth into leadership, involving youth in worship, and planning for ways all areas of congregational life can nurture assets.

In some cases, smaller congregations may have an advantage in creating this kind of intergenerational community. Including youth is more natural in settings where everyone knows each other and where youth can be more visible within the congregation. Larger congregations can easily become segmented by age so that young people rarely even see adults.

Similarly, some communities of color (African American, Native American, and Hispanic American, for example) often maintain a stronger emphasis on the intergenerational community of faith, and they have a stronger tradition of honoring the wisdom of elders. For these congregations, this dimension of asset building is an affirmation of a strength in their culture and heritage.

This chapter highlights four general themes for integrating youth into congregational life: nurturing a welcoming climate for youth; encouraging individual commitment throughout the congregation; building intergenerational relationships; and reshaping congregational leadership. Then it offers ideas for integrating asset building into many specific areas of congregational life: worship, religious education, social activities, congregational care, and facilities maintenance and operations.

nurturing a Welcoming Climate for youth

Just as social climate is an important part of a youth program, it has a great deal of impact on young people's experience of the larger congregation as well. Earlier Search Institute research suggests that a "warm climate" is one of the most important factors in influencing a young person's loyalty to the congregation.[4] Several steps can be taken to make the congregation's climate more youth-friendly.

Evaluate current climate

A first step is to evaluate the current climate. How do youth feel when they are with the whole congregation? Are they ignored? Do they know people? Do they feel as if people are frowning or smiling at them?

At least three groups should be asked these kinds of questions: active youth, those who don't attend regularly, and newcomers or visitors. The active youth will have a deeper understanding of congregational dynamics. But their experiences may be quite different from others. A Search Institute study of youth in The Lutheran Church–Missouri Synod found, for example, that infrequent attenders were only about half as likely to experience a positive climate as regular attenders or those in leadership roles, as shown here:

	Inactive/ Infrequent Attenders	Regular Attenders	Active Leaders/ Volunteers
The congregation has a warm, welcoming, and friendly climate.	24%	42%	57%
Youth often experience the care and support of an adult.	7%	10%	20%
People take time to get to know each other.	25%	37%	60%

Newcomers and visitors can also lend valuable insight, particularly since they notice things that are taken for granted by regular attenders. They can report how many people actually talked with them on their first visit, the times when they felt lost or out of place in activities, and things about the congregation that really made them feel welcome and at home.

Address existing barriers to assimilation

The issue of welcoming youth from the community can be particularly challenging for middle-class congregations that seek to reach out to vulnerable youth, when the young people's only experience with a congregation may have been negative. As Jim DiRaddo, an urban youth work consultant in Pennsylvania, has said, "The church stands as a very imposing figure in the community, representing a whole lot of things which the people in the streets simply aren't comfortable with."[5]

Tipsheet 16 suggests some of the "invisible signs" congregations post that tell youth they are not welcome. Examining these issues and seeking to address those that are problematic is key to developing a welcoming climate for young people throughout the congregation.

Increase youth visibility

One of the reasons youth sometimes don't feel welcome is that they are invisible to many adults in the congregation. Plans are made and activities are led with little or no recognition that young people will—or could—be participating. Adults greet other adults without saying a word to the child or teenager who is accompanying her or his parent. Many of the strategies outlined in this chapter will increase youth visibility. Some specific ideas to try include:

- If the congregation prepares name tags for adults to wear during congregational activities, prepare similar ones for the youth.

- Highlight youth activities and accomplishments to the whole congregation.

- If the congregation has a newsletter, include youth news and activities (even if you also have a special newsletter for youth).[6]

- Give youth opportunities to make announcements, serve as ushers, and perform other tasks that make them visible in the larger community of faith. (See the leadership section later in this chapter.)

- Highlight youth activities and programs as *congregational* activities. For example, when youth go on a work camp or other mission/service trip, recognize them as representatives of the whole congregation, not just the youth program.

T I P S H E E T   1 6

"Youth Not Welcome": A Too-Common Sign in Congregations

Congregations often want to provide quality programs for "our" youth, yet put up invisible but powerful signs that other youth from the community are not really welcome. Here are some of the "hidden" messages that congregations often post.[7]

- **"No trespassing"**—Members become highly protective of their traditions and facilities. The result is that youth get the feeling the congregation is someone else's, not theirs.

- **"No suit, no cash, no service"**—Wayne Gordon, former pastor of Lawndale Community Church in Chicago, Illinois, once asked community members why they didn't attend a congregation. Two of the top reasons were they didn't have nice clothes to wear and they didn't have money to put in the offering plate. Youth programs add similar pressure by charging fees for activities without scholarships or subsidies for those who cannot pay.

- **"Whites only"**—Many white-dominated congregations exhibit subtle racism that keeps youth of color from feeling welcomed. This may range from the jokes youth tell to the cliques they form to the style of worship and leadership in the congregation. Congregations that traditionally serve another specific ethnic community may find similar issues of exclusivity.

- **"One way"**—Traditions are hard to change. Jim DiRaddo describes the problem this way: "Many white churches would love to have a black choir come over and sing on Sunday morning. And they'll tolerate it—even enjoy it—and say, 'Wasn't that neat? The blacks have such rhythm.' ... But if you try to introduce that music into the church, even in an urban setting, folks will defend their right to maintain their traditions to the point where they alienate a vast number of people."

- **"Do not disturb"**—Congregations may want to reach out to youth, but they don't want youth to make any noise or interruptions. Many youth find this attitude to be stiff and confining.

Educate adults and youth

Most of the time when youth are ignored or excluded, it is unintentional—an old habit or pattern that people don't even think about anymore. Raising the issue and challenging those assumptions can be an important first step in creating a more welcoming environment for youth in the congregation. Something as simple as reminding ushers each week to make a special effort to greet children and youth can make a huge difference (particularly when those ushers start greeting kids all the time!). Similarly, youth can be reminded that they, too, can take the first step in saying "hi" to adults they see.

Make youth *essential* to congregational life

Often when congregations involve youth in meaningful ways, they have a backup plan "in case the kids don't come through." Such an attitude of low expectations for youth undermines the fact that they have much to contribute to the congregation (though they, like adults, will not always do it perfectly).

In the young adult choir described by Myers, young people are solely responsible for leading and organizing. Not only are youth in charge of the choir's operations, but the choir is expected to regularly lead music in the worship service—a central role in the congregation's worshipping life. And there's no backup plan. As one youth advisor said: "Many churches mouth the words 'train up a child in the way he should go,' but then expect youth to get it by osmosis. Grace Church's intent is to empower youth now so that we have permanent leaders in the years to come."[8]

Encouraging Individual Commitment Throughout the Congregation

In too many cases, a congregation committing to a new idea means that a handful of individuals forms a committee and takes action on behalf of the whole

---

T I P S H E E T   1 7

A Sample Pledge to Encourage Congregation Members to Build Assets

The following sample pledge is adapted from one developed by St. Luke Presbyterian Church in Minnetonka, Minnesota.

Everyone in our congregation can make a difference in the lives of children and youth. It can begin with a personal commitment to asset building. This asset-building pledge gives concrete ways you can make a difference in the lives of children and youth—whether you're a child, a teenager, or an adult. Please consider signing this pledge. Then, most important, find ways to live the commitment throughout the coming year.

The Asset Builder Pledge

In my congregation, community, and world, I pledge to be an asset builder for children and youth by . . .

A dvocating

S pending time

S howing that I care

E ncouraging and valuing

T eaching and mentoring

Each of these commitments can contribute in an important way to raising healthy, responsible, and caring youth in our congregation and community. Throughout the year, the Asset-Building Team will provide reminders and tips to help you live up to your commitment.

---

congregation. Then the rest of the congregation feels good because of all the good things "we" do.

Some tasks can be done effectively by a small committed group. But asset building is something that needs to permeate as much of the congregation as possible for it to reach its potential. It's important to get people, one by one, to take asset building personally—to say, "This is something I can and will do in my own life."

My congregation asked adults and youth to sign an Asset-Building Pledge. (See Tipsheet 17.) Our goal was to encourage people to begin seeing that asset building isn't really about things "the congregation should do" or another "neat idea." Asset building is really about each adult taking personal responsibility for building assets for all the children and youth whose lives they touch.

Of course, signing a pledge is not enough. The congregation needs to provide a variety of reminders and opportunities to help those who sign the pledge keep their commitment both with youth in the congregation as well as youth in the community. The asset-building planning team could offer classes and tips to help people build some basic skills and ideas for fulfilling their pledge.

In addition to helping individuals commit to asset building, the pledge creates a concrete, shared commitment that has a sense of focus and movement throughout the congregation. It is general enough that people can "plug in" in many different ways. But it is also challenging in asking for specific commitments that may provoke new kinds of commitments and actions.

Building Intergenerational Relationships

The asset-building vision is really a community-building vision. Forming relationships for asset building is a community-building activity. But while congregations have tremendous potential as an intergenerational community, too often they are as age-segregated as our society.

Relationships do not form automatically; they require intentional focus. As James W. White writes: "Persons join the church/synagogue as individuals or as families with little assurance that sustaining 'ties that bind' will be tied. Significant relationships are not guaranteed merely because one's name is on the membership roll."[9]

In an ideal world, perhaps, intergenerational relationships would form naturally. But in this age-segregated culture, you have to be intentional and programmatic— at least to get it started. (See Tipsheet 18 for ideas.) Here are some strategies to consider.

Encourage individual relationships across generations

Congregations can also encourage individual relationships between adults and youth. These may be relatively superficial (greeting each other each week), or they can become significant supportive relationships for many years.

Sometimes an individual adult may develop a relationship with a group of children or youth (or vice versa). Each year, **Mayflower Congregational Church in Minneapolis, Minnesota**, for example, has a Senior Friend Program in which an older member or couple adopts a Sunday school class and then sticks with that class until it graduates. While there is always some turnover, many of these relationships have flourished across the years. The seniors bring treats to the classes, or they read stories from time to time. On special days, all the kids sit with their "grandparent" during the worship service. And if a Senior Friend becomes

Fast Facts

Young People's Connections to Adults in Their Congregation

Search Institute surveyed 1,100 young people in Minneapolis, Minnesota, Durham, North Carolina, and St. Louis, Missouri, about their experiences in their congregations. Most of the youth were involved in a congregation. Here are the percentages of youth who said that each statement is true about three or more adults in their congregation (not including parents, but including staff and volunteers):

There are three or more adults who:

59%
Give you lots of encouragement

54%
Talk with you at least once a month

44%
You look forward to spending time with

19%
You go to when you need advice about a problem or concern

hospitalized or moves to a nursing home, the children send cards or visit as a class. Says Children's Ministry Director Jane Petrich, "The kids know they're valued when there are caring adults around them."

One idea for highlighting the importance of all congregants taking responsibility for youth is to create a bulletin board with the title, "The Asset Builders at _____." Post pictures of all congregants all over the bulletin board. (This is easy if your congregation has a pictorial directory.) Then place a mirror in the middle of the bulletin board.[10]

While all youth need significant nonparent relationships, these relationships can be particularly important for young people who have inadequate support at home because of a crisis or ongoing problem such as divorce, acute illness, poverty, addiction, or other stresses. A proactive, caring relationship with an adult in the congregation can be pivotal in helping the young person (not to mention the whole family) cope with and come through the problem. This support may include an occasional phone call to check in, invitations to attend events together, or offers of a ride to and from a congregational event because parents are not available.

Many congregations find ways to establish mentoring relationships between adults and youth. Sometimes adults are paired with youth through a particular rite of passage (such as confirmation or bar/bat mitzvah). Other times, links are made based on vocational interests. Finally, congregations often encourage adults to become mentors for young people in the community.

In addition to the traditional one-to-one mentoring, Mark Cannister writes in *Youthworker* about the possibilities of "mentoring communities" in which several youth and adults form a small group that serves as a mentoring community. He argues that these mentoring communities address some of the challenges that occur in one-to-one mentoring relationships, such as people moving frequently, anxiety from adult mentors, and difficulty in maintaining accountability.[11]

Equip people with skills for asset building

For some people, relationships seem to come easily. They remember names. They always have something to talk about, even with people they just met. But other people break into a sweat at just the thought of having to introduce themselves to someone new. Part of the difference is personality. But part is also a difference in skills—skills that can be taught.

In our enthusiasm to build assets, we may forget that many people do not have the skills they need to be part of the team. We need to stop and guide them in how to meet other people, how to form friendships, how to articulate and enforce boundaries, how to be affirming of youth, how to talk about their values. The good news is that these things can be taught and learned. Here are some ideas for what congregations can do:

- Whenever encouraging youth or adults to undertake a new activity, provide training or tips for how to do that activity. For example, if you are asking congregation members to get to know youth, include in the congregation's newsletter some tips for how to greet youth and some things they could talk about or do together. Similarly, if you ask youth to serve as leaders, guide them in learning the skills they need to be effective in those roles. Or if you are encouraging parents to set boundaries for their children, help them build the skills they need to set and enforce those boundaries in ways that are positive and most likely to be respected.

- When taking youth into new situations (such as on a service project where they will be with people who are very different from them), coach them in advance on some basic skills they can use in those situations.

- When young people are struggling with a particular problem or issue, help them identify the skills they need to solve that problem. For example, if they are having difficulty getting along with a friend, what skills could they use that would help to turn the friendship around?

T I P S H E E T   1 8

Ideas for Building Intergenerational Relationships in Your Congregation

- Encourage adults to invite a young person to attend a congregational social activity, service project, or worship service with them.

- Use adults as mentors to provide significant adult relationships for youth from confirmation or bar/bat mitzvah or other rites of passage into young adulthood through high school. Suggest actions and activities that adults and youth can do together.

- Involve youth and adults together in projects such as serving midweek meals, cleanup days, and other activities.

- Offer quarterly intergenerational activity nights . Ask youth and senior citizens to help plan them together.

- Continuously encourage adults in the church to reach out to children and youth by saying "hi" to them, sending them birthday cards, helping out with religious education, going to their school events, and other ways of showing they are interested and care.

- Keep a list of adults who can be referrals for youth in times of stress, such as loss of a friend or parent, a move to another city, or family conflict.[12]

Address the question of safety

In advocating forming intergenerational relationships, we must address safety issues that surface when you begin talking about connecting young people with nonfamily adults. Many youth programs and congregations have extensive policies and guidelines to protect against youth workers who might violate the trust of the congregation and the youth by physically or sexually abusing young people. Highly publicized incidents of clergy and youth-worker involvement in abuse with young people have heightened awareness and a sense of caution.

It needs to be said that abuse will never be a problem in the vast majority of relationships between youth and adults in a congregation. But it is also important to exercise appropriate caution in order to protect the well-being of the young people involved. Failure to do so could lead to serious consequences for the congregation and, most important, to the young people involved, interfering with their ability to develop assets for the rest of their lives. An excellent guide titled *Reducing the Risk of Child*

S N A P S H O T

Musings of a Mentor

The following article was written by Robert V. Stewart, a member of **Grace Lutheran Church in Wenatchee, Washington,** who became a mentor for young people in his congregation when he was in his 80s. His story illustrates the potential of mentoring for both youth and adults.

He approached me one day after worship service. I knew him casually as one of the kids who attended church with his family. "Mr. Stewart," he began, "would you be my mentor?"

"Gosh, I don't know. What's involved?" I replied.

"Well, you're supposed to be sort of a spiritual friend to me during my confirmation."

"How long will that take?"

"Three years."

"Boy, that's a long time. I don't know whether I'll be around that long," I answered. I was 80 at the time.

"At the rate you're going I think you'll make it," he said, smiling.

"Might be OK," I said. "By the way, what's your name?"

"Shane Craven. Our name is in the directory."

"Let me think it over, and I'll call you," I replied, departing with his "thank you" ringing in my ears.

On the way home, my wife and I discussed his request. "You should be honored," she said. "You've always enjoyed teaching Sunday school. Why not give it a try?"

I accepted his invitation. I've enjoyed a fine experience, one well expressed in this bit of philosophy Shane later sent me: "Some people come into our lives and quietly go. Others stay for a while and leave footprints on our hearts, and we are never the same."

It took about a year to find a comfortable relationship. My awkward questions and his "yep" and "nope" answers did not move the process rapidly. I didn't want to invade his lifestyle too much, and he wasn't sure just what this old geezer was like.

But we worked at it, chatted about odds and ends when we met, and exchanged greeting cards at appropriate times. I took pictures of his confirmation class and of soccer games he refereed.

I began seeing his name in the local paper on school honor roll lists and in the church bulletin as an acolyte or usher. I put these things and others into a scrapbook, which we presented to him at his confirmation.

We are still going strong seven years since he asked me to be my mentor. He stops by once in a while for Coke and cookies, sometimes with his girlfriend.

Last fall he went off to college. We'll still be good friends, he assures me. But my wife and I miss him, just like when our kids left the nest. That's life. So long, good buddy.

This article originally appeared in *The Lutheran* (May 1997). Used with permission of the author.

Sexual Abuse in Your Church: A Complete and Practical Guidebook for Prevention and Risk Reduction, describes the problem this way:

> Child sexual abuse robs children of their childhood and can potentially scar its young victims for life. Too often in the past, the effects of abuse were minimized or dismissed. Children were viewed as being resilient. Recent research has shown that children can suffer significant pain from even a single abuse incident. . . . When church leaders, pastors, and respected congregational workers perpetuate the abuse, lifelong religious confusion and deep feelings of enmity toward God and the church can occur.[13]

At the same time, we cannot be paralyzed by these concerns, but need to respond thoughtfully. The key is to find a balance of appropriate caution to minimize risks without such tight restrictions that they hamper healthy, beneficial relationships. Being intentional also protects the reputations of adults in the face of inaccurate, malicious allegations that might arise. Tipsheet 19 suggests some appropriate ways to balance these concerns.

Infuse asset building into existing activities

There are probably numerous times when youth and adults are together in your congregation, but many of these occasions may provide little opportunity for relationship building. By adding time for small-group discussion across generations or shaping activities so generations can spend time together, you can increase cross-generation contact without adding more activities or programs. (This chapter ends with dozens of ideas for infusing asset building into all areas of congregational life.)

Plan group programs and activities

Plan group activities that focus on building relationships across generations. These may include social activities, recreation, music, service projects, dances, education events, and many other opportunities. Structure them so that people share experiences that form a foundation for conversation and reflection.

My congregation produces an annual intergenerational drama and music event. People of all ages participate in planning, building the set, acting, singing, and dozens of other activities that are involved in the event. Many people comment on how much fun they have together in getting ready for the performance. The relationships formed during each production are reinforced the following year when preparations for the next show begin.

Reshaping Congregational Leadership

Most leadership structures in congregations are designed (inadvertently, one would hope) to segregate or exclude youth. A typical congregation might have a worship committee, an education committee, a mission committee, a social committee, a properties committee, and . . . a youth committee. With the exception of the education committee (which often puts most of its energy into education for younger children), all the committees have a *de facto* focus on adults, since everything for youth is the responsibility of the youth committee.

To be fair, most youth committees were formed so youth would not get lost in the shuffle. The committee gives a structure, focus, and direction to activities and programs for youth. But the side effect is that youth are routinely neglected when the corporate life of the congregation is being discussed. The structure also has the effect of letting other groups "off the hook" when it comes to providing leadership opportunities for youth: "That's the youth committee's job." What can be done? Here are some areas for action.

Congregational planning and leadership

In a typical congregation, the leadership board rarely addresses youth issues. Similarly, staff who don't have direct responsibility for youth may pay little attention to them. Unless intentional efforts are made, the congregation's leaders may inadvertently concentrate their energy on programs and activities for adults—unless there's a "youth problem" to deal with.

TIPSHEET 19

Providing Safety in Relationships Between Youth and Adults[14]

Marilyn Sharpe, confirmation director at **Mount Olivet Lutheran Church in Minneapolis, Minnesota**, recently completed an extensive process for establishing her congregation's policies and procedures for "the care of children and vulnerable adults" that seek to place safeguards against physical, sexual, and emotional abuse. Some of her suggestions include:

- **Minimize or eliminate time alone**—The greatest danger lies in relationships where one adult spends time alone with one child. As wonderful as these times can be for forming relationships, they can also be the most damaging. Sharpe recommends never having one child and one adult together. Furthermore, it's best to always have more than one adult.

  An additional precaution is to have people meet in public places (such as at the congregation's facilities). Encourage one-to-one interaction during congregation activities such as eating together at picnics or congregation meals, sitting together in worship, etc. If people want to do activities together away from the congregation (go out to eat, go to a game, etc.), encourage them to pair up with others. Then drop off the kids before either of the adults so that one adult is never alone in a car with a young person.

- **Be sure you know participating adults**—Sharpe says sexual predators may come to a congregation if they hear it is focusing on forming intergenerational relationships. For this reason, she encourages a policy that says someone has to have been active in the congregation at least six months before getting into a planned adult-youth relationship.

- **Set clear ground rules and expectations**—Adults, youth, parents, and others in the congregation (whether or not they are in an intentional mentoring relationship) need to have a shared understanding of what is acceptable and what is not acceptable in adult-youth relationships. Some appropriate ground rules include:

  1. Have clear guidelines for appropriate and inappropriate touch.

  2. No secrets are acceptable between a young person and the adult (such as an adult saying, "Let's just have this be our little secret"). If, however, a young person reveals abuse or neglect at home, that issue should be reported to appropriate authorities (the police) and/or to the congregation's senior clergy.

  3. If an adult-youth pair wants to do something together away from the congregation, they should team up with others for the activity.

- **Connect families with the adults**—It's important for parents to know and be in touch with the adults who are spending time with their children. Provide opportunities for them to get together and build relationships.

- **Screen adults, particularly for individual relationships**—If there is little chance that an adult will spend time alone with one youth, screening may not be needed. But as the opportunities for one-to-one time alone increase, the level of screening also needs to increase. Thorough background checks are appropriate if you expect an adult to spend time alone with individual young people.

  One of the problems, Sharpe says, is that sexual predators appear, on the surface, to have many of the qualities of a great asset builder. They tend to be great listeners. They know what's important to kids. And they meet kids on their own terms. But then they cross the line and violate the youth's trust and person.

  Once relationships have begun forming, don't ignore them. Periodically check to see how each relationship is going, and watch for warning signs.

- **Have a clear procedure to deal with problems**—Make it clear that anyone who believes one of the ground rules has been broken must report the violation. Intervene quickly if you see or hear about any warning signs that a relationship may not be healthy. And make it nonthreatening for young people to report any concerns they have.

  Note: These suggestions do not represent legal advice. In developing a congregation's policy, it is important to seek the services of knowledgeable legal counsel.

These ideas focus on keeping asset building on the agenda and keeping a youth voice at the table.

- Educate congregational leaders (e.g., staff, board) about asset building.

- Survey the congregation on needs, interests, and priorities related to youth and asset building.

- Invite leaders to participate in asset-building events in the congregation and community.

- Invite youth to serve on the congregation's board.

- Include a regular report on youth work and asset building on the board's agenda.

- Develop a shared statement of core values for youth and adults in the congregation.

- Highlight asset building in the head of staff's responsibilities.

- Set up a youth internship opportunity to work after school with the head of staff (imam, pastor, priest, rabbi, etc.) or another staff member.

Budgeting and fund-raising

Another symbol of the isolation of youth from the larger congregational context is that many congregations have no budget for youth activities. Whereas there may be a sizable commitment of congregational resources (through contributions or dues) to adult activities, young people are expected to raise their own funds for youth activities. In addition, in traditions that ask for pledges and contributions, youth are rarely included in that process (even though many may have sizable incomes from part-time jobs).

A challenge, then, is to reintegrate youth activities into the congregation's budget in a way that the congregation claims and supports youth activities as integral to its mission, not something to do only if the youth can make enough money through fund-raisers. At the same time, youth must be challenged to see their own responsibility to contribute to the congregation as members of the community.

Integrate responsibility for youth into the leadership structures

I propose that the following question be posted and articulated whenever a decision is being made in the congregation: WHAT ABOUT THE YOUTH?

T I P S H E E T   2 0

Integrating Responsibility for Youth Through a Matrix Leadership Structure

The following chart illustrates what a leadership committee structure might look like if a congregation used a matrix model to integrate age-specific concerns within each programmatic area in the congregation.

	WORSHIP	EDUCATION	SERVICE	PROPERTY	SOCIAL
Children	Seth	Laura	Vicki	Ann	Jack
Youth	Alfred	Deborah	Richard	Joe	Jessie
Adults	Marta	Ken	Terrance	Maria	Rebecca

Planning a worship service? *What about the youth?* Planning a congregational service project? *What about the youth?* Choosing members for a committee? *What about the youth?* Planning a congregation-wide visitation program? *What about the youth?*

There may be times when a group will decide that "this really is just an adult activity," but, more often than not, the question will remind the group to think a little differently. (And, of course, it will be easier to ask and answer the question if young people are in the room at the time!)

One model for integrating responsibility for youth without losing an age-specific focus would be to develop a "matrix" leadership style. In this model, you would have essentially two integrating structures, as shown in Tipsheet 20. People might meet with their programmatic team one month (for example, the service group—Vicki, Richard, and Terrance), then meet with their age group leaders the other month (for example, the youth leaders—Alfred, Deborah, Richard, Joe, and Jessie).

I have never encountered a congregation that uses this model, but it is similar to the matrix organization model that is being touted for complex organizations. Implemented in a congregation, it could have the potential for sparking creative connections across ages as well as a balance across many programmatic areas of congregational life.

Involve youth in leadership roles

One of the dangers in any effort that seeks to benefit youth is that youth become the passive recipients of kindness, not active contributors to the process. John P. Kretzmann and Paul H. Schmitz put it powerfully in their critique of many efforts to help young people:

> In the cliché, people (adults) in villages act to "raise" young people. Young folks are the objects of the action, never the subjects. They are passive and useless. They are defined as deficient—of knowledge, of skills, of any useful capacities—and relegated with their cohorts to the filling stations we call schools. The assumption is that, magically, at age 18 or 21, young people will emerge from their years of being filled, and re-enter the community as full and useful contributors. . . . Our villages suffer when we fail to empower all members of our society, but especially when we fail those who represent our future.[15]

We often talk about the importance of involving youth in congregational leadership. But those efforts can backfire if youth are not adequately equipped for that role. William Myers tells the story of the pastor of Grace Church, a large congregation church in Chicago, who actively involves youth in leadership for worship, including having them preach every fifth Sunday. At first he got a lot of resistance to it, because people wanted to hear the pastor preach.

But he stuck with it (and stopped announcing in advance who was preaching, so people would show up no matter what!). He put a lot of effort into educating the congregation about its responsibility for nurturing leadership in youth. Just as important, though, the congregation spends a lot of time working with the youth to help them be successful in their task. This involves having them work together on the sermon and practice in advance so the pastor can give feedback and guidance. The pastor says: "Now I can sit there without having a heart attack, because I know someone has worked with the speaker. We train them—and some of the most powerful messages in this church are preached by youth."[16]

An asset-building perspective calls congregations to involve youth in leadership and service in many areas of congregational life. Here are some possibilities:

- Whenever you ask youth to lead, train them in what they can expect and how they can be effective in their role. Provide ongoing support and guidance.

- Include youth in the center of leadership of youth programming. "One reason youth involvement works," asserts a report from the National Assembly, "is because it creates a sense of ownership on the part of the young. Programs they are directly involved in are no longer something adults do for them, they are their programs which they do with adults."[17]

- Provide opportunities for youth to serve in leadership roles in the larger congregation. This could include serving on committees, providing leadership in worship and other activities, organizing special events for the congregation, and leading programs and activities for younger children.

- Offer regular service opportunities that youth can plan and lead.

Equip adults for youth involvement

Just as young people need to be prepared to participate in leadership with adults, adults need training in how to include youth in leadership and decision-making roles. Otherwise, they can be condescending or timid in their interactions with youth. The result is a negative experience for everyone. Tipsheet 21 gives tips for leadership groups that include both youth and adults.

Ideas for Integrating Asset Building into Congregational Life

While asset building can have implications for all areas of congregational life, it's sometimes a stretch to think of specific ways to do it. It may be easy to integrate asset building into worship, but it can be more challenging (and creative!) to think about how it fits with property and maintenance. Here are dozens of ideas for how asset building might be addressed in major function areas in typical congregations. (Some of the ideas may not be workable within some faith traditions because of congregational structure and restrictions.)

Use this idea list as a springboard to think about what might work in your own congregation. Take the ideas to the groups responsible for each area and find out how they see this focus fitting into their responsibilities.

Worship services

In most congregations, young people are expected to participate in worship alongside adults. And, indeed, worship services are the most consistent and visible times when the intergenerational community of faith gathers. These experiences can connect youth with the resources of their faith tradition, offering a sense of purpose, hope, and direction. In addition, services offer an opportunity to build community across generations, while also calling the community to action for children and youth. As Roland Martinson writes, "If a congregation is to faithfully join young people in their life with God, that congregation needs to develop its services into significant and welcoming places for youth."[18]

Each faith tradition has its own worship format, structure, and requirements. And there are strong arguments against changing the flow, structure, and basic elements of worship that have a rich history and deep meaning. But, as James W. White writes, "The basic integrity of worship need not be compromised. What persons in charge of the liturgy can do, though, is pay greater attention to the language, action, pace, and so on of services so that they communicate and resonate with as broad an age spectrum as possible."[19] He goes on to describe what an age-inclusive worship service (which is highly compatible with asset building) might involve:

> Responsive liturgies, for example, might include lines to be spoken by children-under-twelve, parents, single persons, retirees, and so on, thus recognizing congregational distinctions while being one body. There would be time built in during services for sharing between and among people of all generations.... [S]uch might include questions or topics to be considered more than just saying, "Hello . . . nice to meet you." There certainly should

---

T I P S H E E T   2 1

Tips for Leadership Groups That Include Both Youth and Adults

Getting started

- Expect some adults to be resistant to involving youth in decision making and leadership positions; most are not used to working side by side with youth. Discuss openly people's feelings and be creative in developing ways that youth and adults can begin to work together.

- Be creative and sensitive about meeting times and places. For example, if late afternoon and evening meeting times interfere with youth's after-school jobs, consider meeting on a weekend morning or on a weekday at lunchtime in the school cafeteria.

- Understand the needs of youth participants. If they come to a meeting straight from school, you might need to serve snacks. Since most youth probably don't carry calendars with them, you might need to make reminder phone calls a day or two before each meeting. (If you don't know the youth's needs, ask them! Then ask again after you've had a meeting or two.)

Communication and language issues

- Talk openly about language issues. Will you all go by first names? Is the term "kids" offensive to some participants? What about statements like "You're too young to understand" or "You're too old to understand"?

- Become aware of and confront adult bias. Watch for unconscious stereotyping of youth by age, by appearance or clothing style, or by gender, race, ethnicity, or economic class.

- Give each participant—youth and adult—a chance to talk and give each speaker your full listening attention.

- Be intentional about taking youth seriously and be ready to redirect the conversation if adult participants talk too much, interrupt or ignore youth, or are critical or scolding.

- If youth are hesitant to speak up or tend to respond "I don't know" to questions you're sure they have an answer for, help them learn how to identify the reasons for their reticence (e.g., shy, afraid of put-downs, difficulty telling when people are done talking) and be encouraging and supportive when they do speak up.

Training, support, and process

- Make sure to bring new people—youth or adult—up to speed. Review the group's goals and provide premeeting training about basics such as meeting structures, discussion ground rules, and agendas and reports.

- Be aware of the developmental needs of young people and accommodate the preferred learning styles of all group members. This may mean adding more experiential meeting elements, augmenting written and verbal communication with visual aids, and breaking into small groups.

- Start off with a game or other fun activity that helps all participants with the transition from other activities to the meeting.

- Plan concrete projects, give youth responsibilities early, and expect achievement. Let youth learn from their own mistakes, too.

- Be clear about each participant's role and level of authority, the time and number of meetings, and the expected duration of the commitment.

- Consider having mentors for young people. An adult mentor could build a one-on-one relationship with one youth participant, meet with her or him before and after meetings, send reminders about meeting times, provide the youth with access to resources (e.g., copy machine, fax, computer), encourage the participating young people to rely on each other, back youth decisions and actions, and assist and support the youth during meetings.

- Have youth and adults periodically evaluate the role of youth (e.g., are youth being given only insignificant or peripheral tasks?).

be more drama in the ritual, and there would be visual, audible, and kinetic dimensions which take the "whole person" into account.[20]

Here are some additional ideas for integrating asset building into worship, which you can use and adapt to fit with the specifics of your faith tradition.

- Ask children and youth what they like and don't like about worship. Get their ideas for making it more interesting, meaningful, and relevant.

- Have a sermon series that ties asset building to the congregation's faith tradition and beliefs.

- Involve youth on a worship planning team.

- Involve youth as readers, lay liturgists, or other roles in worship, as appropriate for your faith tradition. In some traditions, it is also appropriate for youth to provide leadership for a whole worship service.

- Assign youth a regular responsibility in worship. This might include having them be responsible for collecting the offering every week. Or a youth choir might be responsible for regularly providing music.

- Regularly feature children and youth choirs.

- Include bulletin inserts on asset building in the bulletin for several weeks. (See Appendix A for reproducible bulletin inserts on asset building.)

- Ask youth to create banners or other worship visual aids.

- Ask youth to provide leadership through puppetry, clowning, drama, mime, liturgical dance, or other art forms appropriate to your faith tradition.

- Include at least one hymn in each service that is familiar to children and youth.

TIP SHEET 22

Start a Study-into-Action Education Program

In the book *Welcome the Child: A Child Advocacy Guide for Churches*, Kathleen A. Guy and the Children's Defense Fund offer a model for adult study groups that focuses on an issue and, over four sessions, helps groups move into action, particularly around an advocacy issue. The basic format is:

Session 1: Exploring the issue both in terms of its theological and its societal dimensions;

Session 2: Focusing on the issue in your own community;

Session 3: Examining the issue in the larger (national, global) context;

Session 4: Moving into action (either education, service, or public advocacy).[21]

While the CDF resource guide primarily focuses on problems facing children and youth (e.g., poverty, teen pregnancy), the format could be adapted for asset building. For example, if you were discussing the issue of empowerment, the sessions might flow as follows:

Session 1: How are young people viewed in scripture and in society? Are they valued and given useful roles?

Session 2: What opportunities are there for leadership in your community? A community youth worker might tell about a strong youth leadership program in a community center.

Session 3: What are the national and global issues related to youth empowerment? You might focus, for example, on the ways in which the media promote stereotypes of youth as problems and rarely focus on their contribution to society.

Session 4: How can congregation members address this issue, both individually and collectively? Action ideas might include things to do at home, opportunities to get involved in the community, and ways to advocate change in corporate or political policies.

This format is only one example of how asset building could be integrated into educational opportunities (for adult, youth, and intergenerational settings).

- Tie worship themes to youth activities such as service projects and special trips.

- Evaluate the language and symbols in worship to discover whether they are communicating with youth. If not, either adapt them, or educate youth so they can participate more fully.

- Always include stories and examples relevant to youth in sermons and liturgies. Celebrate their successes, address their struggles and questions, and connect the faith tradition with their world.

- Include an Asset-Building Minute during announcements or at other times during the service. Invite people to tell what they are doing to build assets or give tips for how members of the congregation can build assets.

- Sponsor a Children's Sabbath or Day[22] or similar youth-focused worship service.

Religious education

Chapter 5 addresses ways asset building can shape youth education, and Chapter 6 advocates providing educational opportunities for parents. But these aren't the only ways in which asset building can shape educational opportunities in congregations. It is just as important that other congregational members have opportunities to learn about and build skills for asset building. Here are some ideas:

- Involve youth on the educational leadership committee or team.

- Invite youth to present to adult classes on topics that affect them. (Have them develop a skit or presentation to introduce asset building to adults in the congregation.)

- Focus special seminars or congregation-wide workshops on asset building.

- Offer adult classes in which they learn about developmental assets and their connection to your faith tradition's theology and practice.

- Engage youth as leaders or assistants for children's education.

- Plan intergenerational educational events or classes.

- Highlight the needs of children and youth in the community through adult classes (see Tipsheet 22 for a sample format).

- Have a book study group that gives adults opportunities to read and reflect on books related to youth and asset building.

- Offer classes for adults to help them build skills for asset building (e.g., relationship skills, advocacy skills).

Social activities

In addition to providing care in times of crisis, most congregations often have community-building, fellowship, or social activities. These may include refreshments after a worship service, mid-week dinners, dances, and picnics. Some ways to give these activities an asset-building emphasis include:

- Involving youth in planning and/or leading congregation-wide social activities.

- When providing refreshments, being sure they are appropriate for children (for example, serve juice as well as coffee).

- Planning games at picnics and other events that are appropriate for all ages, not just for children or those who are physically fit.

- If an activity requires entertainment, asking youth to lead it.

- Having mixers that intentionally help generations mingle and get to know each other.

- Creating simple placemats for congregational meals with "trigger questions" that give people ideas for how to start talking and getting to know each other better.

Congregational care

Most congregations have a strong emphasis on providing care and support for members, particularly in times of crisis. This care may be expressed by lay caregivers (e.g., deacons) or by clergy through counseling or pastoral care. Often the people who provide this care think of their role as primarily caring for adults. If a young person needs help or support, a youth worker is deployed for the job.

While it is certainly important for those who work directly with youth to provide support and care, it is also important that the congregation integrate youth into these systems of support. It becomes an important bridge to the larger community of faith, signaling to youth that the whole community cares for them and values them. Here are some steps to take:

- Train youth to be caregivers to others (children and adults as well as other youth).

- If the congregation assigns caregivers to families, be sure they provide support to all members of families, not just adults.

- When caregivers visit homes, take time to talk with children and youth.

- Help caregivers remember and celebrate milestones in young people's lives (e.g., birthdays, learning to drive, end of a school year, special holidays).

- Educate clergy and others providing counseling about asset building so they can integrate the framework into their care.

Facilities maintenance and operations

At first glance, it might seem as if the operational functions of a congregation's facility have little to do with asset building. But they can and do. Sometimes you only see the relationship when something goes wrong: The janitor gets upset that the youth room is messy. The congregation's board resists a plan to invite neighborhood youth to programs or activities in the building because "they might mess things up." Here are some ways to get youth involved in the "nuts and bolts" of congregational life:

- Design some facilities maintenance or building tasks as service projects for youth.

- Make facilities available for a youth "hangout" or a homework room on a regular basis.

- Set and communicate clear policies about how everyone in the congregation is expected to treat the facilities—and the consequences for not respecting those policies.

- Evaluate facilities to ensure they are accessible to children. (For example, can younger children reach the water fountains?)

- If you use volunteers to do cleanup after events or activities, include youth.

Service in the community

All faith traditions include a call to service and action for all ages. In many cases, youth groups are the most active in living out that commitment, with only a handful of adults regularly engaging in active service to the community.

In fact, service opportunities can be a powerful vehicle for nurturing intergenerational relationships. **Glendale Heights United Methodist Church in Durham, North Carolina,** involves youth and adult congregation members in local service projects through an ongoing relationship with Oxford Manor, a local housing project. This partnership provides the youth of the church an opportunity to form intergenerational relationships and to make friends with kids who have socioeconomic backgrounds different from their own. (Chapter 7 focuses on how asset building can shape a congregation's service in the community and world.)

Transforming Congregational Life

In some ways, it is easier to focus attention on creating an asset-building youth program than trying to get the whole congregation involved in integrating asset building into all of congregational life. So many issues and turf battles can arise. So many people have to get involved. So much needs to change. And, indeed, it would be counterproductive to try to introduce too much change too quickly.

When my congregation began thinking about asset building, we focused a lot of our energy on just getting adults to notice that young people were around. We encouraged people to get to know the names of youth. We talked a lot about giving children and youth a voice in the congregation.

We still have work to do. Too often, including youth is still an afterthought. But things are changing. Not long ago, an older church member told me that he now makes a special effort to greet kids on Sunday morning. "I never bothered before," he admitted. The greeters are careful to kneel down and say "hi" to my six-year-old son, something that rarely used to happen. And young people are beginning to stand up during congregational prayer times to share concerns from their lives, asking the community to pray for them and their friends.

Each of these examples is a small thing. But together they are adding up to a new climate for children and youth in the congregation. Not long ago, a visitor noted that the congregation seemed especially welcoming of children and youth.

I don't think he would have said that a few years ago.

Integrating Asset Building Throughout Congregational Life

Key Points

- The asset-building vision pictures the whole community of faith—not just youth workers and parents—as having responsibility to care for young people.

- There are four major areas to address in integrating asset building throughout congregational life:

  1. Nurturing a welcoming climate for children and youth.

  2. Encouraging individual commitment to asset building throughout the congregation.

  3. Building intergenerational relationships between adults and youth and between youth and children.

  4. Reshaping congregational leadership in ways that include and integrate youth.

- There are practical ways to integrate asset building into all areas of congregational life, including worship, religious education, social activities, congregational care, facilities maintenance and operations, and service in the community.

Questions for Reflection and Discussion

- How well does your congregation integrate youth into the intergenerational community of faith? Do young people feel like they are part of the whole congregation or just the youth group?

- What opportunities do you have in your congregation to connect people across generations? How can asset building help strengthen those opportunities?

- In what ways are young people already involved in congregational leadership? What other opportunities might be available?

Suggestions for Getting Started

- Ask young people about their experiences in your congregation. How many adults do they know well? Do they feel welcomed and included in congregational activities? Do they think there are enough opportunities to be involved in congregational leadership?

- Analyze your congregation's activity calendar. What proportion of activities include all ages?

- Talk about assets with leaders in different areas of congregational life. Identify ways they can support asset building in their areas.

CHAPTER 5

Integrating Asset Building into Programming for Youth

hen leaders of the LOGOS Program saw the framework of developmental assets, lightbulbs went on. "This is what we've been doing," the leaders realized. So this mid-week program for children and youth—which is active in 5,000 Christian congregations in 25 denominations across the United States (as well as other countries)—began using the assets to support the value of their efforts. According to promotional literature: "LOGOS provides an arena of time in which quality relationships can be experienced and practiced in a systematic and sustainable way. It is our contention that church communities which conscientiously apply the LOGOS principles will build 30 of the 40 assets in the lives of their young people."

LOGOS is one example of how asset building can provide a helpful foundation for developing a comprehensive youth program. Many of its components are directly concerned with asset building. For example, a comprehensive LOGOS program in a congregation includes, among other things:

• Active involvement of parents;

• Involvement of many other adults in the congregation;

• Structured activities, including music, service, and leadership;

• A focus on nurturing values and giving young people appropriate guidance and boundaries; and

• Opportunities to build positive relationships with peers.[1]

Many youth programs in congregations include these elements. So why bother introducing asset-building language into the mix? Asset building offers at least three unique things to your youth program:

1. A framework and rationale that helps draw all the programmatic elements in a congregation's youth program into a coherent whole—with a clear focus on making a difference in the lives of youth.

2. A tool to use in evaluating what programs, activities, and/or curriculum to emphasize or develop for youth that meet a range of developmental needs. It also challenges you to think about program gaps.

3. A tool that motivates people to get involved in working with youth in the congregation as they see that their involvement can really make a difference for kids. Similarly, emphasizing asset building may also increase youth participation, as more parents recognize the critical importance of congregational involvement for all areas of life, not just for learning basic religious beliefs.

This chapter focuses on some of the practical issues and possibilities for integrating asset building into age-specific activities for youth within the congregation. As you read, you may find yourself thinking that this, surely, must be the main thrust of asset building in congregations. The youth program, after all, has been the whole universe of youth work in most faith traditions. Yet keep in mind that the youth program, though important, is only one piece of an asset-building congregation.

Planning a Youth Program That Builds Assets

While many programs build assets, asset building is not a program. There isn't a set curriculum for it. You can't buy and implement the package. Instead, asset building is a way of focusing and shaping a youth program so that it optimally meets the developmental needs of youth. Asset building is about changing some core assumptions about how we work with children and youth and about using our new understanding to more effectively and consistently give young people the tools and resources they need to grow up strong and healthy.

There are two ways of thinking about how asset building can be integrated into a youth program.

1. One approach is to develop activities or use curricula that directly address one or more of the assets. For example, you could plan a series of classes designed to nurture each of the values outlined in the asset framework.

Many congregations and communities that have begun using the assets find this selective approach to be very helpful. First, it raises consciousness about the importance and the specifics of the asset framework. It also focuses on specific, concrete, and understandable topics. Finally, it can help to provide opportunities for building specific skills youth need for growing up healthy.

However, the pick-and-choose approach has its pitfalls:

- As emphasized in Chapter 2, a key quality of the asset framework is that it provides a comprehensive foundation for youth. Picking a few topics here and there does not necessarily help to build this solid foundation.

- Second, the goal is not to have young people *know about* the assets, but for them to *experience* and *internalize* the assets.

- Third, this approach creates the danger of forgetting about asset building when you run out of specific topics. If, for example, your asset-building efforts consist of a series of youth-group meetings on specific topics, how do you keep the emphasis alive after you've covered the topics? Asset building can easily become "old news"—eventually abandoned for more interesting topics.

- Finally, the assets are not a list in real life. They mix together, with one leading to others and each reinforcing others. One activity could build several of the individual assets at the same time, particularly if you consciously designed the activity to do so.

2. The second, more powerful approach is to infuse the assets into all aspects of the youth program, so that they become a foundation that guides and undergirds everything that's done. With this perspective in mind, let's look at specific ways to integrate asset building into your youth-program planning process.[2]

Build assets while planning

First, it's important to recognize that the planning process, in and of itself, is a key asset-building opportunity. It offers an ideal way to involve youth in leadership and decision-making roles in the congregation. There are two problems with having adults develop a youth program without involving youth. First, there is a substantial risk that the programs will not meet youth needs. Second, not involving youth in planning undermines the entire asset-building philosophy. Involving youth in planning empowers them, helps them feel valued, and nurtures many important life skills.

Integrate asset building into the youth-program mission

An asset-building emphasis provides a focus that can be integrated into your youth program's mission. If your congregation has a mission statement for youth work, it may be important to revisit that statement to determine whether and how asset building fits. If your congregation doesn't have a mission statement for youth work, asset building can provide a starting point for developing one.

Involve many people—from the congregation's board to parents to youth to other adults—in revisiting and shaping your mission statement. Not only will you gain their insights, but you deepen their understanding of asset building and develop a stronger commitment to the asset-building focus within the congregation.

Identify and build on asset-building strengths

As you begin the planning process, discuss with your planning group (e.g., youth committee) what asset-building youth programs look like. Review Tipsheet 4 (Chapter 2) to focus on key characteristics that should be in place to ensure that the whole youth program builds assets.

An asset-building focus does not necessarily mean adding new activities to your schedule. A first step should be to identify how programs and activities already build assets, as well as their untapped potential. Begin by listing all the activities your congregation offers for youth during a typical year. Then evaluate each activity in light of the following questions, which build on the eight categories of assets. How does the program or activity intentionally:

- Provide youth with support, care, and love through relationships with peers, adults, or younger children?

- Empower youth to contribute to the congregation, community, and/or world?

- Reinforce appropriate boundaries and guide youth in their choices?

- Offer constructive, enriching opportunities?

- Undergird a commitment to learning and education?

- Nourish positive values?

- Build social competencies?

- Enhance a sense of positive identity and self-worth?

Every activity does not have to do all of these things in order to be asset building, and some activities may emphasize particular types of assets more than others. But in many cases, a single activity can contribute to many of the assets, particularly if it is designed that way intentionally.

Take a typical religious education class, for example. In too many congregations, it involves an adult who lectures to the young people, who are expected to sit quietly and listen. That class may do little to nurture any assets. But think about the asset-building potential if young people are involved in planning the curriculum (empowerment), spend time talking about the topic with each other and with adult leaders (support and social competencies), and focus on the implications of the subject matter for guiding their life choices (boundaries and expectations) and shaping their values (positive values). Through that process, they probably enjoy the learning (commitment to learning), and it enhances their own sense of identity and purpose (positive identity).

This scenario shows how to tap the asset-building potential of one particular activity and also suggests a useful planning exercise. Have your class or group form small groups or pairs, and assign each group one of the activities that regularly occurs in your congregation. Using Worksheet 6, have the group brainstorm ideas that can become the basis for planning and leadership training. In addition, this same information can be used to celebrate the ways your congregation already builds assets through the youth program.

One important note: Asset building does not replace, but complements, the congregation's commitment to nurturing faith and traditions in youth. Asset building can inform the teaching methods used, while the faith tradition provides much of the specific content. For example, a typical religious education class may involve studying scripture or other sacred writings. Asset building reminds you of the importance of respecting youth in that process, encouraging relationships to develop in that context, helping young people apply the learning to their own life choices, and giving them skills to live out what they learn.

Fill major gaps

Once you've reviewed existing programs in light of their asset-building potential, you may see some important gaps. For example, you may have many activities that offer youth support, but none that really empower them to contribute to the congregation and community. Your planning group will then have to decide whether, how, and when to fill that gap. You might begin by enhancing current activities with new emphases on leadership training. Or you may begin a process to introduce new activities to meet those needs.

The planning process in my congregation involved doing both. We identified a number of activities within the youth program where asset building was already happening—from youth group to summer trips to leadership and service opportunities—and activities that needed reshaping to become more effective in asset building. For example, young people were not always involved in planning their programs.

We also discovered some gaps that were difficult to fill within existing opportunities. One is that there are relatively few opportunities for youth to get together for fun social activities (an important way to provide youth with a sense of community and support). Part of the problem is that the congregation's facilities are not well equipped; there's not really a good room for indoor group activities during cold Minnesota winters. And there's not a kitchen for preparing snacks (not a developmental asset, but an essential ingredient for social activities!). So we must now examine options for addressing that need.

Nurturing an Asset-Building Climate

Offering quality programs or activities is not enough to create an asset-building program. Just as important is the climate or atmosphere. Just as comfortable weather adds energy and enthusiasm, a comfortable and safe "climate" in youth activities enhances the asset-building potential of your congregation. If, for example, young people are ignored or teased during activities, they will remember little of the programming content because it is overshadowed by the way they were treated.

Thus, while it's important to plan quality programs, it's just as important to focus on creating a climate in which asset building can flourish. Some characteristics of an asset-building climate in a youth program include:

Warmth

The young people and leaders are friendly and welcoming.

Caring

Young people feel that other people (youth and adults) care about them.

Thinking

Young people are challenged to think and grow; it's stimulating and interesting to be there.

Valuing

Young people are valued and respected.

Dealing constructively with conflict

While some conflict is inevitable in a youth program, it's important that it be dealt with constructively, not allowed to fester and infect relationships among the youth and leaders.[3]

Everyone has a role to play in creating a positive climate. The adults who are involved can set a tone of openness and acceptance. Through their attitudes and actions toward each other, young people also contribute to a positive climate. And the whole congregation—in the way members treat youth—also can enhance the climate.

One area where congregations may inadvertently create an unfriendly climate is with newcomers or visitors—particularly if the visitors are not familiar with the congregation's traditions, customs, and norms, or if the visitor is very different from others in the group. These issues are important to address both with leaders and youth. They need to be equipped with the attitudes and skills to be welcoming to people who are different from them.

Infusing Asset Building into Youth Activities

As an underlying philosophy for youth programming, asset building has the potential to shape many different types of programs and activities. Virtually any youth activity in your congregation has the potential to build assets in at least the following ways:

- Creating a climate that is warm, friendly, and accepting (support assets);

- Involving youth in planning and leadership (empowerment assets and social competencies assets);

- Giving youth opportunities for positive, constructive, and enriching activities (constructive use of time assets); and

- Having clear expectations and ground rules (boundaries and expectations assets and positive values assets).

In addition, activities with educational content also have the potential for building positive identity and increasing commitment to learning. In short, with intentional efforts and extra planning, any activity you offer for youth in your congregation can contribute to asset building. This section surveys some of the typical types of programs in congregations and suggests some of the ways asset-building might shape the various youth-specific activities.

Leadership opportunities within the youth program

Many congregations have youth councils or other groups that involve youth in program planning and leadership. Too often, however, these groups depend on adults for leadership, direction, and initiative. A focus on asset building recognizes that these meetings are more than planning meetings; they are opportunities to enhance leadership skills and opportunities for the youth who are involved. In addition, these leadership groups need to develop an understanding of the assets so they can effectively create activities that build assets for their peers.

One effective approach to youth leadership is the peer helping model. This approach focuses on equipping youth with leadership and caring skills so they can be resources to their peers. It emphasizes empowering youth to contribute to others, and the young people who participate develop strong social competencies.[4]

T I P S H E E T 2 3

Characteristics of Effective Youth Development Programs

A Search Institute study of research on community-based youth development programs for the YMCA identified the following key ingredients for successful youth programs. While the report focuses on secular organizations, the characteristics easily translate to congregations.

1. A focused and articulated vision.

2. A broad spectrum of services and opportunities tailored to the needs and interests of young adolescents.

3. Services and opportunities that recognize, value, and respond to the diverse backgrounds and experiences that exist among young adolescents.

4. Understanding youth in the context of the family.

5. A supportive, flexible atmosphere for staff and volunteers.

6. Collaboration with other community programs and outreach to families, schools, and other community partners in youth development.

7. A supportive atmosphere for young people and caring relationships between staff/volunteers and young people.

8. Youth workers who are committed and act as vigorous advocates for and with youth.

9. Collective as well as individual efforts to extend the program reach to underserved populations.

10. A feeling among young people that the staff/volunteers care about them, respect them, and can be trusted.

11. A commitment to empowering young people that enhances their role as resources to their communities.

12. Creative problem solving, including working to stabilize funding bases and to adapt or circumvent traditional professional and bureaucratic limitations in order to meet the needs of [members].

13. A solid organizational structure, including energetic and committed leadership.

14. Services that are coherent, easy to use, and offer continuity.

From Nancy Leffert et al., *Making the Case: Measuring the Impact of Youth Development Programs* (Minneapolis: Search Institute, 1996).

Leadership Development Undergirds Youth Program

Nurturing youth as leaders is a major focus for the youth program at
North Shore Synagogue in Syosset, New York. "You go from having it all
done for you to doing it yourself," says Youth Director Jeff Green.

In fifth to seventh grades, youth programming is developed and carried out by staff. In seventh grade, a youth steering committee is formed for youth to give input. In this process, they begin developing leadership skills as they present their ideas to the steering committee. In eighth grade, the steering committee takes a more active role, learning how to write programs, lead groups, and monitor what other young people like and don't like.

By ninth grade, Green says, the young people run the youth group, with the youth director serving primarily an advisory role. Through this process, they also learn general leadership skills such as program management and budgeting. Furthermore, Green looks for opportunities for the youth to participate in congregational leadership roles. For example, the president of the youth group goes to religious school classes for fifth to seventh graders to talk about upcoming activities in the youth program. In addition, some of the youth are trained to be board members for regional and national youth organizations.

Peer helping is a basic component in the youth program at **Annunciation Catholic Church in Minneapolis, Minnesota**, according to youth worker Mark Conway. Youth who participate in the peer ministry program commit to active involvement. One evening a month, they receive training. Then they serve as small-group leaders and large-group facilitators in the youth program. In addition, they lead a retreat for junior high youth.

Religious education

Religious education (e.g., Sunday school, scripture study, Hebrew school) is the most common youth activity in most congregations. Because of its focus on religious or theological content, it is sometimes assumed that it has little potential for asset building. But, as noted earlier in the chapter, while you may never "study" asset building during religious education classes, the philosophy can infuse the curriculum in many ways.

At the same time, it may also be useful to develop a series of classes that focus explicitly on asset building. While there is not yet a youth curriculum available that takes this approach,[5] it could be empowering for youth to develop an understanding of assets. Each week could focus on a different category of assets, with youth sharing about their own experiences and connecting the assets to themes in your faith tradition's scripture and theology. This approach gives youth a better understanding of each category while also presenting, over time, the bigger picture of the assets framework. (One way to do this would be to read stories from scripture and then have young people discuss the assets—or lack of assets—that appear to be present in each character's life.)

Youth groups

Youth groups are often the core of a congregation's work with youth. At their best, they provide a warm, accepting community for youth that integrates many different types of assets. Indeed, all four types of external assets (support, empowerment, boundaries and expectations, and constructive use of time) can be integral to youth-group activities.

Often, however, youth groups can be unfocused social cliques that appeal only to "insiders." The assets can provide a sense of direction and purpose for youth groups. Tipsheet 24 gives some ideas of ways assets can be integrated into youth-group activities both as a content focus and a context for other content.

Sports and recreation

Many congregations find that sports and recreation programs are one of the best ways to reach out to unconnected youth. These programs offer constructive activities through which young people also can build relationships and skills.

T I P S H E E T   2 4

Ideas for Integrating Developmental Assets into a Congregation's Youth Group

This chart illustrates how each category of developmental assets can be integrated into a congregation's youth group, both as a content focus and as a context for other content.

ASSET CATEGORY	CONTENT FOCUS (MEETING TOPICS)	CONTEXT FOCUS
Support	• Getting along with parents • Friendship issues • Getting along with adults • How to show people you care • Where to go when you need help	• Create a supportive climate • Welcome newcomers • Adult leaders/sponsors form strong relationships with youth • Parent involvement in programs
Empowerment	• Learning about your gifts and talents • How youth can make a difference in their families, communities, and world	• Youth involvement in planning and meetings • Use of service as an experiential learning activity
Boundaries and Expectations	• Issues such as sexuality, alcohol and other drugs, violence • Positive peer pressure	• Clear ground rules and expectations for youth who participate • Communication with parents about activities
Constructive Use of Time	• How to find balance in your life • The importance of staying involved in the congregation • Art, music, and literature in your faith tradition	• Avoiding scheduling conflicts with other activities • Making sure programs are enriching and interesting to youth • Integration of music, art, and literature into youth-group activities
Commitment to Learning	• Your faith and school • Choosing a college or vocational school • Finding your vocation or career	• Clear expectations for learning • Opportunities for additional learning on topics of interest
Positive Values	• What your faith tradition says about service and justice • What values are important to you? • What is integrity? (or honesty, etc.)	• Leaders who model positive values • Articulate values even when they are assumed
Social Competencies	• How to make good decisions • Friendship-making skills • Other cultures and religions • Nonviolence and conflict resolution	• When focusing on a topic, teach skills for addressing the topic effectively • Use role plays and other methods for practicing skills
Positive Identity	• What does the future hold for you? • Finding your sense of purpose in life	• Create a climate that values youth • Give youth practical ways to address tough issues so that they don't seem overwhelming

---

While sports can meet the needs of many youth, their asset-building potential depends on a number of variables. A Search Institute report on effective youth development programs found that sports and recreation programs are most effective for positive development when:

- The coach/leader has a positive attitude;

- They are balanced with involvement in other activities at school, home, and elsewhere;

- Parents are involved and supportive; and

- They actively encourage older youth to stay involved.[6]

The same report noted that, while sports involvement can reduce involvement in risky behaviors, a highly competitive environment can actually increase involvement in some negative behaviors (such as alcohol consumption), possibly because of the related stress. Perhaps a key is for coaches to focus their energy on creating an environment that is as (or more) concerned about providing a positive experience for young people as it is about winning. This emphasis would influence how the coaches treat team members, how decisions are made about who plays, the kinds of team building that is done during practice, and expectations of players at practice and in games about how they treat each other.

Social events and activities

From hay rides to pizza parties to dances to amusement park trips, social activities are important ingredients in many youth programs. Not only do youth have fun, but they also have opportunities to build friendships and share experiences with each other. When designing social activities and events, keeping the following emphases in mind will enhance their asset-building potential:

- Select activities that provide youth with lots of opportunities for building relationships with each other and with the adults involved. (For example, watching a movie may do little to enhance relationships unless you build in time to talk about the movie.)

- Select or design activities that are not "fun" at the expense of group members or others. ("TP-ing" a person's house may be fun, but it is also a lot of work to clean up and may be embarrassing for the "victim.")

- Be sure they are affordable and accessible to all youth. (Provide discreet ways for those with less money to participate and provide transportation for those who need it.)

Retreats, camps, and trips

When they grow up, many adults' most life-shaping memories from their congregation focus on an away-from-home experience: a trip to Israel, a national youth conference, annual youth-group retreats, and work camps. These opportunities to leave the routines and familiar settings can provide ideal laboratories for learning, enrichment, growth, and relationship building. These activities are most likely to build assets when they:

- Balance fun with learning and relationship building;

- Expose young people to other people and cultures;

- Involve youth in leadership and planning;

- Make it possible for any youth to participate, regardless of her or his ability to pay; and

- Relate the experiences from the trip to life at home.

While camps, retreats, and trips are often viewed primarily as fun experiences by the youth, Judi Ratner, youth director at **Temple Emanu-El in Dallas,** sees them as formative experiences for the young people. She recalls one year when she took her group on a ropes course that included a 50-foot climbing tower. One of the girls

---

T I P S H E E T   2 5

Involving Unconnected Youth in Congregational Youth Programs

A common complaint in congregational youth programs goes something like this:
"We put a lot of energy into designing a great program. We publicized it for weeks.
But then only the regulars showed up. No matter what we do, the other kids just won't come to anything."

There are a lot of reasons why some youth don't participate in youth activities in a congregation. Sometimes things are going on in young people's lives that make religious involvement a low priority. But it is premature to write off all but the most committed youth because they are "too busy" or "don't care." There may be things about your congregation's youth programming that inadvertently keep many youth away.

Edward A. Trimmer notes that most youth programs design activities that address the needs and interests of only a small portion of youth.[7] For example, they focus on the interests of the most committed youth (the ones who plan the activities), and those activities may have little appeal to those who are less involved. Or they develop activities designed to attract a lot of youth from the community, but do not provide activities that meet the needs of the most active youth. The result of this type of program may be that the most mature youth never participate because activities are not stimulating.

As you develop programs and activities, keep in mind a balance of activities that address the needs of the youth who participate regularly as well as those in the community whom the congregation is reaching out to involve. For this last group, a key challenge is to provide a climate where they feel comfortable and where they will not be embarrassed because they are unfamiliar with religious concepts, language, or traditions.

In addition, it is important to educate the congregation and youth-group members about welcoming youth who are not aware of the expectations and traditions that are second nature for those who have been in the congregation for years. Otherwise, longtime participants quickly become frustrated and angry about all the things the newcomers do that they're not "supposed to do."

Here are six specific suggestions for helping visitors and unconnected youth feel welcome and comfortable in your congregation:

1. Plan for visitors

If you assume that everyone knows everyone and everything, then visitors are sure to feel unwelcome. If, however, you assume there will be visitors, you might be sure people always wear name tags, provide music books—even for the songs "everyone knows"—and other things that help visitors participate fully in activities.

2. Pay attention to them

There's nothing worse than going to an unfamiliar place and having no one notice you. You end up awkwardly standing or sitting off to the side, reading bulletin boards or handouts. Yet, newcomers often have that experience in youth activities. Regular attenders are often busy catching up with their friends. Thus, everyone in the group needs to be encouraged to pay attention to and take time to talk with visitors and include them in conversations and activities.

3. Show them around

While a congregation may be familiar turf to regularly attending youth, it is unknown to newcomers. They may feel lost in many different ways, from knowing what room to go to next, to how to follow along during rituals, music, or activities. You may want to assign youth to be "guides" for any visitors who come, showing them around the facilities and helping with specific traditions or customs in your congregation.

4. Ask what they want to do

When newcomers express interest in becoming regulars, it can be tempting to try to sell them on getting involved in everything that is important to you. That can turn them off or overwhelm them. A better way to start is to ask them what they are interested in doing, then find opportunities within the congregation that fit those interests.

5. Give low-risk opportunities for involvement

As noted earlier, not all young people are ready for or interested in deep commitments. Evaluate your overall youth program to ensure that you have some relatively low-risk "entry points" through which young people can get involved at their own pace.

6. Follow up with them

When a young person visits, have someone (preferably a young person) follow up to answer questions and to invite the visitor to future activities. If someone attends several activities, then stops, check to be sure everything is okay. The absence may be insignificant, but the call is an expression of care that will increase the odds that they will come the next time.

made it halfway up, then stopped and wouldn't go any further. Her partner kept climbing, but she said she couldn't make it to the top.

When it became clear what was happening, Ratner climbed up to talk with the girl. "What you have to look at is not your goal of getting to the top. . . . Can you take two steps?"

"Yes," the girl said, and began climbing. That process continued, and some of the other group members came to help. And the girl made it to the top.

But that wasn't really the point, Ratner concludes. The experience became a teachable moment. "Sometimes our kids see life that way"—always having to reach the top. Then she asked: "Does the goal always have to be the top of the tower?"

Rituals and rites of passage

Each faith tradition has rituals that are important parts of congregational life. These may focus on rites of passage, such as confirmation, bar/bat mitzvah, or baptism. And while the purpose of these activities is primarily spiritual or religious, these events also can build assets for youth, particularly when intentional efforts are made. For example:

- Confirmation, bar/bat mitzvah, or baptism empowers youth when it emphasizes the young person's growing responsibility and contribution to the community of faith.

- Worship, prayer, meditation, and other rituals enhance young people's identity and sense of purpose.

- Because of their communal nature, many rituals underscore the intergenerational community of support, care, and guidance.

- In many traditions, youth involvement in leadership during rituals enhances their sense of contribution and self-confidence.

Service learning activities

Service learning—the intentional integration of service to others with learning objectives—may be one of the best opportunities for asset building in congregational life. Not only does it build on the emphasis in every major faith tradition on service to others, but it also helps young people learn about themselves, their faith, and the world through active engagement in making a difference.

In her experience, says Ratner, service experiences are one of the best ways to get older and younger youth doing things together. Service gives everyone a role. The 10th-graders feel good that they can help the younger youth, and the 6th-graders feel good being included. "This is one thing that has become highly successful," Ratner says.

Whether youth are involved in service within the congregation, in the community, or in another part of the country or world, service activities can be infused with an asset-building perspective. Key elements include:

- Involving youth in planning and leading the activity;

- Developing intentional opportunities to reflect on what is being learned through the experience;

- Nurturing positive relationships throughout the experience;

- Developing service activities that also address the asset-building needs of the people being served; and

- Identifying and focusing on assets that can be built through the service experience.

Many congregations make service an integral component of their youth program. **Mount Olivet Lutheran Church in Minneapolis, Minnesota,** for example, includes four hours of service as a requirement of the confirmation program. In addition to whole-group service activities, young people also work with adults in the congregation to offer service, such as helping in the church nursery and working on food drives.

A complete guide to service learning in congregations from an asset-building perspective is under development by Search Institute.[8]

Community/drop-in centers

In addition to structured programs and activities, young people may also value safe, supervised places to spend time after school, on weekends, and when school is not in session. Through drop-in and community centers some congregations offer (or cosponsor) these opportunities for youth who are active in the congregation as well as others in the community. These centers may just provide a safe place to hang out, or they may also offer youth a variety of services (health, counseling) or enrichment opportunities (access to computers, study rooms, tutors).

Drop-in centers can be particularly valuable in providing a low-risk opportunity to youth in the community. They may see these centers as safe, comfortable places where they can spend time. Staffing the center with caring adults (paid or volunteer) provides an important service and point of connection between the congregation and community.

In addition, community centers can also serve as an informal gathering place for youth in the congregation or tradition. For example, Jewish community centers see it as central to their mission to offer "a place in the community where all Jewish teenagers, regardless of belief or background, can socialize in a Jewish environment."[9] Some Christian traditions have a similar emphasis when forming youth coffeehouses and other low-risk, safe places.

Some congregations develop their own after-school programs for community youth. For example, **Bethel Temple in Philadelphia, Pennsylvania,** sponsors an after-school program for children and youth that includes tutoring and a weight-lifting program. In addition, the congregation uses the gym in the middle school across the street for a basketball program.

While individual congregations may not have the resources to sponsor a community or drop-in center on their own, these centers provide a natural opportunity for cosponsorship by many congregations (as well as secular youth-serving organizations), with staffing and supervision by trained volunteers from the various congregations.

Educational enrichment/work preparation

Some congregations, particularly in urban areas, have a strong emphasis on serving youth in the community and congregation with various educational enrichment and/or work preparation activities. These may include a tutoring program (staffed with volunteers from the congregation), computer training, a

Assessing Youth Activities Through an Asset-Building Lens

In order to continually increase the asset-building strength of youth activities, take time to debrief or reflect on youth activities using the eight categories of developmental assets. Complete this worksheet after an event, then refer to it the next time you plan a similar activity.

Description of Activity: _____

Date: _____

ASSET CATEGORY	HOW THE ACTIVITY BUILT THESE ASSETS	OTHER WAYS IT COULD BUILD THESE ASSETS
Support: How did the activity reinforce caring relationships and a warm climate in which all youth felt welcomed and accepted?		
Empowerment: How did the activity empower youth to serve and lead? How well did it offer physical and emotional safety?		
Boundaries and Expectations: How did the activity support appropriate boundaries for behavior? How did it challenge youth to be their best?		
Constructive Use of Time: How did the activity use young people's time for enrichment and growth?		
Commitment to Learning: How did the activity reinforce curiosity, learning, and discovery?		
Positive Values: How did the activity reinforce and articulate positive values?		
Social Competencies: How did the activity build young people's life and relationship skills?		
Positive Identity: How did the activity nurture in youth a sense of purpose, value, and possibility?		

homework hotline, or job mentoring (youth matched with adults in the congregation to learn about interesting careers).

Almost by definition, these activities build the commitment to learning assets. In communities with few opportunities for youth, they also contribute to a sense of hope for the future, and they often provide a chance for significant relationships with adults. Their asset-building potential can be enhanced by:

- Emphasizing the value of adult-youth interaction beyond "the task";

- Giving youth an opportunity to shape the activities;

- Having older youth volunteer to tutor younger youth;

- Holding youth responsible for maintaining agreed-to boundaries; and

- Having high expectations for participating youth.

Academic enrichment can go far beyond opening a building for study hall, particularly in communities with low expectations for education. A notable example is the work of **First Church of the Brethren in Brooklyn, New York**. Youth worker Phill Carlos Archbold and the pastor actively encourage young people in the primarily Hispanic community to continue their education through college. Tutoring begins in elementary school and continues all through high school. Often parents encourage their children to quit school to earn money for the family, Archbold says. But the church tries to counter the need for immediate money by emphasizing the long-term benefits of education.

The church also meets specific economic needs of students that might otherwise mean their dropping out of school. This may include buying shoes and covering bus fares for those who have trouble getting to school because they don't have enough money.

The clergy also help the young people apply for college admission and scholarships. "They want to go to college, but there are no funds," Archbold says. "We dig up the funds. We check out the books. . . . We help them find the funds from various agencies, and we get them through school."

In addition, Sunday school teachers and the pastors check up on kids in school. "We, as leaders of the church, feel we should make our presence felt for these children, so we make periodic visits to the schools," Archbold explains. They check with principals, teachers, and counselors about their students' progress. Archbold believes that "these kids have done very well and have received more attention because of the interest we have shown in them."[10]

Counseling

Many congregations offer formal or informal counseling to members and others. Like psychotherapy in general, this counseling often focuses heavily on addressing problems in people's lives. Developmental assets can provide an added focus in these situations—not only pointing young people and their families to the kinds of resources they need to overcome problems, but also focusing energy on building a positive foundation. Asking people in counseling to reflect on the assets in their own lives can open up new strategies that empower them to take action.[11]

Teaching? A Chance to Build Assets

You're sitting down at your kitchen table after another long day. You pull out your teacher's guide for the youth religious education class, telling yourself that you've got to do a better job of preparing to teach this week. You ask yourself: *Why did I say yes when they asked me to teach this year? Does what I do really make any difference?*

Chances are good that one reason you agreed to teach a children's or youth religious education class is that you care a lot about kids and you want to see them grow. And your commitment to and involvement in the lives of young people can be an important, positive influence in their lives—particularly when you pay attention to how you build developmental assets.

What do we mean by developmental assets? Identified by Search Institute, developmental assets are the essential influences, opportunities, and commitments that children and adolescents need to help them grow up healthy, caring, and responsible.

These assets aren't built by investing in stocks or stashing money in savings accounts—or even by spending more money on equipment and curriculum. Developmental assets are built through relationships—by investing ourselves, our time, and our energy in the lives of children and youth. And research shows that this kind of investment pays off: The more assets young people have, the more likely they are to grow up making positive, healthy choices.

EIGHT TYPES OF ASSETS

As teachers in your congregation, you have wonderful opportunities to build these assets for children and youth. Let's look at the ways you can build all eight types of assets:

Support

Children and youth need to experience support, care, and love wherever they spend time—at home, in school, in their congregation, in the neighborhood. You help build support assets by showing care to each young person in your class, taking time to greet each of them personally, noticing when they don't come, sending them birthday cards, saying "hi" in the hall, and listening to them talk about the things that are important to them.

Empowerment

Children and youth need to be valued by their community and have opportunities to contribute to others. In religious education, empowerment can begin with creating a climate in the classroom where young people's opinions and experiences are valued and respected. But it also extends to giving children and youth a voice in selecting and adapting the curriculum (something that rarely happens). And many people are finding ways to connect classroom learning with service to others—a great opportunity to empower young people.

Boundaries and expectations

Children and youth need to know what is expected of them and whether behaviors are "in bounds" or "out of bounds." Setting and enforcing clear and fair ground rules is an important part of teaching. In addition, you can help young people learn the "boundaries" on behaviors that are integral to the life of discipleship.

Constructive use of time

Children and youth need structured opportunities for growth through creative activities, youth programs, congregational involvement, and quality time at home. Young people experience these assets whenever they participate in religious education. Through your planning and leadership, you ensure that this use of time is constructive, enriching, and enjoyable.

Commitment to learning

Children and youth need to develop a lifelong commitment to education and learning. When you make lessons interesting, engaging, and relevant, you help children and youth internalize the commitment to learning. A congregation reinforces this commitment by emphasizing lifelong involvement in religious education.

Positive values

Children and youth need to develop strong values that guide their choices. Part of making lessons relevant to the young people in your class is to tie the learning to their life experiences and to emphasize the values at stake.

Social competencies

Children and youth need skills and competencies that equip them to make positive choices, build relationships, and succeed in life. You can help young people build these skills by giving them opportunities to practice (for example, role-playing how they would respond in different situations) and helping them find new skills in the lesson (for example, what does the scripture passage say about how we build friendships?).

Positive identity

Finally, children and youth need a strong sense of their own power, purpose, and promise. Much of what you do in helping young people internalize their faith and discover their own sense of purpose or mission is foundational in helping shape their identity.

CELEBRATION AND CHALLENGE

You may already be doing many of these things that build assets. If so, remember that the effort you make is an invaluable contribution to the lives of the young people you teach. You are an asset builder!

At the same time, there may be some areas where the asset framework challenges you to try some new things in the ways you work with children or youth. Talk to other teachers and resource people in your congregation to get ideas about what might work. Try some things. But, most of all, remember that each young person in your class benefits immeasurably from the time you take getting to know her, spending time with him, and showing her that you care. That is the best reason for saying yes to teaching that class!

Equipping Adult Volunteers and Teachers for Asset Building

Most congregational youth programs rely on volunteer youth workers and teachers to provide quality activities, programs, and relationships. Yet many of these volunteers receive little or no training.

A Search Institute study of religious youth workers found that only 49 percent of volunteers had participated in youth work training in their congregation during the past year.[12] Another study found that 55 percent of religious education teachers in mainline Christian denominations had received no training in effective teaching methods, and 49 percent said they never meet together with other teachers to talk about specific problems and challenges.[13] In short, too often congregations ask volunteers to work with youth with little or no training and support.

Efforts to integrate an asset-building focus will not be effective if volunteers are not trained and skilled in relating to youth and providing leadership and education consistent with asset building. Here are some recommendations for ways to strengthen their abilities:

T I P S H E E T 2 7

Some Skills Volunteers Need to Be Effective in Building Assets

Here is a preliminary list of the kinds of skills volunteers need to develop to be effective in nurturing each type of assets, adapted from the skills-building approach from Boy's Town.[14]

To Provide . . .	Youth Workers Need to Know How to . . .
Support	• Greet a young person and start a conversation. • Listen to a young person.
Empowerment	• Invite youth to share their gifts and talents. • Praise effectively.
Boundaries and Expectations	• Discipline in a way that teaches. • Set limits with youth.
Constructive Use of Time	• Connect topics to young people's lives and interests. • Integrate physical activity into educational sessions.
Commitment to Learning	• Develop activities for different learning styles. • Model a positive attitude toward and interest in school and learning.
Positive Values	• Model and articulate their own values. • Teach problem-solving skills.
Social Competencies	• Integrate skills building into curricula and activities. • Teach social skills to youth (e.g., listening, asking for help, negotiating, controlling anger).
Positive Identity	• Give a compliment. • Help youth identify their own talents and abilities.

Equip with the asset-building philosophy

Sometimes it's tempting to get straight to the "practical stuff." Yet learning is most effective when people understand both the how and the why—particularly for some learning styles. Focusing only on skills gives neither the larger vision (which motivates and gives a sense of direction) nor the context in which the skills make sense. The information in the first three chapters of this book can provide the grist for training.

In addition, Tipsheet 26 is a reproducible article to distribute to religious education teachers, which shows how they can build assets in religious education classes. The principles apply to other settings as well.

Equip with skills—At the same time, it is not enough simply to give people the larger vision without also addressing the specific skills needed to be effective. (Of course, some volunteers will already have the skills, which they can incorporate into the asset-building vision—particularly when the skills are articulated.) Tipsheet 27 suggests the kinds of skills you may want to focus on in training and other learning opportunities.

Practice and reflect—Just as youth learn best when they get involved, adult volunteers internalize knowledge and skills best when they have opportunities to practice them. Thus, introducing the asset framework is most effective when participants have a chance to work with it and apply it to their own responsibilities and lives. Similarly, having opportunities to practice skills in a safe environment (through exercises or simulations) begins to make people feel more comfortable and natural in using them.

In addition, volunteers need opportunities to reflect on their knowledge and skills once they have been working with them a while. Thus it's important to offer multiple opportunities, throughout the year, for volunteers to talk together about what's working and what's not.

Be a partner for learning—One of the best ways to learn is to work or teach alongside a more experienced leader. Find ways to pair a new volunteer with an experienced volunteer in a peer-mentoring relationship. The mentor will enjoy sharing what he or she has learned through the years, and the mentee will build understanding, skills, and confidence by watching and practicing in the context of a supportive relationship.

Evaluate—Many congregations don't bother to do any real evaluation of their volunteers. Indeed, too often leaders are delighted that somebody agreed to help. But when viewed as a tool for growth and development, evaluation actually encourages and motivates volunteers to stick with their assignment. Through evaluation (including establishing expectations through a job description, watching the volunteer in action, talking about impressions, and working on a plan for growth), you clarify skills and practices that need to be developed and help the volunteer build those skills.

Prompt and reinforce—One way to help volunteers continue to increase their understanding and work on their skills is to prompt them through the year with tipsheets, reminders, refresher discussions in meetings, and other opportunities. In addition, affirming and recognizing increased competencies reinforces the learning and helps to make it stick.

When training volunteers and teachers, it is important not to forget that a great deal of asset building—and effective youth work—depends on the volunteer's commitment to, and care for, young people. While skills are needed to effectively express that commitment and care, no amount of skills training can take the place of those personal qualities and commitments. As veteran youth worker Jim Burns writes:

> In order to have an important influence in the lives of young people, you do not need to be a dynamic speaker, know all the latest rock musicians, or even dress in the latest fashions. You must, however, love kids and be willing to spend time with them. . . . Caring for your students is the primary prerequisite for working with them. All the competencies one could list would never compensate for a lack of genuine love for students.[15]

Building Connections

This chapter has focused on age-specific programs and activities for youth in the congregation. Infusing the asset-building philosophy into youth programs is an important way for congregations to build assets in young people. Yet it's far from the whole story. A youth program cannot live up to its full potential for asset building in isolation from other areas of congregational and community life. Here are some other important connections to make:

Other age-specific programming

Young people's experiences in the congregation don't begin when they become part of the youth activities. Most have been involved in some form of programming for children (usually religious education). Those experiences—either positive or negative—set the stage for their experiences in adolescence. Similarly, assets don't magically start forming when a young person turns 12. Rather, they begin

---

TIP SHEET 28

Finding Resources for Training Volunteers

You don't have to do all the training of volunteers in your congregation by yourself.
Here are some possible resources, many of which can be free or inexpensive.

Workshops in the community—Take a team of volunteers from your congregation to workshops in your community sponsored by interfaith groups, secular youth organizations, or colleges, universities, or seminaries. Or check if your team can join in a staff development training that another organization is offering to its own staff and volunteers.

People within the congregation—Don't overlook people in the congregation who have talents and gifts that could be shared. These may include teachers, counselors, professional trainers, parent educators, and many others.

Youth workers in other congregations—By networking with youth workers from other congregations in your community, you will learn about programs that have been successful for them as well as particular skills they have. Consider bartering your time: They come train volunteers in your congregation in a particular topic area, then you go train in their congregation in another topic area.

Denominational resource people—Your denomination or judicatory body may have particular resource people assigned to congregations. Check if they have areas of expertise that match your volunteers' needs and interests.

Youth workers in other organizations—Youth workers in organizations such as the YMCA, YWCA, and Boys and Girls Clubs often have expertise and experience in many areas related to asset building and may be willing to help train in your congregation.

Shared learning—One of the best ways to learn new information and skills is to teach it to others. Consider forming a "shared learning" team (like a seminar) in which each person investigates new topics, finds and synthesizes good sources of information, and then trains the others in what he or she has learned.

Print and video resources—Design a training event based on high-quality magazine articles, books, videos, or other resources you find or have in your library. (Then offer to do the same training event in another congregation!)

---

developing at birth and are gradually nurtured across the years.[16] Thus, connecting with children's programming in the congregation seems like a natural extension of an asset-building approach. Some connections may include:

- Coordinated planning that reinforces similar asset-building emphases across all ages;

- Joint training of volunteers and teachers for all ages in asset building; and

- Intergenerational activities that connect youth with children.

This understanding of the continuity and connections between childhood and adolescence permeates the youth program at **Temple Emanu-El in Dallas, Texas.** "What we want to do with kids can't just start in ninth grade," says Judi Ratner, the synagogue's youth director.

According to Ratner, program leaders ask this question about first-graders: What do we want them to be when they graduate from high school? Then they plan the program for all ages with that focus and children's developmental needs in mind. "I look at the whole thing as a trajectory and ask how you build bridges across the groups."

In first to fifth grades, the youth program offers fun activities for children three times per year, Ratner says, "to create fellowship and a sense of Jewish continuity." This time is important for forming community because otherwise the children— who attend many different schools—never really get to know each other or form strong friendships.

In seventh and eighth grades, more energy is spent on keeping the young people interested and excited about their involvement, even while their attention is focused on bar/bat mitzvah. By ninth grade, the youth program is more focused on service projects, special outings and retreats, Jewish education, and leadership development.

Families, congregation, and community

Age-specific youth programs and education have been at the heart of congregational youth work in recent decades. As a result, we have learned a lot about how to make them effective.

But the asset-building paradigm challenges us to look beyond the youth program as well to see that congregations can have the most impact on youth by combining strong age-specific programming with a larger vision that includes the families of youth, the larger congregation, and the community in which young people live. The next two chapters explore the details of this expanded vision.

Integrating Asset Building into Programming for Youth

Key Points

- Asset building offers youth programming a focus and framework, a tool for shaping and strengthening programming, and motivation to get people involved in working with youth.

- While asset building isn't a program, programs can build assets.

- Creating a positive climate in youth activities is essential for asset building.

- Asset building can be infused into existing youth programs, including religious education; youth groups; sports and recreation; social events and activities; retreats, camps, and trips; rituals and rites of passage; service-learning activities; community/drop-in centers; educational enrichment/work preparation; and counseling.

- Adult volunteers and teachers need to be trained and supported as asset builders.

Questions for Reflection and Discussion

- What are you trying to accomplish in your youth programming? How might asset building help focus your efforts?

- What types of age-specific programming do you offer for youth? How might assets be infused into these activities?

- How do you work to ensure a positive, caring, and encouraging climate for all youth in your youth programming?

- How well equipped are adults who work with youth to build assets?

Suggestions for Getting Started

- Share the assets with the youth and adults who are responsible for planning and leading youth activities. Brainstorm ways asset building can strengthen what you already do.

- Use Worksheet 6 to assess how well an existing youth activity already builds assets. Brainstorm ways to strengthen its asset-building potential.

- Introduce adult volunteers and teachers to the assets during a volunteer training event. Ask them what information, tools, and skills they need to be better asset builders.

Integrating Asset Building into Work with Families

"It is within the family that we imbibe and incorporate the skills and knowledge that will one day enable us to live outside it....The family is the earliest, most basic environment in which we learn about what things we are—or are not—entitled to, and about whether people are reliable and trustworthy."[1]

—*Psychologist Maggie Scarf*

"Society should be spending less time on the structure of the family questions like divorce, marriage, and the number of children and more time on finding ways of helping families create warm, loving environments."[2]

—*Sociologist Charles V. Willie*

"In today's complex world no family has within itself all of the knowledge and resources necessary to meet all of its members' needs. Parents in different circumstances need different kinds of help and different kinds of support, but all parents need some kind of help at one time or another."[3]

—*The Children's Defense Fund*

 congregation's commitment to asset building will be incomplete if it does not include a strong focus on strengthening and equipping families as partners in asset building. Indeed, there is a growing awareness that any efforts to work with youth must also include their families. Yet despite the widespread call for congregations to provide support, education, and advocacy for families, little has changed in most congregations. Consider the following three studies:

- A 1995 survey of 500 religious youth workers found that only 45 percent see supporting and educating parents as a "very important" goal in their youth program; only 6 percent say they do this "very well." (Fortunately, 59 percent were very interested in training and resources to help in this area.)[4]

- A study of adults in one Christian denomination found that 52 percent of adults say "the congregation intentionally strengthens family life." However, only 20 percent of the parents surveyed said "the congregation helps parents learn how to nurture the faith of their children."[5]

- Search Institute's study of 11,000 adults and youth in congregations in six major Christian denominations found that only about 9 percent of congregations provide education for parents of youth on effective parenting or communication.[6]

While there are certainly many congregations that have developed innovative approaches to serving youth and their families, it is clear that there is a significant gap that must be addressed. Because of its positive, practical focus, asset building can open new doors for working with families. As Glenn Seefeldt, pastor of **Nativity Lutheran Church in St. Anthony Village, Minnesota,** says: "[The asset framework] gave us some easy handles to hold on to that are motivating. . . . People can see how they fit in quickly, and that has motivated parents to get involved."

After a brief overview of the importance of, and barriers to, working with families, this chapter examines strategies for integrating families into the congregation's asset-building vision.

Opportunities That Emerge Through Connections with Parents

Too often, congregations (and other organizations) have a hands-off policy about families: leave them alone and don't interfere. But the lack of connection between the congregation and the families of young people misses unmatched opportunities for contributing to young people's healthy development.

Addressing a critical need

The first opportunity is to address a critical need. Perhaps more now than ever, many families really need the support and guidance a congregation can offer. The Children's Defense Fund describes the need this way:

> Many parents are isolated, without strong ties to their neighborhood and with few kin to call on. With the recent increase in divorce rates and rates of births to unmarried women, more and more women are raising their children without a partner, which makes a difficult job even harder. . . . Parents face a continuous struggle to balance the demands of family life and the jobs necessary to make ends meet. . . . Parents used to be able to depend to some degree on society to reinforce the values they taught at home. . . . Today a barrage of messages from mass culture promotes and glamorizes the opposite values, meaning that parents constantly struggle against the tide to teach their values to their children.[7]

In short, as the demands on parenting have increased in a more complex culture, families face increasing isolation with fewer of the traditional sources of support and guidance in place to draw upon. Because of their connections to both youth and parents, congregations have the potential to contribute significantly to addressing parents' needs. (Tipsheet 29 highlights the benefits of the asset-building perspective for parents.)

Parental support for growth in their teenagers

You've probably experienced this scenario: A young person goes on a youth trip or to a national event. It's a life-changing experience, and the teenager comes back home ready to try new things or "turn over a new leaf."

At home, however, a parent tells the young person: "It's just a phase. You'll get over it." The teenager's commitment and energy deflate like a popped balloon.

Much of what congregations seek to do with youth is to nurture positive change. But that change will be difficult to sustain without support and encouragement at home. "The challenge," writes Leif Kehrwald, "is to help families adjust to the changes the programs are trying to encourage in the lives of individuals. Families resist change, even if it is a positive one. If ministers cannot help them adjust, then the changes for individuals will not be lasting."[8]

Consistency

Another opportunity offered by connecting with parents is the opportunity to develop consistent, mutually reinforcing messages and opportunities for youth related to asset building and healthy development. Setting boundaries in the congregation regarding use of alcohol and other drugs is much more likely to have an impact when that message is reinforced—and enforced—at home.

Parental involvement

Extensive research has underscored the value of parental involvement in school. The same principles hold true for parental involvement in a congregation's work with youth. Young people are more likely to internalize and apply what they learn in their congregation when their parents are involved.

Parental support for asset building

Finally, connecting with parents builds their support for asset-building efforts in the congregation. When they know and support what is happening, they can be influential in broadening support throughout the congregation. If, however, they become antagonistic, they can seriously hurt your efforts.

Barriers to Working with Families

While there are clear benefits and opportunities for working with parents, there are also significant barriers. Some of the most common include:

T I P S H E E T 2 9

What Asset Building Offers Parents

The asset-building approach gives a concrete, sensible perspective for thinking about parenting and family life. Rather than offering a laundry list of "stuff you should do," it suggests priorities and perspectives to shape the parenting task. The book *All Kids Are Our Kids*, by Search Institute president Peter L. Benson (San Francisco: Jossey-Bass, 1997), highlights the following benefits of asset building for parents.

A focus for parenting

The asset-building framework reminds parents of the "bottom line" in their child rearing. Rather than focusing on "getting ahead" or avoiding problems, the assets help parents see that their primary role lies in raising caring, competent, and responsible young people.

Affirmation and motivation

Asset building affirms parents' important role in their children's lives. It reminds them that what they do makes a big difference. Furthermore, it motivates them to stay actively involved in their children's lives throughout childhood and adolescence, rather than assuming that teenagers no longer need their parents when they begin becoming independent.

A positive perspective

Many parent educators say they struggle to get parents to come to workshops because parents are afraid of being labeled as having problems with their kids. By emphasizing the positive things all young people need, asset building can break down the barriers and reduce the stigma of seeking support and guidance.

Partners in parenting

Because asset building seeks to nurture a shared responsibility in the community for raising the youngest generation, this approach promises to provide families with a supportive, caring network of partners in raising their children. In short, it begins to recreate the kind of informal community that previous generations of parents depended on for support and guidance.

No one shows up

Often when congregations begin thinking about serving parents, the first thing someone says goes something like this: "Well, I offered a parenting class last year, and only four people showed up." Then people notice that no parents showed up for this particular meeting either. "Maybe families don't really want anything from the congregation," the group concludes.

Perhaps not, but I doubt it. Something else is probably going on. Perhaps activities are scheduled in ways that make it impossible for parents to participate. Perhaps no child care or activities for youth are provided, so parents either have to scramble to "do something with the kids" or not attend the meeting. Perhaps the topic is not one that interests them.

The point is that you shouldn't jump to conclusions about why parents don't participate. And it's even more important to find ways to support and educate families without adding to their already hectic lives. The goal of connecting with families is not to add more programs and commitments, but to reshape opportunities to ensure that they are nurturing families. As Leif Kehrwald writes, "Instead of lamenting that age-old question, 'How can we get more parents involved with our program?' ask first how you might be more involved with parents."[9]

Parents only ask for help in a crisis

Like everyone else, parents often rely on the squeaky-wheel method: Only worry about things when they are a problem or crisis. And society has exacerbated the problem by shaping most resources for parents around crises and problems. The result is that we offer classes on "Your Teen and Drugs" and other hot topics that may be of little interest to the parent for whom most things seem to be going okay.

Asset building offers a positive perspective and focus for parent education beyond the crisis, and many parents find the positive emphasis refreshing. Furthermore, congregations can develop opportunities for parents around the natural or transitional life stages, when parents are more receptive and eager to learn without the problem-focused stigma.

Kids don't want their parents around

This is a common theme among youth workers. As young people test boundaries and assert their independence, parents assume that they are no longer really needed or important, though extensive research shows otherwise. And when teenagers feel embarrassed to have their parents around and resist signs of affection, it's easiest simply to let the generations keep their distance.

The challenge for congregations is to help adolescents and their parents sort out their changing relationship as it develops and matures. Sure, youth sometimes need to be away from their parents. But it's just as important that they have opportunities to be together to renegotiate roles and expectations of each other.

It's someone else's job

Because congregations are often organized in age-specific categories, it is easy for youth workers to defer family support to whoever is responsible for adults in the congregation. While high-quality adult programming can be valuable for parents, it doesn't address the need for parents and youth to interact together. Furthermore, youth workers can offer parents a unique perspective on adolescence.

The parents aren't active in the congregation

A final barrier in some congregations is that the parents are not active in the congregation, which means connections may be difficult to make. In fact, some parents may be hostile toward religion and the congregation, making constructive support even more difficult to offer.

It is much more difficult to reach parents who are not involved in the congregation, and there are no simple solutions. But it is important to take the initiative in building a trusting relationship with the parents (who may have developed a mistrust of religion or institutions in general). A first step is to listen to the parents and their needs. That dialogue may help to identify opportunities and needs. Or it may help you discover that the parents are not involved for logistical reasons or because they participate in a different congregation. Whatever the case, the conversation will not only have opened the door for a positive relationship, but could also set the stage for future involvement.

With these barriers in mind, let's now turn to some strategies for involving families in the congregation's asset-building efforts.

Shifting Perspectives

One thing that can emerge through family involvement (and should be a philosophy undergirding the efforts) is the need to address some false assumptions about the role of the congregation and the family. These assumptions shape both the way the congregation works with families as well as the expectations that families have of congregations. Some of the shifts in thinking that need to be addressed include:

T I P S H E E T   3 0

Principles of Effective Family Support

A report from the Children's Defense Fund outlines 10 principles of effective family support programs that are relevant to congregations' work with families.[10]

1. **Emphasize the family unit**
   Work with parents and youth together.

2. **Build on family strengths**
   Recognize that all parents want the best for their children and all parents have skills and abilities to build on.

3. **Make participation voluntary**
   Coercion does not build cooperation and a sense of partnership.

4. **Address family needs comprehensively**
   Issues and needs are intertwined. Addressing one without addressing others will have little impact.

5. **Develop parenting skills**
   Providing relevant information and skills enhances parents' self-confidence and effectiveness.

6. **Provide nurturing connections with others**
   Provide opportunities for parents to build relationships with other parents.

7. **Respond to individual and community needs**
   While addressing individual needs is important, there may be larger congregational or community needs that must also be addressed (transportation, etc.) in order to effectively support families.

8. **Work to prevent crises**
   Asset building calls for a focus on building strengths early so that crises are less likely and less common.

9. **Respect individual and cultural differences**
   All families do not have to look alike in order to be strong and healthy.

10. **Coordinate and cooperate with other agencies**
    Work with other family-serving agencies and organizations that can be resources to the families you serve.

FROM . . .	TO . . .
The purpose of involving families is to get more support for congregational programs and activities.	The purpose of involving families is to support them in their primary role as asset builders for youth at home.
Efforts are most successful if a lot of people show up for activities.	Efforts are most successful when you see a positive difference in family life.
Teenagers don't want to be with their parents.	Teenagers and parents need to learn new ways to relate to each other as the young person grows up.
If a lot of people don't show up for an activity, they must not want support from the congregation.	If a lot of people don't show up, perhaps they are too busy, or perhaps the time was inconvenient, or perhaps the topic didn't really address their needs, or perhaps. . .
Asset building is something families need to add to their already busy lives.	Asset building is a tool to help parents examine priorities and be more effective in their role as parents.

Each of these shifts in thinking affects the way you develop strategies for working with families. For example, instead of focusing on "getting a lot of parents to come to a workshop," the focus should be on finding the best ways to support and equip families to address a topic. Perhaps a workshop is a great strategy, but there may be other ways that are more effective in serving families.

Getting to Know the Families of Youth

A first step is to get to know the families—not just their names, but their interests, needs, and realities. This information will not only help to shape your approach, it will also send an important signal that you are there to serve and support them, not to try to coax them into taking on yet another responsibility in the congregation. As Kehrwald writes, "The better you know parents, the easier it is to know just how to invite their participation. They will also be motivated to contribute."[11]

Getting to know parents can happen on two levels. First, you can gather information from them. Survey them about their interests and needs. Have focus groups to talk about ideas. But even more important is for them to have a personal connection to the congregation and those responsible for youth work. A survey can never replace the relational value of a conversation over coffee in the workplace, a visit to the home, or a casual conversation in a hall.

Respecting Limits on Parents' Involvement

Since families are already stretched and stressed, a key priority in involving families in asset building is to respect limits on involvement and make the times parents are involved enriching, giving back to the family more than is taken away.

Sometimes we equate an effective family emphasis in the congregation with lots of activities for families in the congregation. If a lot of families participate in a lot of activities, then a program is successful. But while some activities provide the opportunities needed to connect with families, the true measure of success is what happens in the home. If efforts to support and educate families result in parents and teenagers spending more time together, communicating more openly and clearly, and living out their faith and values together, then the efforts have succeeded—regardless of how many people show up for a particular event.

Finding the best ways to help parents balance their involvement will require creative experimentation. Here are some ideas to get started.

- Keep expectations reasonable. While it might be great to meet weekly to plan a big event, it might be better for families to have just one meeting each month, with the rest of the planning taking place over the phone.

- Don't expect parents to provide all the volunteer support and leadership for youth activities. While they certainly should be encouraged to be involved, one way the rest of the congregation can show its support for families is to give parents an opportunity for their own enrichment while other caring adults lead youth activities.

- Increase the benefits of participating. For example, have a shared meal (that parents don't have to cook) on committee meeting nights so that families can all come together, have social time with others in the congregation, and then participate in meetings and other activities. In this approach, building relationships becomes an additional draw that makes it easier to make time for meetings or other activities.

- Find ways to get parents and youth to do things together without coming to the congregation's building or meeting place. As an example, Kehrwald suggests sponsoring "an electricity fast" during which families are encouraged to spend time together without using electricity. "You'll be amazed how creative folks can be," he notes.[12]

- Coordinate activities within the congregation so that families only have to make one trip.

T I P S H E E T 3 1

Some Ways Parents Can Build Assets

What are the implications of asset building for families? While the possibilities are endless, the underlying shift is that parents become proactive and engaged, focusing attention, energy, and resources on the things their children need to grow up healthy. Some specific ways parents can and do build assets include:

- Developing a family mission statement that focuses on building assets, then using it as a guide for family decisions and priorities.

- Modeling and talking about the values and priorities they wish to pass on to their children.

- Taking time to nurture their own assets by spending time with supportive people, using their time constructively, and reflecting on their own values and commitments.

- Regularly spending time with their children doing things that both of them enjoy, which might include projects around the house, recreation activities, and service projects.

- Actively seeking support from the extended family, neighbors, the congregation, and others in their networks of friends.

- Eating at least one meal together as a family every day.

- Limiting television watching.

- Being active in their children's education through school activities, monitoring homework, and talking with their children about school and learning.

- Negotiating boundaries and consequences for behavior for the whole family.

- Modeling involvement in structured activities in the community or in a congregation. In the process, keep a balance so that activities do not overwhelm the parents' ability to meet other needs.

- Plan opportunities for parents simultaneous with youth activities, so that parents will not have to find other opportunities or care for their children in order to participate.

- Offer child care during parent activities and meetings. (Even though you are focusing on parents of teenagers, they also may have younger children who need attention.)

- Offer opportunities for involvement that don't involve going to meetings or leaving home. (See Tipsheet 32, which lists six different ways parents can be involved.)

- If a number of parents work in the same area, provide support and education opportunities over a lunch break during the work week. (Breakfast meetings typically are hard because parents have to help their children get off to school.)

Providing Opportunities for Parent-Teen Interaction

When we talk about supporting and educating families, often the first things that come to mind are parent education classes and support groups. While opportunities for parents play an important role in an overall system, it's perhaps even more important to find opportunities to support and educate families together through parent-youth events, activities, and classes. These family events are important for several reasons, including:

- They keep the family together rather than pulling them apart.

- They give families an experience that everyone shares together.

- They provide a safe environment where parents and youth can develop new understandings of each other.

- They give families practice in communicating with each other in safe ways.

While these activities can have many benefits, they can also be difficult to pull off effectively. As Dub Ambrose and Walt Mueller write: "Families are so busy that it's sometimes difficult to get them together. Different generations have different needs

---

T I P S H E E T 3 2

Six Types of Parental Involvement

The Center on Families, Communities, Schools, and Children's Learning at Johns Hopkins University has identified six ways parents can be involved in school. These six types translate easily into ways congregations can involve parents in the congregation's youth work.[13]

1. **Parenting**—Equipping parents with parenting and family life skills.

2. **Communicating**—Telling parents what is happening in the congregation with youth and how their child is doing.

3. **Volunteering**—Involving parents as volunteers in youth programming.

4. **Learning at home**—Involving parents in their teenager's learning (for example, offering ideas or assignments for working together on projects for a religious education class).

5. **Decision making**—Involving parents in planning and setting policies for the congregation's work with youth and families.

6. **Collaborating with community**—Coordinating support for families in and through other organizations in the community.

Building Assets in Congregations

and interests. Different types of families have different needs. But when your programming works, it has a significant impact on families that participate, making it worth the effort."[14]

There are many different opportunities for facilitating parent-youth interaction in a congregation. Here are some of the possibilities:

Education

There are dozens of asset-building topics that can be addressed to youth and parents together. These might range from positive family communication to effective decision making. And these can occur in many environments, from a standard religious education class to a special event to a family retreat setting. (Tipsheet 33 offers guidelines for effective family programming.)

Mark DeVries describes a model in which each year parents and teenagers take a four-week religious education class together. In seventh grade, for example, the topic is community building, in ninth grade, they focus on sexuality, and in twelfth grade, the emphasis is on preparing for college/adulthood. "The focus," he writes, "is not so much informational as bridge-building, giving teens repeated opportunities to know an extended family of . . . adults."[15]

While your education could focus on asset-building themes and family relationships, another approach to consider is offering classes and workshop, on hobbies and interests that parents and teenagers can learn together. While it wasn't offered through a congregation, one of my fond memories as a teenager was taking a photography darkroom class with my dad. Neither of us knew anything about photo development, but we were both interested. Our relationship grew as we learned side by side, compared notes, and practiced together. There are likely many people in your congregation who have specific hobbies and skills that they could teach to a class designed specifically for parent-teenager partners.

Service and action

A powerful shaper of young people's faith and values is the opportunity to serve others together with their family. Yet it is a rare experience. Search Institute's study of mainline Christian youth found that only 36 percent of youth sometimes or often participate in family service projects. Furthermore, when youth are the only ones in the congregation active in service projects, they get the message that service is "something teenagers do, something like proms and student government, and that they expect to grow out of it."[16]

Designing service opportunities that allow parents and youth to spend time together, talk about what motivates them, and share their values has tremendous potential for both enriching family life and also strengthening faith. The challenge is helping parents see that service is not "just for kids," but can be a formative experience for adults as well.[17]

Worship

While families may sit together in worship, too often the service does little to draw them together or to focus on strengthening the family. One key is to shape the service so young people themselves feel engaged and interested (see Chapter 4).

Guidelines for Effective Family Programming

In their book *Ministry to Families with Teenagers*, Dub Ambrose and Walt Mueller
outline 16 guidelines for effective programming for families.[18]

1. Remember basic programming principles regarding preparation and engaging activities.

2. Focus on common family concerns, not just concerns of parents or of youth.

3. Be sensitive to different family situations.

4. Facilitate family cooperation so that families work together, not compete.

5. Let families communicate, don't just talk to them.

6. Begin with nonthreatening activities.

7. Don't let parents dominate.

8. Remember that parents are adults.

9. Avoid addressing just one generation.

10. Help each generation respect the other.

11. Be sensitive to participants without all family members present.

12. Keep costs down.

13. Recognize physical limitations.

14. Plan for other ages, such as younger children.

15. Include time for relaxing.

16. Use different leaders, both parents and youth.

Other opportunities include:

- Addressing family issues in sermons.

- Including in the bulletin take-home discussion starters based on the service.

- Involving families in rituals that acknowledge milestones or rites of passage.

- Asking families to be involved in leadership together (for example, reading scripture in dialogue, lighting candles together, providing special music).

Celebration and fun

One of the best ways to strengthen relationships in a family is to have fun together. Family sports teams, game nights, camping or canoe trips, and dozens of other activities can be great, nonthreatening ways for parents and teenagers to spend time together—particularly if the activities are cooperative instead of competitive. Competitive activities can be problematic. If parents and teenagers are on the same team, the parent may revert to the role of a pushy coach. If they are on opposite teams, fierce competition can drive them apart.[19]

Empowering Parents Through Educational Opportunities

Beth El Synagogue in Minneapolis, Minnesota, has made family support a focal point for its youth programming. The congregation regularly offers workshops and study sessions for parents and sponsors mini-retreats for families. The result is that families are actively involved and supportive of the congregation's other activities for youth.

Many congregations find that parent education is a valued and valuable way to serve families and engage them in asset building. Because nuclear families are often isolated from their extended families, they may not have access to the "wisdom of generations" for parenting. In addition, some parents may be determined not to repeat the mistakes of their own parents, but do not have the skills or know the alternatives.

The asset framework is filled with specific themes to address in parent education. An obvious series would be a class that explores the parenting implications of each of the eight types of assets. Or there may be specific assets that parents feel a need to examine.[20]

Another approach is to identify some of the underlying themes and skills for asset building and focus sessions on building these skills. (See Tipsheet 31 for some of the basic ways parents can build assets.) For example, communication is a parenting skill that is necessary for building many of the assets. Similarly, an understanding of basic adolescent development will allow parents to be more comfortable with—and build assets during—the changes occurring in their family as their teenager grows up. And by tying educational opportunities to the asset framework, parents see, for example, how a workshop on positive discipline relates to a class on helping your teenager choose a college.

Finally, an important opportunity for parent education is in conjunction with major youth activities or programs, such as confirmation, bar/bat mitzvah, retreats, a new year, a pilgrimage, work camps, and mission trips. These times not only help parents understand what their child will be doing, but can also prepare parents to understand what changes might begin in their child and how they can support those changes.

Whatever the specific topic, a key goal should be to help parents gain a healthy understanding of adolescence as a normal stage of development that does not have to be rife with conflict. Their understanding of the changes in their teenager—and themselves—can help them respond in healthy ways to changes and challenges that occur.

T I P S H E E T 3 4

Parent Workshops That Make Them Want to Come Back for More

All workshops and classes are not created equal. Not only does the content you include need to be relevant to parents, but the process you use will make a big difference in how well parents learn and whether they will be eager to participate the next time. Here are seven tips for designing and leading effective educational experiences for parents.

1. Create a supportive, caring environment for learning. Greet parents, provide time for them to get acquainted with one another, and encourage mutual support during and after the experience.

2. Actively engage parents in the learning. The amount they learn will be in direct proportion to how much they put into the experience.

3. Let parents be the "experts." Show that you value their knowledge and experience by giving them opportunities to contribute to the learning experience.

4. Tie the learning activities around parents' experiences and values so they know "this is for me and about my family."

5. Focus the content on real needs, issues, or concerns, not just on content that parents "ought" to know. If, for example, you want to address nurturing positive values, first identify the ways this connects with parents' needs or concerns regarding values, then develop the experience to reflect those concerns.

6. Include information and skills parents can put into action immediately. Such application reinforces and helps parents internalize what they learn.

7. Pay attention to logistics. Schedule at a time that is convenient for parents. Always begin and end on time. Be sure positive opportunities are available for their children during the class or workshop.

In thinking about educating parents, keep in mind the many ways you can help them learn new skills and perspectives:

- Classes or workshops with many parents together. (See Tipsheet 34 for ideas for making these positive learning experiences.)

- Small groups of parents who might study a book, watch a video, or have another form of ongoing, peer-led discussion.

- Resources (e.g., tipsheets, newsletter articles, bulletin boards, videos, books) given to parents for self-learning at home.

- Instead of (or in addition to) sponsoring your own educational events, alert parents to parent education opportunities in the community. Have parents sign up, go as a group, then discuss the topic in a follow-up conversation.

Providing Support for Parents

As important as education can be to equip parents for asset building, it is equally important to provide support and relationships. (Indeed, one of the best ways to educate parents is within the context of a supportive peer group!) And because parents come together in the congregation, it provides a natural context through which they can find support.

In the same way that supporting youth is primarily about building relationships, parent support comes through relationships—with other parents of youth, with parents whose children are now adults, and with other members of the faith community. While clergy and other staff also have a role, the primary support best comes from the community of faith.

Providing empowering support

The goal of providing family support is to empower families to build their own strengths and resources, not to make them dependent on the congregation, its staff, or other service providers. As Richard P. Olson and Joe H. Leonard, Jr., write: "The term 'family support' involves ministering with families in a way that puts them in charge of the care or services they are receiving. It involves respecting the needs, aspirations, and goals families have identified, rather than imposing your pastoral care or programs on them."[21]

T I P S H E E T   3 5

Skills and Attitudes for Empowering Families

Joan M. Patterson of the University of Minnesota identifies seven skills and strategies for working with families in order to build their strengths.[22]

1. Listen to the family's story.
2. Use the family's language as you interact.
3. Acknowledge and validate emotions.
4. Ask questions versus providing answers.

5. Provide information in a clear, timely, and sensitive manner.
6. Cocreate solutions with the family.
7. Advocate for social policies that support families.

Addressing the Needs of Diverse Families

Today's families are diverse and varied. Effective support for families involves addressing the specific dynamics of their family situation. In their book *A New Day for Family Ministry*, Richard P. Olson and Joe H. Leonard, Jr., identify many ways to respond to a wide array of dynamics facing families.[23] Here are a few of the variations and implications for congregations.

Families Dealing with Divorce

- Give couples support as they struggle with the decision. Olson and Leonard suggest a "clearness meeting" in which couples meet with friends who pray and ask open-ended questions together.

- Create a support circle for each family member in the midst of a divorce, particularly addressing the guilt, anger, depression, and other feelings that are common among adolescents whose parents divorce.

- Offer rituals that bring dignity and closure.

Families with Remarriages (or Blended Families)

- Offer premarital and early marriage counseling for all family members.

- Establish opportunities for the whole family to talk together to learn each other's heritage, rules, and other things that are typically taken for granted.

- Offer support groups for people in remarriages.

Two-Career Families

- Give opportunities to plan and renew. The authors recommend a retreat setting in which families can explore how to "build into their lives both fun and meaningful interaction."

- Provide (or cooperate in) after-school activities and other strategies to ensure young people's safety and enrichment in the after-school hours.

Research on various types of help has identified a number of factors that are empowering. These factors are highly consistent with an asset-building approach, which focuses on the positive and seeks to build the family's capacities not only to build assets for the children, but to undergird the whole family with a web of resources to build its own strengths. Researchers Carl J. Dunst and Carol M. Trivette identify the following positive characteristics of help for parents (with examples added from an asset-building approach in congregations):

- The help is both positive and proactive, given by people who display caring, warmth, and encouragement.

- The help is offered, rather than waiting to be requested.

- The person seeking help is the primary decision maker (including whether to accept the help in the first place and options for following through).

- The help is consistent with the norms in the help seeker's own culture.

- The help offered is congruent with the help seeker's perceptions of her or his own needs or problem. If parents are struggling with concrete issues such as curfews, for example, the support should help them address those issues from an asset-building perspective.

- The help offered is not more costly (in terms of money, personal control, dignity) than the benefits of receiving the help.

- The help can be reciprocal in that the help seeker can in some way "repay" the help giver. For example, parents may be offered opportunities to volunteer in the congregation, or they may be willing to share their experiences with other parents.

- The effort bolsters the help seeker's own sense of success and self-esteem. One way to do this is to encourage parents to reflect on their progress and affirm each other.

- The help promotes the family's existing support networks and does not replace them with professional services. Within a congregation, this may mean that parents are encouraged to tap a class or small group in which they participate.

- There is a sense of cooperation and partnership in the help offered.

- The help promotes positive behaviors and skills in parents that decrease the need for help and increase the help seeker's own competence. In an asset-building context, this might include training parents in how to talk with their teenager and how to use positive discipline.

- The effort helps the help seeker see not only that problems are solved, but also that he or she plays a major role in solving those problems.[24]

These guidelines give some broad parameters for the kind of support congregations can provide families. And they provide an important filter for evaluating the various support opportunities for families to determine if they are truly empowering parents or making them feel dependent.

Opportunities for providing support for families

One of the challenges in providing support is that sometimes "no one shows up." There seems to be a need, yet no one comes to classes, groups, or other opportunities. What's going on?

We've already noted the scheduling issues that may be involved. In addition, parents' sense of need may not be high enough to motivate them to seek support, particularly if they do not already have positive relationships in the congregation.

TIP SHEET 37

Making the Congregation Welcoming to Unconnected Families

Sometimes it's easy to think about ways to work with families who are part of the congregation already. But what about the families of youth who never participate—or who are antagonistic to the congregation? There are no simple ways to build connections with them, but here are some "do's and don'ts" to consider:

- **Do** begin by building relationships. It may be with a staff person or a volunteer, but the goal is for parents to get to know someone in the congregation whom they trust.

- **Don't** assume you know why the parent isn't involved or interested. Let them tell you when they are ready.

- **Do** focus on building on family strengths and capacity rather than focusing on what's missing in the family.

- **Don't** ignore external forces that are stressing families, such as illness, job loss, or economic pressure. By assisting families in addressing those issues, you provide a significant service that will increase their trust in and commitment to the congregation.

- **Do** provide information about congregational youth and family activities, goals in the youth program, expectations of participating youth, and other information that will help parents understand your congregation's efforts.

- **Don't** ignore serious problems or concerns you notice. If, for example, you have a concern about abuse or neglect, talk with a qualified counselor about your concern.

- **Do** keep good, up-to-date records. Many unconnected families may face considerable change that is important to know about as you seek to serve them.

- **Don't** expect them to come to your "turf." Go to where they are comfortable. Often, sponsoring activities in neutral sites (a park, a community center) will be less threatening than asking them to come into an institution that is unfamiliar or alienating to them. Or set up a family resource center (with, for example, materials to check out, counseling, workshops, support groups) in a comfortable, convenient location.

- **Do** pay attention to stresses and changes in the family. Often, a crisis may provide an opportunity to serve the family in a way that is meaningful and opens the parent to more connections.

- **Don't** make it a goal to get them into the program or congregation. Rather, focus on how the congregation can best support and equip the parents to fulfill their role in the home.

- **Do** offer a variety of opportunities to connect that meet different needs and interests.

Thus, one foundational task is to provide opportunities for parents to get to know each other. Integrating sharing time into educational events and other congregational activities can open these connections. As they grow, these relationships can open doors to providing support for parents.

Second, a critical time for providing support is in the midst of crisis. During these times (when they most need support), families often withdraw and isolate themselves and feel powerless in the midst of their circumstances. In some cases when there is a stigma associated with the stress (e.g., divorce, alcoholism, teen drug use, financial problems), they are even less likely to articulate their needs because of feelings of shame.

A proactive, nonjudgmental effort to reach out to them with a web of support and care can be the buoy that keeps them afloat through the crisis. Furthermore, researchers have found that one of the main reasons people leave congregations is that they failed to receive care and support in the midst of crisis, and they feel angry and estranged.[25]

Finally, an excellent window of opportunity for providing support is in the midst of family, parent, or child transitions. Whether the birth of a child, a move to a new community, entering adolescence, or leaving home for college or work, transitions are times when families are more in need of support. Intentional efforts to create supportive networks around these times can build a foundation that provides support through and beyond the transition.

Ways to provide support for families

Too often in congregations, the clergy or staff are called on to do most caregiving. Because of its focus on relationships as the primary vehicle for transmitting assets, an asset-building philosophy challenges this pattern and calls for highlighting and strengthening other ways of providing support and care. Tipsheet 38 gives specific ideas of ways congregations can support parents. In addition, there are four structures through which congregations can provide this support.

First is to *nurture individual peer support,* where one parent (or another adult) provides support to another parent (old-fashioned friendships!). While it seems simple to encourage friendships in a congregation, it has to be an intentional effort. If, for example, a parent only attends worship for an hour each week and rarely participates in other congregational activities, how does he or she form supportive friendships with other members? Or if all the opportunities for parents are centered on a leader speaking, then how will parents find time to get to know each other?

Thus, whenever parents are involved in events or activities in the congregation, there should be time built in for people to get to know each other. Furthermore, since many parents may not have strong social skills themselves, it may also be important to give them tools, structures, and skills that make it easier to "break the ice" and form friendships. Training parents in peer-helping or caregiving skills can make them more aware of the times when families need support and help them become better able to respond.[26]

Second, many congregations *form support groups* for parents. While these groups have many functions, a survey of support group participants found that the main benefit is that they "made you feel like you weren't alone."[27] This can be particularly valuable to parents who are seeking to respond in healthy ways to the changes in their growing teenager and their family.

Support groups can also be invaluable in offering support to families with particular life experiences, such as divorce, chronic illness, depression, a family member with a disability, interreligious families, and many others. Furthermore, small groups may provide the foundation for connecting parents with the larger community. In reporting on a major study of small-group involvement in the United States, sociologist Robert Wuthnow writes:

> The members of small groups are quite often prompted to be more active in their communities, to help others who may be in need, and to think more deeply about pressing social and political issues. . . . [S]mall groups may help to integrate people with their families or neighborhoods and to make them more aware of the larger society.[28]

A third way congregations can support families is through *counseling services*. These services need to be staffed by trained clergy and/or counselors. And while it can play an essential role in supporting families in times of crisis and stress, counseling can also be offered in ways that enrich and strengthen family life for all families. For example, counselors could be proactive in spending time with families of young adolescents to help them understand how their family can maintain its strengths and relationships as changes accelerate through the teenage years.

A final way to provide support for families is by *connecting them to resources in the community*. For example, rather than trying to meet every specific need within the congregation, find out what kinds of support groups might be sponsored by other congregations or organizations in the community. And provide information on groups in your own congregation that might be of interest to people from other congregations. While it doesn't necessarily contribute to building your own

---

T I P S H E E T   3 8

15 Ways Congregations Can Support Parents

1. Connect them with other parents experiencing similar life issues.

2. Release them from congregational responsibilities that interfere with family life.

3. Provide services that give parents a break (such as baby-sitting).

4. Sponsor a shared meal during the week so that parents don't have to cook.

5. Get other adults in the congregation to teach religious education classes and staff other programs for children.

6. Sponsor after-school programs for children and teenagers of working parents.

7. Honor parents during worship services for their central role in shaping the lives and faith of young people.

8. Ask parents whose children are now adults to be partners with or mentors for other parents, starting when a child is born and continuing through high school.

9. Sponsor support groups for parents around specific needs.

10. Ask retired people in the congregation to be "on-call volunteer sitters" to relieve parents when one of their children is sick and they need to go to work.

11. Arrange for volunteers to provide meals and spend time with the children when a parent is ill or faces another type of crisis.

12. Hold intergenerational family events that bring together members of all ages to socialize and get to know each other as families.

13. Provide an information booth or table with literature about local resources for families such as parent education, health care, financial planning, housing, counseling, and support groups.

14. Organize a new baby support team to bring meals, clean house, play with older children, and provide information and support to new parents.

15. Ask retired congregation members to volunteer as "grandparents" for families with grandparents who live far away or who are deceased.

program or congregation, this kind of mutual sharing does contribute to the ultimate goal: assuring that families have the support and resources they need to build a solid foundation for their children and teenagers.

Advocating on Behalf of Families

Support and education are at the heart of an asset-building approach to nurturing families in the congregation. In addition, however, congregations can also play an advocacy role in the community to address issues that get in the way of parents' abilities to build assets. Advocacy might include:

- Supporting public awareness efforts that challenge negative messages about parenting and highlight ways parents seek support simply to increase their effectiveness.

- Calling on businesses and corporations to provide flexible work schedules, on-site daycare, and other family-friendly policies for parents.

- Lobbying for public policies that make it easier for families to build assets.

- Taking on other causes that strengthen families and their abilities to support young people's healthy development.

An Essential Shift

In an interview with *Group* magazine, veteran youth worker Ben Freudenburg said:

> In all the studies we've accumulated over the years regarding what influences teens, parents continue to be the most influential shapers of a person's life—either positively or negatively. I'm not sure we've responded in our structure and programming to address that concept. . . . Here's the major paradigm shift—How do we build strong homes and families? And how do we make the church the support system for the home, which is the center of nurture? So it's a shift from church-centered, home-supported ministry to home-centered, church-supported ministry.[29]

An emphasis on reaching out to and including families in asset-building efforts broadens the typical focus of most congregations' youth work. It raises questions about who is supposed to do what. It raises questions of workload and skills. It raises questions about priorities. But it is an essential shift in youth work if congregations are to be optimally effective in building assets in youth.

Integrating Asset Building into Work with Families

Key Points

- Building connections to parents provides important opportunities for asset building. It not only gets parents involved, but better equips them for their own role as asset builders.

- A number of barriers can make connecting to parents difficult. These include parents not showing up for activities, an assumption that youth don't want parents around, and family support not being seen as a responsibility of youth work.

- In working with families, it's important to get to know them and to respect their limits on involvement.

- Families can benefit from opportunities for parent-teen interaction, educational activities for parents, providing support for parents, and advocating on behalf of families.

Questions for Reflection and Discussion

- What are ways your congregation already involves, supports, and educates parents? How might asset building strengthen these activities?

- What kinds of support and education do parents want and need?

- What barriers do you face in trying to serve the different kinds of families in your congregation? What are creative ways to overcome those barriers?

- How does or could your congregation promote parent-teen interaction?

Suggestions for Getting Started

- Talk with parents about the kinds of activities, services, and other opportunities they would most value from your congregation.

- Ask youth about ways they do and don't want their parents to be involved.

- Present the assets to a group or groups of parents in your congregation. Find out what interests them.

- Identify and plan one new activity that you can do in your congregation to build more connections to parents.

Reaching into the Community for Asset Building

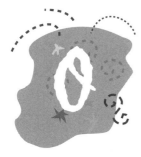

ne of the underlying principles in asset building is that no one can do it alone. While families are important, their efforts can be undermined if other institutions are not also providing consistent messages and a solid foundation. And while congregations can work to create an asset-building climate, many positive opportunities, and a strong, supportive system for families, these efforts can either be enhanced or undermined by young people's experiences in their schools, their jobs, and the community.

Congregations of all faiths have strong traditions of service and advocacy in the community. In some communities, congregations already play a significant role as community leaders, and there already is a foundation of trust and cooperation. In too many cases, however, congregations are isolated from other sectors and may even be antagonistic toward broad efforts in the community. Search Institute's 1995 survey of religious youth workers found that only a tiny percentage of them networked with secular youth workers over the previous year.

While some congregations may think of asset building primarily in terms of "our kids," the paradigm challenges congregations to see their responsibility to all youth in the community—particularly those who are disconnected from all positive socializing systems, including congregations. Ultimately, there is much to gain from cooperating with others who share a positive vision for youth and, in the process, strengthening the community for all youth.

The Value of Reaching Out

Asset building provides a new focal point for developing a congregational commitment to the community. And it has benefits for both the congregation and community. (See Tipsheet 39.) In my own congregation, for example, asset building connects to a historic commitment to social activism and service. In the past, it has taken a major crisis to galvanize the congregation's energy and commitment. Our hope is that we can use the asset model to help us focus on issues that contribute to—or detract from—the healthy development of children and youth.

A commitment to asset building in the community has benefits for everyone involved. Specifically, it has potential in the following areas:

Fulfillment of congregational mission

First, a commitment to asset building can be an important expression of the congregation's commitment to service and justice. By focusing energy on strengthening the developmental foundation for all youth in the community, congregations contribute to rebuilding community and changing the odds that young people will grow up healthy, responsible, and caring.

All major faith traditions include a commitment to serving the most vulnerable members of society. An asset-building filter enriches that service, ensuring that it not only meets basic physical needs, but also equips those being served with support, skills, and opportunities to make positive choices.

This commitment to healthy development does not conflict with, but complements, a commitment to meeting people's basic needs for food, shelter, and health. John M. Perkins, one of the founders of the Christian community development movement, founded the **Harambee Christian Family Center in Pasadena, California,** to address the needs of poor children in that community. When asked what the center was all about, he replied: "We are trying to meet the greatest need in this community, which is the need for care. We are trying to parent these children." Perkins goes on to quote David Claerbaut:

> Humans were created to be whole persons, with physical, mental and spiritual dimensions. Deprivation of any of these dimensions has a deadening effect on the others, since all parts are interrelated and interactive. . . . The soul without a body is a ghost; the body without a soul is a corpse.[1]

In addition to enhancing a commitment to service, congregations can get involved in public advocacy for asset building. Congregations—particularly those with a tradition of public activism—bring important resources to the "public square" in addressing the needs of youth. In a chapter in *Working with Black Youth*, Romney M. Moseley writes:

> The contemporary social situation demands that the church retrieve its militant heritage as an arena for dialogue on any moral, political, economic, and spiritual issues confronting black identity formation. No other institution is equipped to be the locus of authority, the cradle of transforming leadership, and the matrix of symbols and rituals essential to the creation of structures for making meaning for our youth.[2]

This public advocacy may involve both awareness raising and education regarding asset building, as well as political action. For example, congregations could begin monitoring how the media address youth issues (in much the way some organizations have begun monitoring media depictions of violence). Or congregations could educate and mobilize their members to speak out on public policy issues that affect healthy youth development in the community, nation, or world.[3]

Impact on the congregation

Second, an asset-based effort in the community can transform both youth and adults in the congregation. By involving members in the community, the asset-building focus gives them experience in serving others—the kind of experience that transforms both those serving and those being served. In this way, the efforts in the community become the opportunity for putting beliefs into action. In addition, learning about opportunities and resources in the community is a valuable way to help youth and families in the congregation access services or opportunities they need.

Impact on the community

Finally, as highlighted in Tipsheet 39, congregations have many resources to offer the community. The congregation's efforts to build assets in the community, then, have tremendous potential to have a positive impact on community life.

Yet, moving out into the community is not always easy. Congregations may be viewed with suspicion when they reach out beyond their membership. Many communities do not have a tradition of cross-faith and cross-sector cooperation. Furthermore, congregation members may be wary of efforts that appear to deflect energy from building assets "in our own kids." The challenge is to find innovative ways to take the first steps that build on the congregation's identity and values while building bridges into the community.

T I P S H E E T 3 9

Why Join with Others in Your Community?

Linking with other sectors in the community and with community-wide initiatives takes time and effort, and congregational leaders already have plenty of other things to do. Why add something else? Here are some benefits such an approach brings both to the congregation and the community.

WHAT CONGREGATIONS CAN GAIN FROM COMMUNITY INVOLVEMENT

Commitment to service—All major faith traditions include a commitment to serve others. Reaching out to build assets in the community's youth (particularly those most vulnerable) can be a significant and lasting outreach.

Connection—Connecting with teachers, youth workers, city leaders, social service agencies, and other residents can help you identify resources for the young people and families in your congregation, while also providing opportunities for personal support and professional growth.

Coordination—A common complaint is that different sectors in a community don't know what others are doing, so conflicts in schedules and priorities inevitably emerge. Partnerships can ease some of these problems.

Community climate—As more and more sectors in a community adopt the asset-building vision, the whole community is strengthened, creating a better place for all youth and families, including those in your congregation.

Clout—Joining with people in other sectors can heighten your congregation's visibility and influence in the community.

Credibility—In many communities, congregations maintain an important leadership role. Their support of an asset-building vision can be important in gaining community-wide support for the efforts.

WHAT THE COMMUNITY CAN GAIN FROM CONGREGATION INVOLVEMENT

Compassion—Congregations are filled with many willing and motivated hearts and hands that want to make a difference—and that can be mobilized effectively.

Community—Congregations model intergenerational community in action. Congregations can provide settings where children and youth can learn from an older generation's wisdom and values.

Contact—More parents and other adults are involved in congregations than in any other institution in a community. Congregations can access these adults to bring them onto the asset-building team.

Clarity—The congregation provides an ongoing safe place for people to test, reflect on, and articulate their values.

Catalyst—As congregational energy and excitement grow around asset building, the energy becomes contagious to others in the community.

From Glenn A. Seefeldt and Eugene C. Roehlkepartain, *Tapping the Potential: Discovering Congregations' Role in Building Assets in Youth* (Minneapolis: Search Institute, 1995).

Approaches to Community Action for Asset Building

One of the problems that emerges when you talk about congregational action in the community is that it can mean many different things. For some, it may mean service projects that the congregation does for the community. For others, it may mean getting involved in a major collaboration for youth with dozens of other organizations. It is helpful, then, to examine the different types of community action that can grow out of asset building.

Encouraging individual member involvement

Many members of congregations are already active volunteers in community-based organizations or have professional commitments that involve them in the community (e.g., through civic clubs, corporate community commitments). One way a congregation can extend its reach into the community is to identify, encourage, and celebrate this involvement.

Supporting community programs

One of the most common ways congregations get involved in building assets for community youth is by supporting community youth or family programs, either by providing volunteers or funding. These efforts might include after-school programs, recreation centers, health clinics, parent centers, mentoring programs, and many others. This commitment is relatively low risk, and it avoids duplicating activities that may already exist. However, because it is low risk, the commitment and benefit can also be less. For example, if a congregation simply provides funding for a computer training center for youth, the members may never get to build relationships with young people or other adults at the center.

Sponsoring community-based programs for asset building

Another way to build assets in community youth is to sponsor recreational, educational, social, or other activities and programs in the community. One model for this is Project SPIRIT (which stands for Strength, Perseverance, Imagination, Responsibility, Integrity, and Talent), a program of the Congress of National Black Churches. This program—which targets youth, parents, and clergy—includes a daily after-school program for youth led by elder volunteers from the congregation. Activities include:

- Snacks, prayer, and time for meditation;

- Tutoring in reading, writing, and mathematics;

- Activities that teach practical life skills through games, skits, songs, and role plays;

- Activities to develop cultural and ethnic pride; and

- A weekly rite of passage curriculum that culminates in a year-end ceremony.[4]

Congregation-sponsored programs may also be run by young people in the congregation. For example, the youth from **Ginghamsburg United Methodist Church in Tipp City, Ohio,** coordinate and lead an after-school and summer activity program that serves 50 children each week in inner-city Dayton.[5]

Opening the Congregation for neighborhood Youth

North Shore Baptist Church in the Uptown community of North Chicago opens its doors to young men from three neighboring HUD buildings. With the help of staff from After School Action Programs and local residents, the church provides sports activities and educational programming. Youth Minister Ezelle Sherrod says one of the most important things about this partnership is altering the perception youth have of the church. "We wanted the local young people to know we are not just here on Sundays. They don't think churches have a function other than saving souls, but we wanted to make it clear we're there for them in all aspects of life."

Dedicating staff to community youth

Some congregations build into their youth worker's job description responsibility for working with youth in the community. This may involve just "hanging out" with them in parks to build relationships, coaching sports, or assisting with other youth programs. While this commitment helps to meet important needs, it risks letting the congregation's laypeople "off the hook" in terms of their own personal involvement with youth in the community.

networking with other congregations

Congregations can also connect with other congregations to work together on asset-building efforts in the community. This approach is often used to help congregations do things that they could never do alone. Some of the ways congregations can network for asset building include:

- Cosponsoring programs and activities targeted to community youth who are not connected to congregations. Many congregations cosponsor after-school programs and drop-in centers to provide community youth with positive activities in the afternoons.

- Cosponsoring activities for youth from all the congregations. For example, congregations in Albuquerque, New Mexico, work together to sponsor a New Year's Eve party for youth that keeps them safe while providing fun activities.

- Working together on community-wide events. For example, congregations in Santa Clara County, California, sponsored a community-wide rally to focus community attention on the needs of children and youth and on how everyone in the community shares responsibility for addressing those needs.

- Joining together to advocate for asset-building policies in the community and nation.

networking with other youth-serving institutions

In the same ways congregations can network together, they can also broaden the circle to network with other youth-serving systems in the community, such as YMCAs, YWCAs, Boys and Girls Clubs, 4-H, and others. This networking can result in congregations providing financial support and volunteers for these programs, as

A Different New Year's Eve Celebration

Every year, congregations in Albuquerque join together to provide a safe New Year's Eve celebration for area youth. The young people travel on buses to a concert, a worship service, ice skating, dancing, and rollerblading, and wind it up with a "late, late, late show" movie at 5:30 in the morning. Adults from participating congregations provide supervision for the event. Youth worker Toni McNeill is part of the New Year's Eve committee. "We want our kids to see there is a good way to have fun and it doesn't have to be trouble," she says. "And we're really excited that this interfaith event keeps growing. Our goal to is make it the 'in' thing for youth to do in Albuquerque on New Year's Eve!"

noted earlier. In addition, networking can help to identify opportunities for youth in the community.

Partnering with other organizations can allow congregations to do things that would otherwise be difficult, if not impossible. Several years ago, **First Baptist Church of Los Angeles, California,** made a major commitment to serve youth in its neighborhood through a recreation and arts center. The congregation wanted to give youth a safe place and constructive ways to spend their time.

But despite good intentions, programs, and supervision, the center itself became a gang hangout. "We had hoped to build an accepting environment of safety," youth worker Jim Hopkins said. "But they saw it as just another safe place to continue gang and drug activities." So the center had to close down.

Rather than giving up on what it saw as an important outreach, the congregation looked to partnerships to meet the needs. It began working with the YMCA to develop a more structured and controlled program that would include more values education and drug education. The new program didn't reach as many youth, but Hopkins hoped it had a much greater impact on those involved.[6]

Participating in community-wide partnerships

Finally, congregations can be active participants in community-wide efforts for asset building. As word of asset building has spread across the country, literally hundreds of communities are beginning to explore how to form a multisector partnership around the asset-building vision. By joining in these efforts, congregations not only contribute to the movement, but also enhance relationships and connections in the community.

In some cases, the impetus for these community-wide partnerships has come from the faith community. Glenn Seefeldt, pastor of **Nativity Lutheran Church in St. Anthony Village, Minnesota,** convened community leaders to begin developing a community-wide vision for asset building. From this meeting, an initiative is taking shape that involves all sectors of the community, from the police to schools to businesses.

Guidelines for Asset-Building Partnerships in Your Community

One of the reasons congregations are sometimes viewed with suspicion when they begin moving into the community is that people's perspectives are colored by negative memories and preconceptions. Perhaps they know of times when congregations have misused a partnership as a tool to promote themselves or to try to convert others to their own faith. Perhaps they have experienced well-meaning service projects that were paternalistic or patronizing. Or their only experiences of faith communities in the public sphere have revolved around particular religious agendas or issues.

Because asset building represents a framework and vision that can be shared across many sectors of a community, it has the potential of opening doors for congregations to connect in the community in positive ways. For such partnerships to be successful, however, several guidelines should be kept in mind.

Recognize the necessary investment

Building partnerships in the community takes work and time. And it's not always comfortable. As Carl S. Dudley and Sally A. Johnson write: "Congregations highly value their independence, and the typical church has little experience in sharing decisions or working closely with others. . . . Partnerships among churches require effort, creativity, and risk. But without venturesome and imaginative combinations, ministries must depend on the limited resources of a single congregation."[7]

Build connections between asset-building efforts within and beyond the congregation

Congregations often operate out of a false dichotomy that might be illustrated like this:

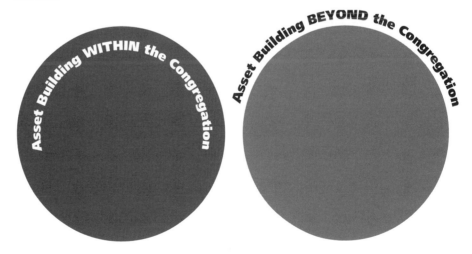

In this image, service in the community is quite separate from other "internal" congregational asset-building activities such as youth programming and parent education. This perspective can set up competition between those who want the congregation to "take care of our own kids" and those who say "we're called to reach out to others." It is important, then, to find ways to bring the circles together, like this:

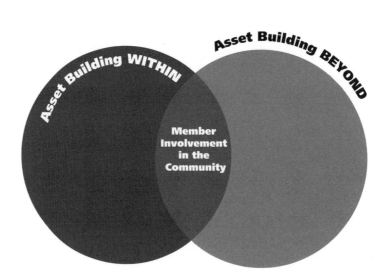

In this vision, there are certainly still activities that emphasize efforts either within the congregation or beyond the congregation. However, efforts are made to build bridges between the two. This might be done, for example, by planning service projects that connect to educational emphases in the congregation, combined with opportunities to reflect on the experience during religious education classes. Or a congregation's youth program or family emphasis could tie its service activities to a community initiative so that members are actively involved in the community in ways that bring them growth and nurturing.

In short, the challenge is to see that community efforts are reciprocal so that the congregation receives as much as it gives. For example, a middle-income congregation might offer services and support to a lower-income congregation or organization, and the members might benefit from a new understanding of the world and enriching relationships with the people in the community.

Another approach is to develop activities and programs with a dual focus on serving youth and families in the congregation while also welcoming youth and families not connected to the congregation. In this approach, parenting classes might be held in a neutral location where both congregation members and community members would learn together. Or an after-school program would actively seek to involve both congregational and community youth.

Connect to the congregation's strengths and values

Your congregation is unlikely to sustain its commitment to action in the community unless that action ties in with the congregation's deep values, traditions, and strengths.

In a fascinating, groundbreaking project led by Carl Dudley, **Chicago's Center for the Church and Community Ministry** worked across several years with a wide variety of Christian congregations in establishing ministries in their communities. One of the things the researcher-consultants discovered was that almost any type of congregation had the potential for community action—so long as that action was consistent with the congregation's identity.

The researchers identified five basic congregational images that shaped the type of action they undertook. While the study was limited to Christian congregations, the findings seem relevant across the faith spectrum. Here, briefly, are the five types of congregations and the kinds of activities they are most likely to do in the community:

1. *Pillar congregations* are like the stable pillars of a community that take responsibility for strengthening the whole community. They can mobilize significant resources to meet needs, and they are most likely to support ongoing programs and initiatives.

2. Often founded by immigrants, *pilgrim congregations* emphasize relationships, and congregational life binds them to one another and to their cultural heritage. While members don't think of themselves as activists, they are often very involved in services of compassion aimed at long-term improvement in people's lives—the kind of hope that drew them to emigrate.

3. *Survivor congregations* are ones that always seem to struggle, but they have surprising energy to address the problems they face, often in declining neighborhoods. The struggle creates a sense of unity that gives them strength to rally around crises in the community. Furthermore, their experiences have taught them never to give up.

4. *Prophet congregations* are the ones most ready to risk for their sense of calling and justice. These congregations tend to be proactive and impatient, and ready to make partnerships and coalitions with other congregations and agencies committed to the same cause.

5. Finally, *servant congregations* respond primarily to individual needs. They are less inclined to get on board with the latest issue; rather, they offer steady, consistent service to address the needs around them.[8]

Of course, no congregation fits any one of these pure types perfectly; most blend elements of several. However, the images are helpful reminders that community action can take many forms and still be consistent with a congregation's identity and purpose. The descriptions also underscore the value of involving many congregations in a shared vision for asset building so that the strengths of each can complement the others and contribute to the well-being of young people in the community.

Start by nurturing relationships

Whenever you begin working with new people and organizations, it's important to establish a foundation of trust and respect. People need to know and value each other. Each time you meet, take time to build relationships, listen to each other's stories, and see each other's worlds. And as you're designing your first joint efforts, emphasize opportunities that will help form and solidify relationships and trust.

Focus on common ground

Every congregation and faith tradition has its own theological emphases and beliefs—often, they conflict with other congregations even within their own denomination. Furthermore, congregations have specific faith commitments and goals that are quite different from the commitments and goals of secular organizations.

This diversity can make the idea of cross-faith and community partnerships seem daunting. And, indeed, any attempt to resolve these differences as a prerequisite to taking joint action will end in failure. Instead, forming partnerships in the community requires setting aside differences and focusing on shared commitments and goals. As Dudley and Johnson write: "The key to unity that transcends differences lies in finding common ground. Although churches are inclined to work alone, they overcome their barriers and achieve cooperative strategies when they realize how much they need one another to reach a common goal. The prize must be worth the effort."[9]

In our experience, the framework of developmental assets provides a starting place around which all faith traditions can gather for joint learning, dialogue, and action. Because they share a commitment to youth, congregations from many perspectives can enter a dialogue about the assets and how to build them together. Still, some asset-building strategies may not be shared across all traditions. For example, some congregations may see political action as an essential part of asset building, while others argue that political lobbying is inappropriate for congregations. A genuine dialogue should produce several acceptable and worthwhile alternative strategies.

In forming partnerships, it's important to distinguish clearly between shared community action for youth and proselytizing. As we have begun working with interfaith youth-worker networks, many youth workers have been reluctant to participate for fear that other congregations will try to "steal" their youth.

While seeking converts is important in many faith traditions, using community partnerships as a vehicle for proselytizing undermines the trust that is essential for a partnership. Congregations that emphasize seeking converts as part of their mission should be up-front in their intentions regarding proselytizing, making it clear that the partnership is part of their service to the community and that they will not use it as a vehicle for converting others.

Involve recipients in decision making

To have a true partnership, all stakeholders must be involved in planning and decision making. Thus, for example, if the partnership focuses on providing activities for community youth, then young people from the community need to be involved. Or if a project focuses on addressing issues in a particular neighborhood, it may be appropriate to include an already existing neighborhood organization.

Involve people from your congregation

Too often, partnerships in the community are designed primarily to involve one or two people from the congregation in an activity or planning group. While this involvement may be important, the potential benefit and impact will be much greater if many people from the congregation are involved, either directly or indirectly.

A study of church-community partnerships by Rainbow Research found that partnerships with congregations are most effective when they involve people from multiple levels within the congregation, from staff to congregation members.[10] This involvement not only builds support for and commitment to the effort, it can provide an enriching experience for congregation members—not to mention the added benefit of their service.

People to include are children and youth, parents, other members, and congregational leadership. Some ways to involve them include:

- Bringing them in on the planning;

- Keeping them informed about what you're doing;

- Providing them with opportunities to become active in the partnership;

- Using their talents and connections to enhance the partnership; and

- Involving them in celebrations of progress and achievements.

When **First Presbyterian Church of Crafton Heights in Pittsburgh, Pennsylvania,** decided to rehabilitate and convert an old movie theater into a community recreation center, a central goal was to have kids involved in the whole process, says former youth worker Dave Carver. Kids sponsored fund-raisers and went along when Carver sought grant money. Then they helped with renovation by hauling cement and busting down old walls. Altogether they spent 18 months on the project.

"The kids most appreciated the fact that they could make a positive contribution," Carver remembers. "The church gave those kids the chance to do something right."

Commit to the community

One of the challenges congregations face in reaching out to the community is a perception that congregations aren't really committed to their own neighborhood, particularly in inner-city areas. Many residents remember the congregations that moved to the suburbs with the "white flight" of the 1960s, and others see congregations that attract members from all over the metro area but are not welcoming to people who live in the immediate community.

A key, then, to being seen and trusted as a partner is for congregations to show that they are truly committed to the neighborhood. **Bethel Temple in Philadelphia, Pennsylvania,** is a congregation that formed out of a split when the original congregation decided to move to a new location in the suburbs. As a result, Bethel has a strong commitment to its neighborhood. "We have become very committed to the community, to persons, and to permanency," says Senior Pastor Luis Centeno. "That is the heart of our commitment to people who are hurting in the community."

That commitment has led to a wide variety of ministries in the community, including formation of an organization called Reclaimers of Hope Ministries, an alcohol and other drug ministry to families. "To earn the right to be heard, we need to move within the felt needs of the community," Centeno says.

Keep it simple

In Search Institute's survey of youth workers, we asked about the major barriers to doing interfaith work in a community. The top responses were not "theological differences" or "congregational opposition." The top responses were "lack of time" (44 percent) and "scheduling conflicts" (31 percent).[11]

These findings are a reminder to keep partnerships in the community simple, particularly at first when people haven't yet become fully invested in the relationships and mission that are part of the partnership. Thus, for example, you may want to begin by planning some joint projects that don't involve a major, long-term commitment.

Build partnerships into job descriptions

Unless they are seen as integral to your responsibilities, partnerships are rarely a priority. Thus, it is important to include community outreach in job descriptions as integral to one or more youth work positions (either professionals or volunteers).

Don't neglect change within the congregation

A clergyperson once mused that it might actually be easier to do asset building in the community than within the congregation. A community-wide focus does not challenge the congregation to look in the mirror and transform its own systems and activities. Furthermore, the congregation isn't held accountable for what does or does not happen.

Whether or not this perception is truly accurate, it raises an important caution about continuing to hold in creative tension the focus on within-congregation change and on community change. Perhaps a commitment to keep, then, is: We will not advocate any changes in the community that we are not also willing to incorporate into our own congregational life.

Give it time to develop

Like any relationship, a partnership in the community takes time to form and solidify. This is particularly true in congregations, which depend largely on volunteers to get things done. The Rainbow Research study found that one of the most frequent complaints among the secular organizations involved in partnerships was that religious organizations tend to move slowly.[12] Thus, it's important to have reasonable expectations and to be clear with all partners about realistic timelines. Beginning simply, focusing on nurturing relationships, and giving time for the partnership to mature and evolve are all components of maintaining a long-term, effective presence in the community.

TIP SHEET 40

Preparing Youth and Other Members for Community Involvement

While it's important to involve congregation youth and other members in community partnerships, it's also important to equip them for their involvement. Otherwise, you risk involving them in a negative experience (for them or the community) from which it can be difficult to recover. Here are some key components in preparing members for community involvement.

- **Provide information**—Let people know as much as possible about the situation they will be entering. This information can challenge stereotypes and answer questions they may have about what it will be like. If the experience is cross-cultural, this information may include background information on the cultures involved, as well as information on the specific project at hand. One effective way to share information is to invite someone from the community to talk with your congregation about the community.

- **Build relationships**—One way to help people be more comfortable getting involved in the community is for them to do it with people they know from the congregation. Providing opportunities for them to get to know each other better before going into the community provides a level of comfort that can make their involvement more positive. (Furthermore, their involvement together can serve to solidify the relationships.)

- **Build skills**—People may not feel ready to get involved because they don't feel they have the skills they need to be effective. These skills may include the specific skills of the partnership (e.g., how to be a good tutor), or they may be more general relational skills (e.g., how to form a relationship across cultures). Training in these kinds of skills may include discussions of case studies, role plays, and simulations.

- **Reflect and debrief**—Just as important as the preparation is the opportunity to debrief and reflect on the experience. This reflecting provides an opportunity to celebrate and tell stories. But it also can allow the surfacing of issues or concerns that need to be explored and interpreted. Otherwise, people may leave an experience with unresolved problems or concerns that inhibit their interest in getting involved in the future.

Support Through the Tough Times

Providing support and care for the young people in the community is a major commitment of **Bethel Temple in Philadelphia, Pennsylvania.** Several times, a congregation member or staff person has "become the temporary foster parent" for a young person whose parents are incarcerated or in treatment for alcohol or other drug addictions, according to Pastor Luis Centeno.

In addition, the congregation becomes an advocate and supporter for the family so that it can put its life back together again. Centeno tells the story of a drug dealer who had a contract on his life and whose children were taken away by the state. The church became a support network for this man, helping him change his life course and rebuild his family. Today he is an active deacon in the church.

Ideas for Asset-Building Efforts in Your Community

There are dozens of specific ways congregations can build assets for youth in the community, either through congregation-sponsored efforts, joint initiatives with other congregations or organizations, or support for and involvement in existing community programs and activities. Some may be extensions of current programs for congregational youth.

Here is a sampling of possibilities for congregations to consider, arranged by the eight categories of assets. (Of course, a particular program or activity may— indeed, should—build several types of assets!) Some ideas are relatively simple; others require a great deal of work or resources. Pick those ideas that work best in your community and congregation and that respond to the interests, capacities, and needs within the community.

General asset building

Here are ways congregations can work with others in the community to raise awareness of and commitment to asset building.

- Join with other congregations or organizations to sponsor a survey of developmental assets among youth in the community.[13]

- Work with community youth to develop a drama or music presentation on their experiences of assets in the community or to introduce key asset-building ideas to various audiences in the community. Then have the group perform in congregations, schools, and other places.

- Sponsor billboards or other public service announcements related to asset building.

- Join with (or start) a community-wide partnership for asset building. Tipsheet 41 gives suggestions for starting a community initiative.[14] (To see if your community has an existing multisector initiative, check the listing on Search Institute's Web site at www.search-institute.org.)

- Offer workshops for parents, educators, and others that introduce them to how they can be asset builders for youth.

Support

Congregations can do many different things to let community youth experience care and support. Here are some possibilities.

- Get congregation members involved in (or cosponsor) a community mentoring program.
- Offer counseling services or peer support groups for community youth.
- Offer workshops on positive family communication and relationships.
- Integrate relationship building into all service and outreach efforts in the community.

Empowerment

Ideas for making community youth feel valued and safe and giving them opportunities to contribute include the following.

- Offer leadership development opportunities to young people in the community.
- Invite youth from the community to participate in congregation-sponsored service projects.
- Challenge messages in the media that stereotype youth or portray them as problems, and affirm stories that reflect an asset-building perspective on youth. Send letters to the editor, meet with editorial boards, and take other appropriate action.
- Become an advocate and partner in community efforts to improve safety for children and youth.
- Involve community youth in planning all activities and programs designed for them.

Boundaries and expectations

Setting boundaries and expectations for youth in the community is an important, difficult task. Some ways congregations can contribute include the following.

- Equip congregation members to clarify boundaries for youth in their neighborhoods.
- Get involved in a community's efforts to limit young people's access to alcohol, tobacco, and other drugs.
- Establish and enforce clear ground rules for activities for community youth.
- Work with community youth to develop a statement of expectations for all youth in the community. Then sponsor conversations among youth and others about these expectations.

Constructive use of time

Congregations already offer many constructive opportunities for youth. Here are possibilities for extending your impact in the community.

- Sponsor sports and recreation activities or music, drama, or other arts programs for community youth, or invite them to participate in existing congregational programs.

- Sponsor or cosponsor after-school activities for community youth (e.g., recreation, study space, tutoring, computer training).

- Advocate for public support for youth programs in schools, parks, community centers, and other places.

- Cosponsor with other organizations and congregations a hotline that youth can call to learn about available positive programs and activities.

- Cosponsor a youth drop-in center with other congregations and organizations. If your congregation has a large facility, make it available for this purpose.

- Coordinate with other youth-serving programs in the community to ensure a variety of activities for youth with different interests and to reduce scheduling conflicts.

TIP SHEET 41

Eight Principles for Starting a Community-Wide Initiative for Asset Building

One of the exciting, though challenging, aspects of launching a community-wide asset-building initiative is that each community goes about it in a slightly different way. Keeping the following principles in mind will help guide your efforts.

1. **Engage people from throughout the community.** Because the asset-building vision calls for community-wide responsibility for youth, involving many different stakeholders is important from the outset. Many communities have developed a "vision team" with representatives from all sectors (e.g., schools, government, law enforcement, congregations, service agencies, business, health care) along with young people, parents, and other citizens, including senior citizens and people from various racial/ethnic and socioeconomic groups.

2. **Start with a positive vision.** A positive vision can energize a community for the long term. It can also help groups lay aside political and ideological agendas to work together because of their shared commitment to the well-being of children and adolescents.

3. **Build on quality information.** Many communities find that surveys of young people can be an important catalyst for creative and sustained action. Quality information gives people a shared reference point for reflecting on the needs, realities, and resources in the community as they shape their vision for the future.

4. **Resist the temptation to create new programs.** Because most responses to youth issues in recent decades have been programmatic, intentional effort will be needed to avoid simply developing another program to respond to a specific need. The most important tasks for the "vision bearers" of asset building are to keep the vision of a healthy community alive and prompt individuals and institutions to discover ways that they can integrate asset building into their own mission and commitments.

5. **Take time to motivate and educate.** Because asset building represents a new way of thinking about communities and youth, it is important not to assume that everyone automatically understands the framework and its implications. Unless people internalize the many dimensions of the asset framework, asset building risks becoming a shallow campaign to "be nice to kids."

6. **Celebrate commitments and successes.** Asset building is a long-term vision, not a quick fix. But as communities embark on this journey, it is important to notice, celebrate, and talk about the landmarks along the way. These stories renew energy and refocus commitment.

7. **Embrace innovations from the community.** Once people are aligned with the vision of asset building, their creativity in finding ways to nurture assets can be startling. Encouraging this innovation is key to breaking out of old patterns and discovering fresh approaches.

8. **Network with other communities.** While many communities have begun asset-building initiatives, the vision is only in its infancy. No one knows all the answers, and no one knows how everything will work. But each community is learning something new each day.

Adapted from Peter L. Benson and Eugene C. Roehlkepartain, *Healthy Communities • Healthy Youth* (Minneapolis: Search Institute, 1996).

Commitment to learning

At first glance, you may assume that a commitment to learning among young people is the responsibility of schools and families. But congregations can also play an important role.

- Sponsor or cosponsor afternoon tutoring or study places for community youth.

- Set up a homework hotline. Ask (and train) older youth and adults to volunteer to answer calls about various subjects. (A retired teacher in the congregation might be interested in coordinating the program.)

- Donate books for youth to community and/or school libraries, or set up a church library and train youth to staff it.

- Advocate for high-quality, safe, caring schools.

Positive values

Congregations have a long history of and comfort with talking about values. With appropriate care, this tradition can be a great resource to a community. Here are ways congregations help advance a focus on the positive values assets.

- Join with other organizations to identify and promote shared community values.

- Honor young people in the community who model positive values. Consider, for example, sponsoring a scholarship or award for youth who exhibit a strong commitment to serving others.

- Highlight positive values in activities sponsored for community youth.

Social competencies

Many of the other activities listed in this section help build social competencies in community youth. Here are other specific ideas.

- Include skills building in after-school activities that your congregation offers or cosponsors for community youth.

- Get involved in community efforts to encourage nonviolence and peaceful conflict resolution. This may include, for example, convening stakeholders (and competing factions in the community) to resolve differences.

- Have youth develop drama, music, or other presentations for teaching social skills to children and youth in the community. Perform them in parks, malls, community centers, and other settings.

- Offer sessions for youth in the community that address skills-building topics.

Positive identity

Helping community youth nurture a positive identity can be done in the following ways.

- Sponsor or cosponsor programs or activities that help young people affirm and connect with their own cultural heritage.

- Work with community youth to paint a mural (or murals) that depict their sense of identity and the kind of community and world they hope for.

- Invite role models from the community who have overcome the odds to talk to groups of community youth about how a sense of purpose and meaning has helped to shape their lives.

- Convene a group of boys and a group of girls to talk about what it means to be male and female today.

Integrating Asset Building into Service and Missions Beyond the Community

This chapter has focused on how asset building can shape outreach into your own community. Yet many of the same principles can apply to many areas of the congregation's outreach beyond the immediate community to the nation and world.

What would it be like, for example, if in the midst of planning every work camp or mission trip from your congregation, you asked the question, "What can we do to make this trip an asset-building experience not just for our kids, but for the community we visit?"

Or what if your congregation identified places to support financially on the basis of whether their efforts intentionally include asset building (even if they don't call it that)? Thus, for example, a building project that focused on forming relationships and equipping families to succeed in their new homes might have a higher priority than a project that simply builds homes without the other components.

Certainly, asset building isn't everything, and it's not the only commitment a congregation has in reaching out to others. Yet, it can offer a new way of thinking about, evaluating, and setting congregational priorities. It can provide an intentional focus on building the relationships and opportunities needed by youth in the congregation and community, across the nation, and around the world.

Reaching into the Community for Asset Building

Key Points

- Asset building can help congregations fulfill their mission of service and involvement in the broader community. This outreach can also help strengthen and energize the congregation.

- Congregations can approach community action in many different ways, ranging from simply encouraging individual commitment among members to sponsoring or cosponsoring activities for community youth and being active in community-wide partnerships.

- Building connections in the community depends on building trusting relationships. It also requires finding common ground for joint action.

- Congregations can build all types of assets through activities, partnerships, and strategies in their community.

Questions for Reflection and Discussion

- In what ways is your congregation already working in the community to benefit children and youth? How might asset building be infused into those efforts?

- How would you characterize your congregation on the basis of the five images of congregations outlined in pages on page 151? How does this focus help to shape the asset-building actions you take in your community?

- What relationships or connections do you and your congregation have in the community that might lend themselves to asset-building partnerships?

- If your congregation is viewed as a strong leader in the community, what might you do to initiate broader asset-building action across the community?

Suggestions for Getting Started

- Develop a list of the various activities your congregation is already involved in to help young people in the community, nation, and world. Brainstorm ways to integrate assets into these activities.

- Work with people in your congregation who are responsible for your congregation's service, leadership, or justice efforts in the community.

- Talk with others in your community (civic leaders, educators, youth organization leaders, and other residents) about their needs and interests related to youth in the community. Identify ways your congregation could help to meet those needs through asset building.

- Talk with other leaders and activists in the community about whether to launch an asset-building partnership either among congregations or across multiple sectors in the community.

Moving Forward ... One Step at a Time

ot long ago, I was sitting in a meeting of my congregation's youth committee, discussing the upcoming program year. The issues were the same kinds of issues youth program planners face every year: finding adult sponsors; scheduling events; coordinating with other areas of the congregation.

For a while, I was frustrated. Why weren't we talking about asset building!? After all, the congregation had officially said it's an important emphasis. Everyone in the room had been enthusiastic about it. So why were we still dealing with the same old things? Had all our work in planning for asset building made no difference at all when it came to what really happens in the congregation?

As I listened and reflected, though, I realized I was overlooking how much had already begun to change, after only a couple of years. First, the group itself had been formed partly to help the congregation be more intentional in its youth work. We had begun to see that more programming wasn't what we needed. Rather, we needed to be thoughtful about selecting activities, events, and programs in light of a larger vision. And asset building was a central part of that vision.

Then I looked around at the six people who had gathered. Two youth were participating actively in the discussion. Not long ago, there weren't any youth at the table. One of the copastors was there, as was a member of the congregation's session (board). An older adult was part of the group, actively finding ways to connect youth with adults. In short, these leaders were a good mix to really make a difference for youth. And they were already going about the work of asset building.

As it progressed, the discussion highlighted the many ways the congregation was beginning to integrate asset building into its ongoing life. We talked about ways to bring adults and youth together for learning. When identifying possible youth advisors, nominees ran the gamut of congregational members—young and old; men and women. We talked about service activities, building relationships between adults and youth, leadership opportunities, and lots of other things that are core strategies for building assets.

So I left that meeting feeling pretty good about the progress we had made. Sure, I wish we were further along. And sure, there are some important themes in asset building that weren't reflected in that meeting. We focused most of our time on the youth program, dedicating less energy to the broader vision of the congregation, of families, of youth in the community. We tended to fall back on old patterns, even if they didn't always serve us well.

But that's reality. Change takes time. And rarely does it look like the neatly organized and edited chapters of a book. Change comes as committed individuals and groups find creative ways to take a step forward in their particular time and place.

Building Assets in Congregations has offered a vision and practical tools for using developmental assets as a vision and tool for congregational transformation. When you put it all together, it's a lofty—sometimes overwhelming—challenge.

Yet, like asset building itself, the task of transformation happens one little step at a time. It begins when one person does something a little bit differently. And it grows as those initial efforts become lasting commitments shared by more and more people.

As you explore the potential of asset building in your congregation, try not to get discouraged by what you don't or can't do. Rather, try to focus on what you've done and can do. Sure, you may need to tackle some of the tougher issues at some point. But for now, it's probably most important to take a step, begin the journey, make a difference where you can in the ways you can.

Perhaps your commitments and actions will seem inconsequential at the time. But as you continue that journey and as others join with you, your congregation can become a powerful resource for youth in your congregation, your families, your community, and ultimately, the nation.

notes

Introduction

1. Carnegie Council on Adolescent Development, *A Matter of Time: Risk and Opportunity in the Nonschool Hours* (New York: Carnegie Corporation of New York, 1992), 52.

2. Peter L. Benson and Dorothy L. Williams, *Effective Christian Education: A National Study of Protestant Congregations—A Summary Report on Faith, Loyalty, and Congregational Life* (Minneapolis: Search Institute, 1990), 50. See also Eugene C. Roehlkepartain, *The Teaching Church: Moving Christian Education to Center Stage* (Nashville: Abingdon Press, 1993).

3. Jonathan Woocher, preface to *Jewish Youth Databook: Research on Adolescence and Its Implications for Jewish Teen Programs*, by Amy L. Sales (San Francisco: Maurice and Marilyn Cohen Center for Modern Jewish Studies, Institute for Community and Religion, Brandeis University, 1996), i.

4. Commission on Jewish Education in North America, *A Time to Act* (Lanham, MD: University Press of America, 1990), 25.

5. This book focuses primarily on congregations within the Judeo-Christian traditions (Jewish, Catholic, Protestant, and Evangelical), though I also seek to address the Muslim context in several places. These traditions tend to have a similar congregational polity and styles of congregational life. (For example, weekly worship services and youth groups are common features in these traditions.) This focus allows for more practical application.

   Furthermore, congregations in the Judeo-Christian tradition represent the vast majority of congregations in the United States. Though all religions of the world are present in the United States (and some are growing in adherents), less than 2 percent of U.S. residents claim a religious affiliation other than Christian or Jewish. (About 7.5 percent profess no religion.) See Jacob Neusner, ed., *World Religions in America: An Introduction* (Louisville, KY: Westminster/John Knox, 1994), 2.

6. Many of the valuable sources of information are not always inclusive, often using "church" or other terms that are specific to their faith tradition. I have maintained the original language in quotations from most such sources.

Chapter 1

1. For more information on how the developmental assets were identified and measured, see Peter L. Benson, *All Kids Are Our Kids* (San Francisco: Jossey-Bass, 1997).

2. See, for example, Emmy Werner and Ruth S. Smith, *Overcoming the Odds: High-Risk Children from Birth to Adulthood* (Ithaca, NY: Cornell University Press, 1992).

3. National Commission on the Role of the School and the Community in Improving Adolescent Health, *Code Blue: Uniting for Healthier Youth* (Chicago: American Medical Association, and Alexandria, VA: National Association of State Boards of Education), 3.

4. Benson, *All Kids*, 11.

5. Mark DeVries, *Family-Based Youth Ministry* (Downers Grove, IL: InterVarsity Press, 1994), 21.

6. Ibid, 116.

7. Steve Farkas and Jean Johnson, with Ann Duffett and Ali Bers, *Kids These Days: What Americans Really Think About the Next Generation* (New York: Public Agenda, 1997), 8.

8. Howard N. Snyder, Melissa Sickmond, and Eileen Poe-Yamagata, *Juvenile Offenders and Victims: 1996 Update on Violence—Statistics Summary* (Washington, DC: U.S. Department of Justice, 1996), 13-14.

9. *An Operations Guide to Project Spirit* (Washington, DC: Congress of National Black Churches, 1989).

10. Robert Michael Franklin, "The Safest Place on Earth: The Culture of Black Congregations," in *American Congregations—Volume 2: New Perspectives in the Study of Congregations*, ed. James P. Wind and James W. Lewis (Chicago: University of Chicago Press, 1994), 257-58.

11. "Renewing the Vision: A Framework for Catholic Youth Ministry," *Origins: CNS Documentary Service* 27, no. 9 (July 31, 1997): 136, 138.

12. Kenda Dean, *A Synthesis of the Research on and a Descriptive Overview of Protestant, Catholic, and Jewish Religious Youth Programs in the United States* (Washington, DC: Carnegie Council on Adolescent Development, 1991), 114.

13. Peter L. Benson, "Spirituality and the Adolescent Journey," *Reclaiming Children and Youth* 5, no. 4 (Winter 1997): 206-9.

14. Peter C. Scales et al., *The Attitudes and Needs of Religious Youth Workers: Perspectives from the Field* (Minneapolis: Search Institute, 1995), 15, 17.

15. Based on the typology of congregation size outlined in Roy M. Oswald and Speed B. Leas, *The Inviting Church: A Study of New Member Assimilation* (Bethesda, MD: Alban Institute, 1987), 31-36. The original typology uses the term "Pastoral Church." I've substituted "Clergy-Centered Congregation" as a more inclusive descriptor. See also UAHC Task Force on the Unaffiliated, *The Life-Cycle of Synagogue Membership: A Guide to Recruitment, Integration, and Retention* (New York: Union of American Hebrew Congregations, 1991), xi-xii.

16. Stephen R. Covey, *The Seven Habits of Highly Effective People* (New York: Fireside, 1990), 31.

Chapter 2

1. National Commission on Children, *Speaking of Kids: A National Survey of Children and Parents* (Washington, DC: National Commission on Children, 1991).

2. Scales et al., *Attitudes and Needs*, 17.

3. Robert Bly, *The Sibling Society* (Reading, MA: Addison Wesley, 1996).

4. David Elkind, "Facilitating Spiritual Growth Among At-Risk Youth," in *The Ongoing Journey: Awakening Spiritual Life in At-Risk Youth* (Boys Town, NE: Boys Town Press, 1995), 72.

5. M. W. McLaughlin and M. I. Irby, *Urban Sanctuaries: Neighborhood Organizations in the Lives and Futures of Inner-City Youth* (San Francisco: Jossey-Bass, 1994).

6. Search Institute, *Five Fundamental Resources for Children and Youth* (Alexandria, VA: America's Promise: The Alliance for Youth, 1997).

7. National Commission on Children, *Speaking of Kids.*

8. From Eugene C. Roehlkepartain, *Youth Ministry in City Churches* (Loveland, CO: Group, 1987), 223.

9. Reed W. Larson, "The Emergence of Solitude as a Constructive Domain of Experience in Early Adolescence," *Child Development* 68, no. 1 (February 1997): 80-93.

10. Carnegie Council on Adolescent Development, *A Matter of Time*, 77.

11. "Religious Leaders Pledge to Support the America Reads Challenge," *U.S. Department of Education Community Update* (June 1997). For information on the America Reads Challenge, call 1-800-USA-LEARN.

12. Tom Dowd, *Teaching Social Skills to Youth* (Boys Town, NE: Boys Town Press, 1995), 4-5.

13. Ibid., 5.

14. Marianne Neifert, "A Strong Sense of Self," *Parenting* (October 1991): 98-109.

15. See Susan Harter, "Self and Identity Development," in *At the Threshold: The Developing Adolescent*, ed. Shirley S. Feldman and Glen R. Elliott (Cambridge, MA: Harvard University Press, 1990), 353-87. See also Alfie Kohn, "The Truth About Self-Esteem," *Phi Delta Kappan* (December 1994): 272-83.

16. Nancy Leffert et al., *Making the Case: Measuring the Impact of Youth Development Programs* (Minneapolis: Search Institute, 1996), 19.

17. Nancy Leffert, Peter L. Benson, and Jolene L. Roehlkepartain, *Starting Out Right: Developmental Assets for Children* (Minneapolis: Search Institute, 1997).

18. Roland D. Martinson, *Effective Youth Ministry: A Congregational Approach* (Minneapolis: Augsburg Publishing House, 1988), 11-12.

19. Carnegie Council on Adolescent Development, *A Matter of Time*, 21.

Chapter 3

1. Thanks to Roland Martinson, professor at Luther Seminary, St. Paul, Minnesota, whose insights helped to identify these roles.

2. Thom Schulz, "An Open Letter to Your Senior Pastor," *Group* (July/August 1997): 13.

3. J. Immerwaher, *Talking About Children: A Focus Group Report from Public Agenda* (Washington, DC: Public Agenda, 1995), 1.

4. Search Institute has a variety of tools to use in the awareness-raising process, including an introductory video on asset building. See the resource listing in Appendix B.

5. An additional resource is a set of newsletter masters, available from Search Institute, designed to be distributed to parents. These include practical tips on building the 40 assets. For information on the *Ideas for Parents Master Set*, call 800-888-7828.

6. Another option is *Sharing the Asset Message*, a Search Institute kit with a script, reproducible handouts, and color transparencies for presenting the basic message on developmental assets. This could be adapted for use in your congregation.

Chapter 4

1. William R. Myers, *Black and White Styles of Youth Ministry: Two Congregations in America* (New York: Pilgrim Press, 1991), 137.

2. Charles R. Foster, introduction to Myers, *Black and White Styles,* xxii.

3. DeVries, *Family-Based Youth Ministry*, 43.

4. Roehlkepartain, *The Teaching Church*, 59.

5. Quoted in Roehlkepartain, *Youth Ministry in City Churches*, 107.

6. Another subtle message that sometimes occurs in newsletters: Activities for adults are labeled as "congregation-wide activities," or a similar name. Youth activities are put somewhere else in the newsletter in a little box, inadvertently reinforcing the message that youth are separate from the rest of the congregation.

7. Adapted from Roehlkepartain, *Youth Ministry in City Churches*, 107-11.

8. Myers, *Black and White Styles*, 157.

9. James W. White, *Intergenerational Religious Education* (Birmingham, AL: Religious Education Press, 1988), 251.

10. This idea is adapted from a poster created by the LOGOS Program (see note 1, Chapter 5).

11. Mark Cannister, "A Look at Mentoring Communities," *Youthworker* (July/August 1997): 28-33.

12. For more ideas for building intergenerational relationships, see Jolene L. Roehlkepartain, *Creating Intergenerational Community: 75 Ideas for Building Relationships Between Youth and Adults* (Minneapolis: Search Institute, 1996).

13. Richard R. Hammar, Steven W. Klipowicz, and James F. Cobble, Jr., *Reducing the Risk of Child Sexual Abuse in Your Church: A Complete and Practical Guidebook for Prevention and Risk Reduction* (Matthews, NC: Christian Ministry Resources, 1993), 14-15. This resource describes a valuable process for establishing policies and includes numerous worksheets, checklists, and other practical tools.

14. For additional information, contact mentoring organizations or volunteer centers in your community, or contact your state's child protection office (or similar agency). Additional national organizations to contact include:

- **Center for the Prevention of Sexual and Domestic Violence,** 936 North 34th Street, Suite 200, Seattle, WA 98103; phone: 206-634-1903.

- **Interfaith Sexual Trauma Institute (ISTI),** St. Johns Abbey and University, Collegeville, MN 56321; phone: 320-363-3931.

- **National Children's Advocacy Center,** 200 Westside Square, Suite 700, Huntsville, AL 35801; phone: 205-534-6868.

- **National Committee to Prevent Child Abuse,** 332 South Michigan Avenue, Suite 1600, Chicago, IL 60604; phone: 312-663-3520; www.childabuse.org.

15. John P. Kretzmann and Paul H. Schmitz, "It Takes a Child to Raise a Whole Village," *Wingspread Journal* 17, no. 4 (Fall 1995): 8-10.

16. Myers, *Black and White Styles*, 131-32.

17. The National Assembly, *Building Resiliency: What Works!* (Washington, DC: The National Assembly of National Voluntary Health and Social Welfare Organizations, 1994), 38.

18. Martinson, *Effective Youth Ministry*, 93.

19. White, *Intergenerational Religious Education*, 164.

20. Ibid.

21. Kathleen A. Guy, *Welcome the Child: A Child Advocacy Guide for Churches* (Washington, DC: Children's Defense Fund, 1991), 58-60.

22. For information, contact the Children's Sabbath Coordinator, Children's Defense Fund, 25 E Street NW, Washington, DC 20001; 202-662-3652.

Chapter 5

1. The LOGOS System Associates, 1405 Frey Road, Pittsburgh, PA 15235; 412-372-1341.

2. This book does not seek to provide a step-by-step guide for planning a youth program (budgeting, recruiting leadership, publicity, etc). These basic program planning principles are available in many other resources and vary considerably depending on the congregation's faith tradition, size, and other factors. This book focuses on specific areas where asset building influences or shapes the planning process.

3. One interesting note: These same characteristics that contribute to an asset-building climate are also important for nurturing faith in youth. See Roehlkepartain, *The Teaching Church*.

4. For information on peer ministry within Christian congregations, contact the Peer Ministry Association, Augsburg Youth and Family Institute, Augsburg College, Campus Box 70, 2211 Riverside Avenue, Minneapolis, MN 55454; 612-330-1624.

5. One available tool that could be useful in planning these sessions is Jolene L. Roehlkepartain, *Building Assets Together: 135 Group Activities for Helping Youth Succeed* (Minneapolis: Search Institute, 1997).

6. Leffert et al., *Making the Case*.

7. Edward A. Trimmer, *Youth Ministry Handbook* (Nashville: Abingdon Press, 1994), 88-91.

8. See also Peter L. Benson and Eugene C. Roehlkepartain, *Beyond Leaf Raking: Learning to Serve/Serving to Learn* (Nashville: Abingdon Press, 1993).

9. Simon Klarfeld and Amy Sales, *Jewish Youth Source Book: A Planning Guide for Youth Programs* (San Francisco: Cohen Center for Modern Jewish Studies/Institute for Community and Religion, Brandeis University, 1996), 47.

10. From Roehlkepartain, *Youth Ministry in City Churches*, 190-91.

11. The framework of developmental assets is not designed or tested as a diagnostic tool and should not be used in that way. Rather, it can be a helpful conceptual framework for beginning discussions and for educating people about what they can do.

12. Scales et al., *Attitudes and Needs*, 30.

13. Roehlkepartain, *The Teaching Church*.

14. For more information on publications and training with a skills-building approach, contact Religious Education, Boys Town Press, 14100 Crawford Street, Boys Town, NE 68010; 800-282-6657.

15. Quoted in Rick Dunn, "What Are the Necessary Competencies to Be an Effective Youth Worker?" *Christian Education Journal* 16, no. 3 (Spring 1996): 25-38.

16. See Leffert, Benson, and Roehlkepartain, *Starting Out Right*.

Chapter 6

1. Maggie Scarf, *Intimate Worlds: Life Inside the Family* (New York: Random House, 1995), xxxiv-xxxv.

2. Cited in Wallace Charles Smith, *The Church in the Life of the Black Family* (Valley Forge, PA: Judson Press, 1985), 73.

3. MaryLee Allen, Patricia Brown, and Belva Finlay, *Helping Children by Strengthening Families: A Look at Family Support Programs* (Washington, DC: Children's Defense Fund, 1992), 13.

4. Scales et al., *Attitudes and Needs*, 15, 17, 19.

5. Peter L. Benson, Eugene C. Roehlkepartain, and I. Shelby Andress, *Congregations at Crossroads: A National Study of Adults and Youth in The Lutheran Church—Missouri Synod* (Minneapolis: Search Institute, 1995), 22.

6. Roehlkepartain, *The Teaching Church*, 177.

7. Allen, Brown, and Finlay, *Helping Children*, 7-8.

8. Leif Kehrwald, "Early Adolescent Ministry through a Family Lens," in *Access Guides to Youth Ministry: Early Adolescent Ministry*, ed. John Roberto (New Rochelle, NY: Don Bosco, 1991), 124.

9. Ibid., 129.

10. Allen, Brown, and Finlay, *Helping Children*, 8-12.

11. Kehrwald, "Early Adolescent Ministry," 129.

12. Ibid., 130.

13. Joyce L. Epstein, "Advances in Family, Community, and School Partnerships," *New Schools, New Communities* 12, no. 3 (Spring 1996): 5-13.

14. Dub Ambrose and Walt Mueller, *Ministry to Families with Teenagers* (Loveland, CO: Group Publishing, 1988), 100.

15. DeVries, *Family-Based Youth Ministry*, 183.

16. Ibid., 180.

17. An excellent resource for developing a family service focus is James McGinnis and Kathleen McGinnis, *Parenting for Peace and Justice: Ten Years Later* (Maryknoll, NY: Orbis, 1990).

18. Ambrose and Mueller, *Ministry to Families*, 85-94.

19. A great resource for fun family activities is Dale N. LeFevre, *New Games for the Whole Family* (New York: Perigee Books, 1988).

20. For more information on asset building in families, see Dean Feldmeyer and Eugene C. Roehlkepartain, *Parenting with a Purpose: A Positive Approach for Raising Confident, Caring Youth* (Minneapolis: Search Institute, 1995).

21. Richard P. Olson and Joe H. Leonard, Jr., *A New Day for Family Ministry* (Bethesda, MD: Alban Institute, 1996), 65-66.

22. Joan M. Patterson, "Promoting Resilience in Families," *Resiliency in Action* (Spring 1997): 8-16.

23. Olson and Leonard, *A New Day*, 103-42.

24. Carl J. Dunst and Carol M. Trivette, "Enabling and Empowering Families: Conceptual and Intervention Issues," *School Psychology Review* 16, no. 4 (1987): 443-56.

25. See C. Kirk Hadaway, *What Can We Do About Church Dropouts?* (Nashville: Abingdon Press, 1990), 41.

26. A helpful model for training lay members to provide care in Christian congregations is found in Kenneth C. Haugk, *Christian Caregiving—A Way of Life* (Minneapolis: Augsburg Publishing House, 1984).

27. Robert Wuthnow, *Sharing the Journey: Support Groups and America's New Quest for Community* (New York: Free Press, 1994), 170.

28. Ibid., 346.

29. "Why Youth Ministry Should Be Abolished," *Group* (July/August, 1995): 20-23.

Chapter 7

1. John M. Perkins, *Beyond Charity: The Call to Christian Community Development* (Grand Rapids, MI: Baker, 1993), 89.

2. Romney M. Moseley, "Retrieving Intergenerational and Intercultural Faith," in *Working with Black Youth: Opportunities for Christian Ministry*, ed. Charles R. Foster and Grant S. Shockely (Nashville: Abingdon Press, 1989), 88-89.

3. For helpful advocacy tools for children's issues, see Guy, *Welcome the Child*.

4. Carnegie Council on Adolescent Development, *A Matter of Time*, 53.

5. Benson and Roehlkepartain, *Beyond Leaf Raking*, 26.

6. From Roehlkepartain, *Youth Ministry in City Churches*, 28.

7. Carl S. Dudley and Sally A. Johnson, *Energizing the Congregation: Images That Shape Your Church's Ministry* (Louisville, KY: Westminster/John Knox, 1993), 102-3.

8. Ibid., chapters 2-6. The identifiers were changed by this author from "churches" to "congregations" to make the images more inclusive.

9. Ibid., 103.

10. David M. Scheie et al., *Religious Institutions as Partners in Community-Based Development: Findings from Year One of the Lilly Endowment Program* (Minneapolis: Rainbow Research, 1991), 4.

11. Scales et al., *Attitudes and Needs*, 41. Overall, "theological differences" were not ranked as a major barrier; however, they were ranked high among Evangelical youth workers. Forty percent of these youth workers rated "theological/ doctrinal differences" as a major barrier compared to 22 percent of Catholic and 13 percent of mainline Christian. "Lack of time" ranked second among Evangelical youth workers at 38 percent.

12. Scheie et al., *Religious Institutions*, 4.

13. Search Institute's survey, *Profiles of Student Life: Attitudes and Behaviors*, was designed for this purpose. For information, call 800-888-7828.

14. See also: Peter L. Benson, *Uniting Communities for Youth: Mobilizing All Sectors to Create a Positive Future* (Minneapolis: Search Institute, 1995); Peter L. Benson, *All Kids Are Our Kids* (San Francisco: Jossey-Bass, 1997); and *Healthy Communities • Healthy Youth Tool Kit* (Minneapolis: Search Institute, 1998).

Reproducible Bulletin Inserts to Raise Awareness of Asset Building

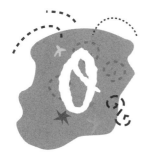

n the pages that follow are ten photocopiable bulletin inserts you can use to raise awareness of the potential of asset building in your congregation. The front and back of a standard-size bulletin insert (5¹/₂ x 8¹/₂ inches) are on facing pages. Some ways to use them include:

- Put one in each week's worship bulletin as you begin your asset-building emphasis to raise awareness of the basic concepts that the congregation is exploring. Photocopy them on bright-colored paper to attract attention.

- If you're hosting adult education or parenting classes on asset building, include the appropriate insert with the bulletin on the week that focuses on the specific topic. (For example, use the support insert on the week the class talks about support.)

- Put one insert in each issue of the congregation's newsletter to members. You could either insert the material or reproduce it on one or two of the newsletter pages.

- Use the bulletin inserts thematically. For example, use the commitment to learning insert (#7) on a back-to-school week, or the support insert (#3) when a service deals with being a caring congregation.

- Photocopy all the inserts and make a small asset-building booklet to distribute to everyone in the congregation. Add a cover and additional information about your congregation's commitment to asset building.

- Make copies of all the inserts and put them in a literature display in a prominent place in the congregation where people can pick them up if they choose. (You will generate less interest this way, but it may be the most consistent with your congregation's style.)

- You may choose to customize the inserts by replacing the second side (which gives ideas) with specific activities and opportunities in your congregation and community.

NOTE: These bulletin inserts may be reproduced for noncommercial, educational use by congregations provided that full credit is given to Search Institute. Additional uses are prohibited.

A Foundation for Success in Life

There is growing interest and concern across the country about our young people. People see too many youth growing up ill-equipped for life and not living up to their potential. They worry about the many young people who make poor choices that lead to violence, drug use, sexual activity, and other problems in adolescence.

What can you do to bring hope in the midst of these difficult problems? What role can our congregation play?

Minneapolis-based Search Institute has developed a framework of 40 developmental assets that offers hope and practical direction for addressing the needs of today's youth. Based on extensive research with youth across the United States, this framework identifies the basic building blocks of life that all young people need to grow up healthy, caring, and responsible. Research has found that these assets are powerful in shaping young people's behavior, yet the average young person surveyed experiences only 18 of the 40 assets.

These assets are things that everyone can build, not just professionals. Whether you're a parent, a grandparent, a neighbor, a volunteer, or a young person, you can make a positive difference for youth by building these assets through your everyday activities.

The framework organizes the 40 assets into eight broad categories, which are listed on the back of this page. People who work with youth in our congregation are exploring how we can focus energy on building these assets in our congregation and community. Everyone can contribute to making our congregation and community a better place for youth.

The Eight Types of Assets: Building Blocks for Life

- **Support**
Young people need to experience support, care, and love from their families and many others. They need organizations and institutions that provide positive, supportive environments.

- **Empowerment**
Young people need to be valued by their community and have opportunities to contribute to others. For this to occur, they must feel safe.

- **Boundaries and expectations**
Young people need to know what is expected of them and what behaviors are "in bounds" and "out of bounds."

- **Constructive use of time**
Young people need constructive, enriching opportunities for growth through creative activities, youth programs, congregational involvement, and quality time at home.

- **Commitment to learning**
Young people need to develop a lifelong commitment to education and learning.

- **Positive values**
Young people need to develop strong values that guide their choices. These include caring, honesty, integrity, justice, and more.

- **Social competencies**
Young people need skills and competencies that equip them to make positive choices, to build relationships, and to succeed in life.

- **Positive identity**
Young people need a strong sense of their own power, purpose, worth, and promise.

What can you do to build these assets in the lives of young people you know? Future inserts will give ideas of what we can do in our homes, congregation, and community.

Search Institute's
40 Developmental Assets

Search Institute has identified the following building blocks of healthy development that help young people grow up healthy, caring, and responsible.

External Assets

Support

1. **Family support**—Family life provides high levels of love and support.

2. **Positive family communication**—Young person and her or his parent(s) communicate positively, and young person is willing to seek advice and counsel from parent(s).

3. **Other adult relationships**—Young person receives support from three or more nonparent adults.

4. **Caring neighborhood**—Young person experiences caring neighbors.

5. **Caring school climate**—School provides a caring, encouraging environment.

6. **Parent involvement in schooling**—Parent(s) are actively involved in helping young person succeed in school.

Empowerment

7. **Community values youth**—Young person perceives that adults in the community value youth.

8. **Youth as resources**—Young people are given useful roles in the community.

9. **Service to others**—Young person serves in the community one hour or more per week.

10. **Safety**—Young person feels safe at home, at school, and in the neighborhood.

Boundaries and Expectations

11. **Family boundaries**—Family has clear rules and consequences and monitors the young person's whereabouts.

12. **School boundaries**—School provides clear rules and consequences.

13. **Neighborhood boundaries**—Neighbors take responsibility for monitoring young people's behavior.

14. **Adult role models**—Parent(s) and other adults model positive, responsible behavior.

15. **Positive peer influence**—Young person's best friends model responsible behavior.

16. **High expectations**—Both parent(s) and teachers encourage the young person to do well.

Constructive Use of Time

17. **Creative activities**—Young person spends three or more hours per week in lessons or practice in music, theater, or other arts.

18. **Youth programs**—Young person spends three or more hours per week in sports, clubs, or organizations at school and/or in the community.

19. **Religious community**—Young person spends one or more hours per week in activities in a religious institution.

20. **Time at home**—Young person is out with friends "with nothing special to do" two or fewer nights per week.

(Continued)

Search Institute's
40 Developmental Assets (continued)

Internal Assets

Commitment to Learning

21. **Achievement motivation**—Young person is motivated to do well in school.

22. **School engagement**—Young person is actively engaged in learning.

23. **Homework**—Young person reports doing at least one hour of homework every school day.

24. **Bonding to school**—Young person cares about her or his school.

25. **Reading for pleasure**—Young person reads for pleasure three or more hours per week.

Positive Values

26. **Caring**—Young person places high value on helping other people.

27. **Equality and social justice**—Young person places high value on promoting equality and reducing hunger and poverty.

28. **Integrity**—Young person acts on convictions and stands up for her or his beliefs.

29. **Honesty**—Young person "tells the truth even when it is not easy."

30. **Responsibility**—Young person accepts and takes personal responsibility.

31. **Restraint**—Young person believes it is important not to be sexually active or to use alcohol or other drugs.

Social Competencies

32. **Planning and decision making**—Young person knows how to plan ahead and make choices.

33. **Interpersonal competence**—Young person has empathy, sensitivity, and friendship skills.

34. **Cultural competence**—Young person has knowledge of and comfort with people of different cultural/racial/ethnic backgrounds.

35. **Resistance skills**—Young person can resist negative peer pressure and dangerous situations.

36. **Peaceful conflict resolution**—Young person seeks to resolve conflict nonviolently.

Positive Identity

37. **Personal power**—Young person feels he or she has control over "things that happen to me."

38. **Self-esteem**—Young person reports having a high self-esteem.

39. **Sense of purpose**—Young person reports that "my life has a purpose."

40. **Positive view of personal future**—Young person is optimistic about her or his personal future.

Champion Supporters for Children and Youth

Who are the champion supporters in your life? These champions are important. They cheer us on when things go well. They stick with us when life throws difficult situations at us. They listen. They question. They smile. They hug. They're people we like to be with.

What kind of a supporter are you to young people in your family, the congregation, and our community? Are you a fair-weather supporter? A stick-with-you supporter? What's your unique way of encouraging and loving the young people in your life?

Search Institute's research on what youth need to grow up successfully has found that a key ingredient is young people having lots of caring people around them—in their families, schools, congregation, neighborhood, and workplaces.

Each of us can provide children and teenagers with care, love, and support. By nurturing and loving the children and youth in our families, congregation, and community, we help our children grow up to be loving, caring people.

The Support Assets

Search Institute has identified the following support assets for youth:

Family support—Family life provides high levels of love and support.

Positive family communication—Young person and her or his parent(s) communicate positively, and young person is willing to seek advice and counsel from parent(s).

Other adult relationships—Young person receives support from three or more nonparent adults.

Caring neighborhood—Young person experiences caring neighbors.

Caring school climate—School provides a caring, encouraging environment.

Parent involvement in schooling—Parent(s) are actively involved in helping young person succeed in school.

What You Can Do to Build Support Assets . . .

. . . In Our Congregation

- Volunteer to help with the children or youth programs. If you're not comfortable being a leader, offer to support a leader. Then use the opportunity to get to know the kids.

- Build an intentional relationship with one or two young people in the congregation. Invite them to do things with you. Send birthday cards. Pray for them. Let them know you care.

- Get to know the names of all the children and youth in our congregation. Invite them to sit with you during worship, social events, or other activities.

. . . In Your Home

- Make having at least one meal together as a family every day a top priority. It's one of the best chances you'll have for connecting, catching up, and showing care.

- Spend focused, one-to-one time with each child every day.

- Make your home a safe haven where young people can—and like to—hang out.

. . . In the Community

- Notice and greet young people you see in your neighborhood or place of employment.

- Volunteer to be a mentor for a young person who may have few sources of positive support. Or volunteer in a school, recreation, or community youth program.

- Advocate for schools, youth organizations, and other youth-serving institutions to be caring places for youth.

The Joy of Making a Difference

"People often talk about what they should do to help others, but never do anything. It makes us feel good to do something."

—Arshia Papa, a high school senior

Teenagers give an estimated total of 2.1 billion hours of volunteer service in one year.

—Independent Sector, 1991

"There is virtually no limit to what young people—with appropriate education, training, and encouragement—can do, no social need they cannot help meet."

—A William T. Grant Foundation report, 1988

Young people are a great resource for our congregation, community, and nation. Recognizing this and empowering them to contribute are keys to nurturing in them a sense that they are valued and valuable and that they can make a positive difference in the world.

The Empowerment Assets

Search Institute has identified the following empowerment assets for youth:

Community values youth—Young person perceives that adults in the community value youth.

Youth as resources—Young people are given useful roles in the community.

Service to others—Young person serves in the community one hour or more per week.

Safety—Young person feels safe at home, at school, and in the neighborhood.

What You Can Do to Build Empowerment Assets . . .

. . . In Our Congregation

- Listen to young people when they talk about their dreams for making a difference—and encourage them to pursue those dreams.

- Support—and get involved in—youth service projects and activities.

- Encourage and affirm young people who take a leadership role in the congregation.

. . . In Your Home

- Do a family service project together. Plan a project as a family, or connect with opportunities that already exist in your community, such as delivering holiday meals or helping with food and clothing drives.

- Give children an opportunity to plan and lead in some family activities.

- Always ensure that your home is a safe place for your children. If you feel overwhelmed with parenting, seek professional help from a counselor or religious leader.

. . . In the Community

- Send letters (or make phone calls) to encourage and affirm youth who contribute to the community in a positive way.

- When planning activities or events, think of ways to include young people as active leaders and participants.

- Speak up when you hear or see young people being put down or devalued by others.

No Limits: Not as Good as It Sounds

Imagine a world without limits or expectations. You could eat whatever you want—whenever you want. You could drive as fast as you want, and you could spend money without any worry about bouncing checks. You could sleep when you want, work when you want, play when you feel like it.

Although a life without limits may sound tempting at times, we know this type of world would be chaotic. No one would know what to expect, no one would seem to care (except about themselves), and we would probably end up paralyzed by the absurdity of it all.

Boundaries give clear message about what's expected. Sleep times. Safety. Mealtimes. Personal care. Homework. Family time. Friendships. Making decisions. Expectations give markers that challenge us to grow and try new things.

Every day young people have many options of how to spend their day. Consistent messages about boundaries and expectations from those around them give them helpful guidelines so that they can grow up healthy.

The Boundaries and Expectations Assets

Search Institute has identified the following boundaries and expectations assets for youth:

Family boundaries—Family has clear rules and consequences and monitors the young person's whereabouts.

School boundaries—School provides clear rules and consequences.

Neighborhood boundaries—Neighbors take responsibility for monitoring young people's behavior.

Adult role models—Parent(s) and other adults model positive, responsible behavior.

Positive peer influence—Young person's best friends model responsible behavior.

High expectations—Both parent(s) and teachers encourage the young person to do well.

What You Can Do to Build Boundaries and Expectations Assets . . .

... In Our Congregation

- Work with youth to establish clear ground rules and expectations for behavior while they are participating in congregational activities.

- If you see young people doing something in the congregation that is inappropriate, ask them to stop. If they persist, be sure parents and youth workers are aware of the situation.

- Be a positive role model for young people by living responsibly and articulating the values that guide your lifestyle.

... In Your Home

- Talk with your children about what you expect of them and come to a shared understanding about appropriate boundaries, rules, and consequences when those boundaries and rules are breached.

- Model responsible behavior for your child. If you do things that are off limits for her or him, be able to give a strong rationale that is not hypocritical.

- Encourage your child to evaluate friends and adult heroes in terms of their positive or negative influence.

... In the Community

- Be a positive role model to young people in your neighborhood or workplace.

- Participate in discussions of community norms or standards (and appropriate ways for enforcing them) for youth regarding use of alcohol, tobacco, and other drugs, staying out late at night, and other behaviors.

- Expect young people in your neighborhood or workplace to treat people and property with respect. Take appropriate action when they do not.

Just Hanging Out ... or Just Hanging On?

The Mall of America in Bloomington, Minnesota, has announced a policy that bans youth under age 16 from spending Friday or Saturday evenings at the world's largest mall unless they are accompanied by an adult. Mall officials say they were forced to implement the policy because thousands of teenagers came to the mall to hang out and, in the process, too many were getting into trouble.

Some young people are so busy doing so many things that they hardly have time to stop for a breath, much less to relax and reflect. Yet many other young people have little or nothing constructive to do with their time. Too often the result is that they get into trouble.

According to Search Institute research, getting involved in constructive activities is vital for healthy growth during adolescence. Yet some youth don't have—or take advantage of—these opportunities, while others get involved in many of them (sometimes too many).

In a time when quality community programs for youth are being cut, congregations have a great opportunity to provide and advocate for providing youth who don't have as many opportunities with the safe, structured, and enriching activities they need.

The Constructive Use of Time Assets

Search Institute has identified the following constructive use of time assets for youth:

Creative activities—Young person spends three or more hours per week in lessons or practice in music, theater, or other arts.

Youth programs—Young person spends three or more hours per week in sports, clubs, or organizations at school and/or in the community.

Religious community—Young person spends one or more hours per week in activities in a religious institution.

Time at home—Young person is out with friends "with nothing special to do" two or fewer nights per week.

What You Can Do to Build Constructive Use of Time Assets . . .

. . . In Our Congregation

- Get involved as a leader or volunteer in our congregation's youth program.

- Share creative talents with young people by offering lessons or working with them in a creative activity (e.g., music, drama, banner making).

- Encourage young people you know to participate in our congregation's youth program. (Help provide transportation if they need it.)

. . . In Your Home

- Encourage your children to get involved in constructive activities that tap their interests, skills, and talents.

- Each week, develop a family schedule that helps keep track of what everyone is doing.

- Set aside two or three nights each week when all family members commit to not scheduling activities outside the home.

. . . In the Community

- Volunteer as a coach or other volunteer in a community youth program or a youth organization (e.g., YMCA, YWCA, scouts).

- Advocate for support for programs in schools and the community that offer constructive activities for youth.

- Offer music lessons to young people in your neighborhood. Or periodically invite neighborhood youth to your home for games, crafts, or other activities.

What Messages Do We Give About Education?

Most people agree that education is a good thing. On the average, the more education you have, the more likely you are to be successful in adulthood. Just about everyone says young people should stick with school and not drop out.

But our attitudes may send a different message. Often we inadvertently send signals that education is a necessary evil, not a rewarding opportunity. Ask yourself these questions:

- If you meet a young person who really enjoys school, do you assume he or she is a nerd or a geek?

- Do you say things like: "So how's school? . . . I bet you'll be glad when summer comes and you won't have to go to school"? Or: "So you have homework. What a bummer!"?

Marie Faust Evitt summarized the issue well in a column for Newsweek. She wrote: "We can talk all we want about the importance of an education, but when we act as though school is a holding tank rather than a launching pad, kids pick up the undercurrent. . . . [My son] David, says he can't wait for the first grade to be over. He's learned the cool response from Mark [his older brother]. But I know he's looking forward to learning 'hard math' and reading long books in second grade. Please encourage him" (June 14, 1993).

The Commitment to Learning Assets

Search Institute has identified the following commitment to learning assets for youth:

Achievement motivation—Young person is motivated to do well in school.

School enagement—Young person is actively engaged in learning

Homework—Young person reports doing at least one hour of homework every school day.

Bonding to school—Young person cares about her or his school.

Reading for pleasure—Young person reads for pleasure three or more hours per week.

What You Can Do to Build Commitment to Learning Assets . . .

. . . In Our Congregation

- Offer to help a young person as a tutor in a particular subject area in school.

- Participate in learning activities within your congregation. Model an attitude that education never ends even if schooling does.

- Be a "learning mentor" to a young person. Take time to talk about new things you are learning, and ask her or him to tell you about what he or she is learning.

. . . In Your Home

- Set aside daily study and/or reading time for everyone in the family. Turn off the television and don't answer the phone during this time.

- Help your child plan and prepare for continuing education after high school.

- Get—and stay—involved in your child's schooling.

- Model a lifelong interest in learning and education by taking courses at a local community education center, reading for pleasure, or learning a new skill.

. . . In the Community

- Maintain a positive attitude about education. Don't reinforce negative attitudes about the value of education by saying things such as, "Won't you be glad when school's out?"

- Advocate for quality educational opportunities for all children and youth.

- If you employ teenagers who are in school, limit the number of hours they can work during the school year. Most researchers agree that working more than 15 hours a week undermines success in school.

Something to Talk About

Talking about values isn't very comfortable for many of us. We'd often rather avoid the topic altogether. But silence about values denies young people powerful assets to shape their behaviors, lives, and futures.

On television or the Internet, at the mall and on the street corner, today's young people face choices and challenges that most adults can't even fathom. Even young people who seek out adults' advice mostly have to depend on their own character, skills, life experiences, and commitments to help them know what to do.

Many things influence how young people make choices. One of the core influences is their set of values. Search Institute has identified six values assets that help shape young people's behaviors in positive ways. Nurturing these and other positive values won't magically solve all the problems youth experience. But it can remind youth what society and their faith expect from them. And it can keep adults honest in "walking our talk" as models and mentors.

The Positive Values Assets

Search Institute has identified the following positive values assets for youth:

Caring—Young person places high value on helping other people.

Equality and social justice—Young person places high value on promoting equality and reducing hunger and poverty.

Integrity—Young person acts on convictions and stands up for her or his beliefs.

Honesty—Young person "tells the truth even when it is not easy."

Responsibility—Young person accepts and takes personal responsibility.

Restraint—Young person believes it is important not to be sexually active or to use alcohol or other drugs.

What You Can Do to Build Positive Values Assets . . .

. . . In Our Congregation

- Talk with others (youth and adults) about the values you hold—and why.

- Participate in activities with youth (e.g., service projects, advocacy) and talk about the values that undergird your commitment to those activities or causes.

- Listen to and guide young people as they talk about and sort through their own values.

. . . In Your Home

- Include children in discussions of family priorities that reflect values (such as recycling, how to spend money and time).

- Talk with children about the values you see portrayed on television, in movies, and in other media.

- Live the values you want to pass on to your children. For example, do service projects together as a family. Talk about why you do it.

. . . In the Community

- Live out the positive values you hold and articulate why you do what you do when talking with children and youth.

- Participate in discussions with others in your neighborhood and community about shared values and priorities.

- Support policies and activities that undergird positive values for youth.

Everyday Skills for Living

Try this child's game: With one hand, pat your stomach. With the other, rub your head. When you get that figured out, try also to whistle. Now, stop before anyone sees you!

It's relatively easy to think about what you need to do to play this game. But it's much harder to actually do it. The muscles just won't do what the mind wants them to do.

Social competencies are sort of like the muscles young people need to make good choices in life. Manuel may want friends, but what if he doesn't have the conversation skills to get to know others? Elizabeth may believe it's important to be peaceful and nonviolent, but what if she doesn't have the coping and analyzing skills to react appropriately in the midst of conflict? Chris may believe it's wrong to use drugs, but what if he doesn't know how to say no to the friend who says, "Everybody's doing it"?

Social competencies like the ones listed below are essential skills young people need for growing up healthy. Without these kinds of skills, they are not adequately equipped for life in a complex and challenging world.

The Social Competencies Assets

Search Institute has identified the following social competencies assets for youth:

Planning and decision making—Young person knows how to plan ahead and make choices.

Interpersonal competence—Young person has empathy, sensitivity, and friendship skills.

Cultural competence—Young person has knowledge of and comfort with people of different cultural/racial/ethni backgrounds.

Resistance skills—Young person can resist negative peer pressure and dangerous situations.

Peaceful conflict resolution—Young person seeks to resolve conflict nonviolently.

What You Can Do to Build Social Competencies Assets . . .

. . . In Our Congregation

- Help youth practice their social skills by regularly interacting with them.

- Support young people when they take leadership roles in the congregation that help them build social competencies.

- If you teach or lead young people in the congregation, teach them skills they can use in applying the values and beliefs of your faith tradition.

. . . In Your Home

- Talk with children about what they can do when they get into various situations where they face tough choices (a rowdy party) or where they feel uncomfortable (going to a new school). Role play the kinds of techniques they could use.

- Involve children in family decisions and planning, showing them the skills you use. Give children opportunities to make decisions on their own.

- Encourage children to build relationships with people from a wide range of races, ages, religions, sizes, shapes, abilities, etc.

. . . In the Community

- Talk to young people you see who you may not know well. In the process, they build their skills in relating to others.

- Get involved in programs and organizations that build social competencies in youth.

- When young people are in conflict situations, don't do all the problem solving for them. Encourage and guide them to develop their own solutions. (Intervention may be appropriate, of course, if there is a danger of physical injury.)

"I Never Had Anybody Tell Me I Was Good"

Ninth grade wasn't a good year for Deon Richardson. He skipped class daily. He scribbled graffiti on walls and school lockers. He fought constantly. By the end of the school year, he'd only earned half of an academic credit.

One of his teachers, Tom Bardal, took an interest in Deon. He often took time to talk with the boy. He noticed that Dean often headed off to shoot hoops with his friends instead of going to class. So Bardal, also the head boys' basketball coach, encouraged Deon to try out for the team. For a long time, Deon refused. But eventually he gave in, tried out, and made the varsity team.

It transformed his life. By his junior year, Richardson had caught up on all his academic credits by going to summer school and attending after-school classes.

"I never had anybody tell me I was good," Deon says. "He was the first coach who told me I could be somebody. He was the first one. And that's why I think I will thank him right now for being there. Otherwise I would still be on that wrong path."

One of the major tasks of the teenage years is figuring out who you are. Without a positive sense of who they are, young people can become powerless victims without a sense of direction, purpose, or hope in life.

The Positive Identity Assets

Search Institute has identified the following positive identity assets for youth:

Personal power—Young person feels he or she has control over "things that happen to me."

Self-esteem—Young person reports having high self-esteem.

Sense of purpose—Young person reports that "my life has a purpose."

Positive view of personal future—Young person is optimistic about her or his personal future.

What You Can Do to Build Positive Identity Assets . . .

. . . In Our Congregation

- Pay attention to young people in the congregation. Notice and celebrate their accomplishments.

- Avoid pessimistic attitudes about the future or about the ability to bring about positive change in the community, nation, and world.

- Get involved in activities that work for a more hopeful future for children and youth.

. . . In Your Home

- Regularly express your love—verbally and nonverbally—to your children.

- Encourage children to pursue their dreams and hopes for their future.

- Give children freedom to make their own choices (as is appropriate for their age), so that they feel they have some control over their own life.

. . . In the Community

- Pay attention to young people you see. Let them know they are an important part of your neighborhood or workplace.

- Challenge media portrayals of youth that show them most often in negative terms.

- Get involved in efforts designed to improve the quality of your community for the future.

Resources for Building Assets in Congregations

Understanding Developmental Assets

he resources in this section give additional background and general ideas about developmental assets and asset building.

All Kids Are Our Kids: What Communities Must Do to Raise Caring and Responsible Children and Adolescents, by Peter L. Benson (Jossey-Bass; available from Search Institute). This foundational book by Search Institute's president outlines the asset vision and how to transform communities for asset building.

The Asset Approach (Search Institute). This eight-page brochure, which is available in bulk quantities, presents basic research and other information about assets and asset building. Ideal for distributing in your congregation or community to build support.

Assets: The Magazine of Ideas for Healthy Communities & Healthy Youth (Search Institute). A quarterly magazine with concrete ideas, real-life stories, and provocative insights about asset building.

The Attitudes and Needs of Religious Youth Workers: Perspectives from the Field, by Peter C. Scales and others (Search Institute). This research report examines the findings of a survey of 500 religious youth workers regarding their experiences, needs, and interest in an asset-building approach in their congregation.

A Foundation for Success: Congregations Building Assets in Youth (Search Institute). This 25-minute video highlights the potential of asset building for congregations, featuring examples from Christian, Jewish, and Muslim congregations. A leader's guide gives ideas for using the video with different groups in the congregation.

101 Asset-Building Actions (Search Institute). This colorful poster gives ideas for how to build assets as individuals and through organizations. Key sections of the poster are in both English and Spanish.

Search Institute's Web Site (www.search-institute.org) has a wide array of information on assets, asset building, and youth. You can sign onto an e-mail discussion group (listserv) on asset building in congregations through the "participate" section of the Web site.

Sharing the Asset Message Speaker's Kit (Search Institute). This kit includes a detailed script, colorful overheads, and ready-to-copy handouts for giving presentations about asset building.

Tapping the Potential: Discovering Congregations' Role in Building Assets in Youth, by Glenn A. Seefeldt and Eugene C. Roehlkepartain (Search Institute). This short booklet presents key ideas about asset building in congregations. Ideal to share with leaders in the congregation.

What Kids Need to Succeed, by Peter L. Benson, Judy Galbraith, and Pamela Espeland (Free Spirit Publishing; available from Search Institute). This quick, practical guide gives hundreds of ideas for building assets at home, in schools, in congregations, and in the community.

Youth Development in Congregations: An Exploration of the Potential and Barriers, by Eugene C Roehlkepartain and Peter C. Scales (Search Institute). This report examines how asset building fits with and builds on the strengths of congregational youth work.

Tools for Asset Building

The resources in this section give insights and practical ideas for the four contexts for asset building that are outlined in this book. Published by many different companies and organizations, most do not explicitly address the developmental assets, and most are aimed primarily at one faith tradition, most often Christian. Addresses for all publishers are included at the end of this resource list.

In the Whole Congregation

Black and White Styles of Youth Ministry: Two Congregations in America, by William R. Myers (Pilgrim Press). Explores the dynamics and differences in youth work between the dominant styles of European American congregations and African American congregations.

Creating Intergenerational Community: 75 Ideas for Building Relationships Between Youth and Adults, by Jolene L. Roehlkepartain (Search Institute). Creative activities for youth and adults to do together, either individually or in groups.

Dry Bones Live: Helping Congregations Discover New Life, by Robert H. Craig and Robert C. Worley (Westminster/John Knox). This book on introducing change and renewal in congregations can give insights into the process of focusing new energy on asset building.

Effective Youth Ministry: A Congregational Approach, by Roland Martinson (Augsburg Fortress). A groundbreaking book that outlines a vision of Christian congregations in which youth are integrated throughout congregational life.

The Equipping Pastor: A Systems Approach to Congregational Leadership, by R. Paul Stevens and Phil Collins (Alban Institute). This book offers a helpful perspective in thinking about congregational leadership from a systems perspective. It offers important insights that can be applied to how to engage the whole congregation in asset building.

Guide to Youth Ministry: Leadership, by Tom East and John Roberto (Center for Ministry Development). Written from a Catholic perspective, this book presents both the theory and practice of a comprehensive approach to youth in congregations.

Intergenerational Religious Education, by James W. White (Religious Education Press, 1988). A unique book that presents the vision and the practical implications of designing religious education as truly intergenerational.

One Kid at a Time: How Mentoring Can Transform Your Youth Ministry, by Miles McPherson with Wayne Rice (Youth Specialties). This book-and-video training course gives practical suggestions for building one-to-one, long-term mentoring relationships between youth and adults in a Christian congregation.

In Youth Programming

Beyond Leaf Raking: Learning to Serve/Serving to Learn, by Peter L. Benson and Eugene C. Roehlkepartain (Abingdon Press; available from Search Institute). Based on Search Institute research, this book gives practical guidelines on engaging youth in service learning—a key asset-building strategy for youth programming.

Building Assets Together: 135 Group Activities for Helping Youth Succeed, by Jolene L. Roehlkepartain (Search Institute). This collection of group activities and ready-to-copy worksheets can be used to introduce the assets to young people in youth groups and other settings in your congregation.

Equipped to Serve: Volunteer Youth Worker Training Course, by Dennis "Tiger" McLuen (Youth Specialties). This video-based training curriculum includes six sessions on basic knowledge and skills for Christian volunteer youth workers.

Hamakor: What You Need to Know About Jewish Living and Leading (North American Federation of Temple Youth). A hands-on guide to basic programming issues for Jewish youth programs.

How to Be an Effective Youth Leader, by Mark Holmen (Augsburg Youth and Family Institute). A manual for training adults in basic skills for effective youth work in a Christian congregation.

Jewish Youth Databook: Research on Adolescence and Its Implications for Jewish Teen Programs, by Amy L. Sales (Institute for Community and Religion, Brandeis University). This book highlights key developmental needs of youth and their implications for programming within Jewish congregations.

Jewish Youth Source Book: A Planning Guide for Youth Programs, by Simon Klarfeld and Amy L. Sales (Institute for Community and Religion, Brandeis University). This guide gives practical ideas for shaping youth development programming in Jewish youth organizations. Among other topics, it addresses leadership development, recreation, sports, social events, community service, cultural arts, and education and family life.

Kids Taking Charge: Youth-Led Youth Ministry, by Thom and Joani Schultz (Group Books). This practical book gives step-by-step ideas for designing a youth program with youth as the leaders.

Lifegivers: A Practical Guide for Reaching Youth in a Challenging World, edited by Steve Games (Abingdon Press). This comprehensive notebook challenges congregations to expand their vision of youth work and offers tools for doing it.

Peer Ministry Training: The Basic Curriculum, by Barbara B. Varenhorst (Augburg Youth and Family Institute). Written by the pioneer in peer helping and peer ministry, this guide outlines 14 sessions for training young people to be peer helpers to each other. (Companion video and personal journal are also available.)

The Practical Youth Ministry Handbook (Group Publishing). A collection of recommendations from youth workers about key topics in leading a Christian youth program.

Sharing Groups in Youth Ministry, by Walt Marcum (Abingdon Press). A helpful guide for engaging youth in supporting and caring for each other.

Teaching Social Skills to Youth, by Tom Dowd and Jeff Tierney (Boys Town Press). This comprehensive guide gives practical tools for building many social skills in youth, which is an important component of asset building.

Volunteer Leadership: Empowering Volunteers for Youth Ministry, by John Roberto and others (Center for Ministry Development). This book collects useful insights and tools for recruiting, training, and supporting volunteers.

Working with Black Youth, edited by Charles R. Foster and Grant S. Shockley (Abingdon Press). This book highlights the unique needs and challenges of doing youth work with African American youth, including a focus on intergenerational community.

Youth Ministry Handbook, by Edward A. Trimmer (Abingdon Press). A basic guide for establishing an effective youth program.

In Family Programming

Building Skills in High-Risk Families, by Jane L. Peterson and others (Boys Town Press). This in-depth book helps you identify and build the strengths families need to promote healthy changes in high-risk situations.

Family-Based Youth Ministry, by Mark DeVries (InterVarsity Press). This provocative and insightful book highlights a practical focus for reshaping youth work to include families.

Four Imperatives: Youth and Family Ministry, by Merton P. Strommen (Augsburg Youth and Family Institute). This conceptual, research-based booklet outlines a vision and key strategies for designing a congregation that supports youth and their families.

Ideas for Parents Newsletter Master Set, by Jolene L. Roehlkepartain (Search Institute). This set includes 50 reproducible newsletters that give parents practical ideas for how to build each of the 40 assets.

It Takes More than Love (Seraphim Communications; available from Search Institute). This four-part video series builds on the developmental assets and helps parents focus on a positive approach to parenting.

A New Day for Family Ministry, by Richard P. Olson and Joe H. Leonard, Jr. (Alban Institute). This book examines many changes occurring in families and offers specific ways for congregations to respond.

130 Ways to Involve Parents in Youth Ministry (Group Books). A collection of creative ideas compiled from youth workers across the United States. Gives ideas for service project, meetings, and other activities.

Parenting with a Purpose: A Positive Approach to Raising Confident, Caring Youth, by Dean Feldmeyer and Eugene C. Roehlkepartain (Search Institute). This booklet highlights the ways asset building can strengthen family life, and how families can contribute to asset-building efforts.

The Youth Worker's Handbook to Family Ministry, by Chap Clark (Youth Specialties). This book identifies specific ways to bring youth and parents together.

In Outreach to the Community

Activism That Makes Sense: Congregations and Community Organization (ACTA). This classic book addresses basic, practical questions about the dynamics of community organizing, including power, controversy, self-interest, and others.

Basic Steps Toward Community Ministry: Guidelines and Models in Action, by Carl S. Dudley (Alban Institute). This excellent guide offers practical insights for focusing a congregation's work in the community.

Better Together: Religious Institutions as Partners in Community-Based Development, by David Scheie and others (Rainbow Research). Based on a four-year evaluation of 28 community development efforts, this report highlights the opportunities and challenges of engaging congregations in community-wide efforts.

Building and Maintaining Community Coalitions on Behalf of Children, Youth, and Families: The Roles of Religious Institutions, by Joanee G. Keith, Martin A. Covey, and Daniel F. Perkins (Institute for Children, Youth, and Families, Michigan State University). This research report shows the ways congregations get involved in community-wide coalitions and the critical roles they play.

Congregation and Community, by Nancy Tatom Ammerman (Rutgers University Press). This cutting-edge book examines the relationship between community change and congregational life, showing the various ways congregations from many faith traditions respond to changes and needs in their community.

Energizing the Congregation: Images that Shape Your Church's Ministry, by Carl S. Dudley and Sally A. Johnson (Westminster/John Knox). This insightful, research-based book shows the variety of ways congregations can and do engage in outreach to their community, whether the congregation takes a role as "prophet," "servant," "pilgrim," "pillar," or "survivor."

Healthy Communities • Healthy Youth Tool Kit (Search Institute). This comprehensive binder includes practical tips, stories, and worksheets to help form a community-wide asset-building effort. It addresses 55 practical topics, from "action plans" to "zaniness."

Welcome the Child: A Child Advocacy Guide for Churches, by Kathleen A. Guy (Children's Defense Fund/Friendship Press). This book focuses on specific strategies for congregations taking an active advocacy role on behalf of children and youth, particularly in addressing issues of injustice and public policy. (Companion video available.)

Contact Information for Publishers

Here is how to contact the publishers whose resources are identified above.

ACTA
4848 North Clark Street
Chicago, IL 60640
800-397-2282

Abingdon Press
c/o Cokesbury
Box 801
Nashville, TN 37202
800-672-1789

Alban Institute
7315 Wisconsin Avenue
Suite 1250 West
Bethesda, MD 20814
800-486-1318

Augsburg Fortress Publishers
Box 1209
Minneapolis, MN 55440-1209
800-328-4648
www.elca.org/afp/afphome.html

Augsburg Youth and Family Institute
c/o Educational Media Corporation
Box 21311
Minneapolis, MN 55421
800-966-3382
www.augsburg.edu/ayfi/ayfi.html

Boys Town Press
14100 Crawford Street
Boys Town, NE 68010
800-282-6657
www.ffbh.boystown.org/

Center for Ministry Development
Box 699
Naugatuck, CT 06770
203-723-1622

Children's Defense Fund
25 E Street Northwest
Washington, DC 20001
202-662-3652
www.childrensdefense.org

Group Publishing
Box 485
Loveland, CO 80539
800-447-1070
www.grouppublishing.com

Institute for Children, Youth, and Families
Michigan State University
Suite 27, Kellogg Center
East Lansing, MI 48824
517-353-6617
www.msu.icyf.msu.edu

Institute for Community and Religion
Brandeis University
140 Balboa Street
San Francisco, CA 94118
415-386-2604

InterVarsity Press
Box 1400
Downers Grove, IL 60515
800-843-9487
www.ivpress.com

North American Federation of Temple Youth
Box 433
Warwick, NY 10990
914-987-6300

The Pilgrim Press
700 Prospect Avenue East
Cleveland, OH 44115-1100
800-537-3394

Rainbow Research
621 West Lake Street
Minneapolis, MN 55408
612-824-0724
rainbowresearch.mtn.org

Religious Education Press
5316 Meadow Brook Road
Birmingham, AL 35242-3315
205-991-1000
releduc@ix.netcom.com

Rutgers University Press
100 Joyce Kilmer Avenue
Piscataway, NJ 08854-8099
800-446-9323
http://rutgerspress.rutgers.edu

Search Institute
615 First Avenue Northeast, Suite 125
Minneapolis, MN 55413
612-376-8955
800-888-7828
www.search-institute.org

Westminster/John Knox Press
100 Witherspoon Street
Louisville, KY 40202
800-227-2872
www.pcusa.org/tpc/

Youth Specialties
c/o ChurchSource
Box 668
Holmes, PA 19043
800-776-8008
www.youthspecialties.com

Reproducible Charts of the 40 Developmental Assets

Search Institute's 40 Developmental Assets

Search Institute has identified the following building blocks of healthy development that help young people grow up healthy, caring, and responsible.

EXTERNAL ASSETS

Support

1. **Family support**—Family life provides high levels of love and support.
2. **Positive family communication**—Young person and her or his parent(s) communicate positively, and young person is willing to seek advice and counsel from parent(s).
3. **Other adult relationships**—Young person receives support from three or more nonparent adults.
4. **Caring neighborhood**—Young person experiences caring neighbors.
5. **Caring school climate**—School provides a caring, encouraging environment.
6. **Parent involvement in schooling**—Parent(s) are actively involved in helping young person succeed in school.

Empowerment

7. **Community values youth**—Young person perceives that adults in the community value youth.
8. **Youth as resources**—Young people are given useful roles in the community.
9. **Service to others**—Young person serves in the community one hour or more per week.
10. **Safety**—Young person feels safe at home, at school, and in the neighborhood.

Boundaries and Expectations

11. **Family boundaries**—Family has clear rules and consequences and monitors the young person's whereabouts.
12. **School boundaries**—School provides clear rules and consequences.
13. **Neighborhood boundaries**—Neighbors take responsibility for monitoring young people's behavior.
14. **Adult role models**—Parent(s) and other adults model positive, responsible behavior.
15. **Positive peer influence**—Young person's best friends model responsible behavior.
16. **High expectations**—Parent(s) and teachers encourage the young person to do well.

Constructive Use of Time

17. **Creative activities**—Young person spends three or more hours per week in lessons or practice in music, theater, or other arts.
18. **Youth programs**—Young person spends three or more hours per week in sports, clubs, or organizations at school and/or in the community.
19. **Religious community**—Young person spends one or more hours per week in activities in a religious institution.
20. **Time at home**—Young person is out with friends "with nothing special to do" two or fewer nights per week.

INTERNAL ASSETS

Commitment to Learning

21. **Achievement motivation**—Young person is motivated to do well in school.
22. **School engagement**—Young person is actively engaged in learning.
23. **Homework**—Young person reports doing at least one hour of homework every school day.
24. **Bonding to school**—Young person cares about her or his school.
25. **Reading for pleasure**—Young person reads for pleasure three or more hours per week.

Positive Values

26. **Caring**—Young person places high value on helping other people.
27. **Equality and social justice**—Young person places high value on promoting equality and reducing hunger and poverty.
28. **Integrity**—Young person acts on convictions and stands up for her or his beliefs.
29. **Honesty**—Young person "tells the truth even when it is not easy."
30. **Responsibility**—Young person accepts and takes personal responsibility.
31. **Restraint**—Young person believes it is important not to be sexually active or to use alcohol or other drugs.

Social Competencies

32. **Planning and decision making**—Young person knows how to plan ahead and make choices.
33. **Interpersonal competence**—Young person has empathy, sensitivity, and friendship skills.
34. **Cultural competence**—Young person has knowledge of and comfort with people of different cultural/racial/ethnic backgrounds.
35. **Resistance skills**—Young person can resist negative peer pressure and dangerous situations.
36. **Peaceful conflict resolution**—Young person seeks to resolve conflict nonviolently.

Positive Identity

37. **Personal power**—Young person feels he or she has control over "things that happen to me."
38. **Self-esteem**—Young person reports having a high self-esteem.
39. **Sense of purpose**—Young person reports that "my life has a purpose."
40. **Positive view of personal future**—Young person is optimistic about her or his personal future.

40 elementos fundamentales del desarrollo

La investigación realizada por el Instituto Search ha identificado los siguientes fundamentos del desarrollo como instrumentos para ayudar a los jóvenes a crecer sanos, interesados en el bienestar común y a ser responsables.

ELEMENTOS FUNDAMENTALES EXTERNOS

Apoyo

1. **Apoyo familiar**—La vida familiar brinda altos niveles de amor y apoyo.

2. **Comunicación familiar positiva**—El joven y sus padres se comunican positivamente. Los jóvenes estan dispuestos a buscar consejo y consuelo en sus padres.

3. **Otras relaciones con adultos**—Además de sus padres, los jóvenes reciben apoyo de tres o más personas adultas que no son sus pareintes.

4. **Una comunidad comprometida**—El joven experimenta el interés de sus vecinos por su bienestar.

5. **Un plantel educativo que se interesa por el joven**—La escuela proporciona un ambiente que anima y se preocupa por la juventud.

6. **La participación de los padres en las actividades escolares**—Los padres participan activamente ayudando a los jóvenes a tener éxito en la escuela.

Fortalecimiento

7. **La comunidad valora a la juventud**—El joven percibe que los adultos en la comunidad valoran a la juventud.

8. **La juventud como un recurso**—Se le brinda a los jóvenes la oportunidad de tomar un papel útil en la comunidad.

9. **Servicio a los demás**—La gente joven participa brindando servicios a su comunidad una hora o más a la semana.

10. **Seguridad**—Los jóvenes se sienten seguros en casa, en la escuela y en el vecindario.

Limites y expectativas

11. **Limites familiares**—La familia tiene reglas y consecuencias bien claras, además vigila las actividades de los jóvenes.

12. **Limites escolares**—La escuela proporciona reglas y consecuencias bien claras.

13. **Limites vecinales**—Los vecinos asumen la responsabilidad de vigilar el comportamiento de los jóvenes.

14. **El comportamiento de los adultos como ejemplo**—Los padres y otros adultos tienen un comportamiento positivo y responsable.

15. **Compañeros como influencia positiva**—Los mejores amigos del joven son un ejemplo de comportamiento responsable.

16. **Altas expectativas**—Ambos padres y maestros motivan a los jóvenes a que tengan éxito.

Uso constructivo del tiempo

17. **Actividades creativas**—Los jóvenes pasan tres horas o más a la semana en lecciones de música, teatro u otras artes.

18. **Programas juveniles**—Los jóvenes pasan tres horas o más a la semana practicando algún deporte, en centros comunitarios, en la escuela o en alguna otra organización comunitaria.

19. **Comunidad religiosa**—Los jóvenes pasan una hora o más a la semana en actividades organizadas por alguna institución religiosa.

20. **Tiempo en casa**—Los jóvenes conviven con sus amigos "sin nada especial que hacer" dos o pocas noches por semana.

ELEMENTOS FUNDAMENTALES INTERNOS

Compromiso con el aprendizaje

21. **Motivación por sus logros**—El joven es motivado a salir bien en la escuela.

22. **Compromiso con la escuela**—El joven participa activamente con el aprendizaje.

23. **Tarea**—El joven debe hacer tarea por lo menos durante una hora cada día de clases.

24. **Preocuparse por la escuela**—El joven debe importarle su escuela.

25. **Leer por placer**—El joven lee por placer tres horas o más por semana.

Valores positivos

26. **Preocuparse por los demás**—El joven le da mucho valor al hecho de poder ayudar a otras personas.

27. **Igualdad y justicia social**—Para el joven tiene mucho valor promover la igualdad y reducir el hambre y la pobreza.

28. **Integridad**—El joven actúa con convicción y defiende sus creencias.

29. **Honestidad**—El joven dice la verdad "aún cuando esto no sea fácil."

30. **Responsabilidad**—El joven acepta y es responsable de sí mismo.

31. **Abstinencia**—El joven cree que es importante no tener actividades sexuales, ni utilizar alcohol u otras drogas.

Capacidad social

32. **Planeación y toma de decisiones**—El joven sabe cómo planear y hacer elecciones.

33. **Capacidad interpersonal**—El joven tiene empatía, sensibilidad y capacidad para entablar amistad.

34. **Capacidad cultural**—El joven tiene conocimiento de y sabe convivir con gente de diferente marco cultural, racial o étnico.

35. **Habilidad de resistencia**—El joven tiene la habilidad de resistir presiones negativas y situaciones peligrosas.

36. **Solución pacífica de conflictos**—El joven busca resolver los conflictos sin violencia.

Identidad positiva

37. **Poder personal**—El joven siente que él o ella tiene el control de "las cosas que le suceden."

38. **Auto-estima**—El joven afirma tener una alta auto-estima.

39. **Sentido de propósito**—El joven afirma "mi vida tiene un propósito."

40. **Visión positiva del futuro personal**—El joven es optimista sobre su futuro mismo.

notes